Latte for One and Loving It!

MELANIE B. DOBSON & TOSHA L. WILLIAMS

Cook Communications

Faithful Woman is an imprint of
Cook Communications Ministries, Colorado Springs, Colorado 80918
Cook Communications, Paris, Ontario
Kingsway Communications, Eastbourne, England

LATTE FOR ONE
© 2000 by Melanie B. Dobson and Tosha L. Williams.
Printed in the United States of America.

1 2 3 4 5 6 7 8 9 10 Printing/Year 04 03 02 01 00

Editor: Wendy Peterson, Julie Smith
Design: Boven Design Studio

Library of Congress Cataloging-in-Publication Data
Williams, Tosha,
Latte for one and loving it/by Tosha Williams and Melanie Dobson
p. cm.
ISBN 1-56476-763-9
1. Young women—Conduct of life. 2. Young women—Life skills guides. 3. Christian women—Conduct of life. 4. Christian women—Life skills guides. I. Dobson, Melanie. II. Title.
HQ1229.W73 2000 99-39734
305.242—dc21 CIP

To our sisters
Christina,
Shannon, and Elisha:
May your lives be balanced, fulfilling, and, most of all,
Christlike.

And to little Anastasha:
You've been with us since the conception of this book.
May you grow into a godly woman
who dares to live her dreams.

CONTENTS

ACKNOWLEDGMENTS

This book has been a team effort, with stories from some, guidance from others, and information from many others. Literally dozens of people have been a part of mixing this *Latte for One*.

Jennifer Cox, thank you so much for continually being available to share a story, proof a chapter, give us feedback, and encourage us. What an invaluable contribution you made to this book.

Sherri, Allison, Elisha, Laura S., Laura C., Julie, Lisa, Sandy, Jenn F., Renee, Holly, Emily, Jacci, Edie, Dori, Shannan, Brenda, Melody, Eleanor, and Betsy: thank you for sharing your stories, perspectives, and opinions with us. Connie, Jennifer F., Lillian, Susan, Jana, Mary, and Stacy, thank you for giving us ideas we could develop. We treasure all of your friendships.

To all the guys who gave us input, including Brian, Jeff, Mike, Jamie, Rod, Robert, Donavan, and Jay, we sincerely appreciate the perspective you've added to this book.

To Jim Beroth, Shannon Misner, Jim Anderson, Karen Holder, Rod Walker, and Dean Dulany, thank you for offering your professional opinions about the contents of the book. And thanks to Leslie, Earl, Doug, Bob, Edie, Katy, and Amy for your input on our career chapter. Our information is more complete and accurate because of all of you.

Jim Weidmann, your recommendation launched our book idea, and we are so grateful for your ongoing encouragement.

Ray and Anne Pokorny, thank you for brainstorming about titles with us, as well as supporting us throughout this project. Your direction has been invaluable.

Jeff and Mindy Kiepke, we thoroughly enjoyed celebrating

the completion of our first book draft at your fabulous restaurant The Mona Lisa. Thank you for this special treat.

Susie and Brianna, thanks for watching Anastasha during the final deadline! Kelly and Jon, thanks for taking "baby nights"!

Our appreciation to Randy Scott, Lee Hough, Julie Smith, Kathleen Campbell-Wright, and Robin Wilson at Chariot Victor for believing in the importance of a book for single women.

Jon and Kelly, thank you for laughing with us (not at us) when some of our chapters weren't quite gelled, providing us with your helpful edits, and always believing that we could do it even when we doubted ourselves.

We would also like to thank our parents for their support in this project. You taught us how to dream big and pursue our goals. Thank you for your encouragement. We love you!

Finally, we thank our Lord Jesus Christ—the giver and fulfiller of all good dreams.

INTRODUCTION

Fall was in the air. The leaves were changing into beautiful yellows, oranges, and fiery reds in the Blue Ridge mountains of Virginia. Our college campus was filled with the anticipation of homecoming, but regardless of the fun that awaited us, we still had to go to class. So the two of us hurried on, unaware that our paths were about to cross.

Broadcast Communication was a required course for every journalism major, and we each dutifully took a seat. For Melanie, a college junior, this class was just another step toward finishing her degree. For me (Tosha), a college freshman, this class was my first peek into a major I hoped to complete.

The professor graciously waited a few minutes after the bell rang to start, giving a little extra time for the stragglers to find the classroom this first day. An uncomfortable hush filled the classroom, since all of us were surrounded by new and unfamiliar faces. As I glanced around, I noticed Melanie, sitting beside me. So I quietly said, "Hello!" She smiled, then introduced herself. Though we could not have realized it at the time, that simple conversation more than ten years ago began a friendship that would last a lifetime.

In the years following that first day in class, Melanie and I earned our degrees and started our careers. We dreamed about the future God had in store for us. Melanie took me on adventures like spelunking and camping, and I asked her to be a bridesmaid in my wedding. We moved several times to different states, and then we ended up moving to the same new city. During dozens of walks through the years, we discussed a million goals, envisioned a thousand dreams, and considered all the aspects of our ever-changing lives.

And that was how the idea for this book came about.

It was during one of those "wouldn't it be fun if . . . ?" conversations that the idea came to us. We had just returned from a walk and were resting on my living room floor. Actually, *I* was the one resting, because six months of pregnancy weighed heavily on my body. Melanie, on the other hand, was a physically fit single woman who had scarcely taken a deep breath.

"Wouldn't it be fun," Melanie proposed after a sip of ice water, "if we could write an encouraging book for single women? Something that would be practical. Like . . ." Mel paused to think of a fitting term, then smiled saying, "Like a guide to life." From my horizontal position, I contemplated her proposition. She continued, "We could do it from our viewpoints as a married woman and a single woman." Now that interested me, because we frequently discussed each other's different perspectives about things.

For the rest of the evening, we discussed the pros and cons of the idea. Neither of us had ever seen a comprehensive resource dealing with a Christian single woman's life. Maybe we could write one—after all, ever since we were little girls, we had both wanted to write books. Now, after saying hello and good-bye to each other more times than we cared to count, God had brought our paths together again. This might be the perfect time for us to take on a challenge and fulfill a lifelong dream together!

So, the next week, with a yellow ledger pad and pen, we went for another walk. We strolled until we found a bench where we could watch the sunset and brainstorm about our book. One by one, we began identifying the many facets of a woman's life. Education, career, and social life are just a few things that are at the top of our lists. Keeping healthy, investing financially, and building relationships are important too. Though we know that life is not going to be perfect, we would still like to be happy and fulfilled.

Completing this delicate balance is our relationship with the Lord. As Christian women who sincerely desire to be Christlike, we want to know more about how God and His Word make a difference in everyday life. We want to end our lives with a feeling of satisfaction, knowing that we did our best, took some risks, and glorified God along the way.

By the time darkness had overtaken the sunset, Melanie and I were ready to start writing. With all these aspects of a woman's life in mind, we were excited about encouraging and challenging women to pursue balance, Christlikeness, and fulfillment. This was a big dream, one that challenged and interested us. God had given and fulfilled big dreams for us before, though, so we talked to Him about this one too.

We began writing, then, not because we have all the answers, but because we like finding them. We talked with dozens of friends, family members, coworkers, and acquaintances hoping to find nuggets of wisdom. E-mail, phone calls, library research, letters, focus groups, Bible study, life experiences, and one-on-one conversations continually added perspective and scope to our work.

With all this in mind, we started writing stories—some of which are true, a few are fictional, and most are composites of several lives. Some names have been changed to protect peoples' privacy. The book of Proverbs became our springboard to dive into some primary aspects of a single woman's life: dating, relationships, wellness, finances, and pursuits. Believe it or not, God's

Word has something to say to us about each of these areas.

One paragraph, one page, one chapter at a time, we labored to fulfill our dream. And now it has come true. You are holding the reality of what we hoped for. You're a busy woman with a lot going on in your life, but you've chosen to stop for a few moments and walk with us through the following pages. The circle of friendship continues to expand as we're honored by your presence. We hope that along the way you'll be encouraged to enjoy your life, enabled to try some new things, and challenged to fulfill your own dreams.

So grab a cup of coffee, find a comfy spot, and get ready to meet some new friends.

Dating

....

Amanda drove slowly down the highway, enjoying the peaceful scenery of colorful flowers, grassy meadows, and horses grazing behind bright white fences. On the right, Amanda passed a creek with a little bridge leading to an island and sighed as she contemplated romance. "What a beautiful day!" She rolled down her window, and the fresh air poured inside.

A look in her rearview mirror showed a black vehicle in the distance, and minutes later, it was right on her tail. Her eyes diverted nervously from the scenery to see what the sports car would do. The woman in the slick car didn't hesitate a moment, flying around Amanda at about ninety miles an hour in spite of an oncoming car. Amanda breathed in relief when the black streak narrowly escaped an accident and then was gone.

On she drove, taking in every detail. Amanda stored photos in her mind's album—the fields filled with wildflowers and the rocks dotting the hills. She didn't want to forget a moment of this amazing ride.

Miles down the road, the traffic suddenly slowed, and she crept along in the line of cars. Instead of getting angry, she put in her *favorite CD and sang along as loud as she could. Nothing was going to ruin her day. She was determined to enjoy this drive.*

Half an hour later, she found out what caused the traffic jam. The black car that had whizzed by her lay beside the road. She saw the owner limping, examining the vehicle that had flown off the road, taken out a fence, and crashed into the side of a rocky hill. It was a miracle that the woman was still alive.

Three miles later Amanda reached her destination and was greeted by friends and family who celebrated her safe arrival.

Dating is a lot like a long highway drive. One woman chooses to speed through the ride while the other carefully and slowly takes in the scenery.

The woman who flies down the dating highway misses both the wonderful details and the glaring danger signs. And, if she crashes and burns, she is back where she started without ever reaching her destination.

The other woman decides to enjoy her ride. She sets her cruise control and gradually learns everything about the route she is taking. All along her drive, she is alert to danger signs, and she turns back when she anticipates problems. As she steadily approaches her destination, she savors every moment, appreciating all she sees and thanking God daily for His blessings.

Are you on the dating highway? If so, which car are you driving?

- *One* -

THE INSIGHTFUL WOMAN
Finding Out What Men and
Women Really Think

THOUGH IT COST ALL YOU HAVE, GET UNDERSTANDING. ESTEEM HER,
AND SHE WILL EXALT YOU; EMBRACE HER, AND SHE WILL HONOR YOU.
PROVERBS 4:7B–8

We girls like to talk about guys. We talk about them late into the night on the telephone, after church, in the cafeteria, or sitting around the living room with our roommates. We ask: "What do you think of Paul?" "Evan called last night. Does that mean anything?" "I'm not sure if Jason is exactly my type." "Do you think I should ask John to that pizza party next week?" So many questions fly around in our minds: What do guys really think? Should we ask them out? Does it mean anything if he does call?

Instead of just wondering, we decided to ask. In order to get the inside scoop, we invited a few of our quality, single guy friends over for an evening of pizza and talk. Armed with a list of questions compiled by us and several girlfriends, we were ready to start. Almost . . .

GIRL TALK
Before we talked to the guys, we wondered what you thought. What are you looking for in a man? What do you love and absolutely hate about the dating process? Can men and women "just be friends"? And what is your ideal relationship?

We invited a group of single girlfriends over who ranged in age from eighteen to thirty to discuss these questions. Everyone got comfortable, lounging on the couch or pillows on the floor, with our pizza and Cokes in hand to talk about men. For the next two hours, no one seemed to be at a loss for words. What follows is a combination of their thoughts and opinions.

What are you looking for in a man? "I want a man who has integrity with God and with people," Jenny jumped in right away. "Someone who is tactful but truthful."

The women nodded their heads, and then more answers started rolling. "A good communicator, responsible, initiator, intelligent, and a guy with a sense of humor."

Stacy, who loves skiing and hiking in the mountains, said, "I don't want a 'Joe couch potato.' I want a man who spends his free time outdoors."

"A man passionate for God is so important to me," Amy told us. "Someone willing to listen to God's still small voice." "I also want someone," Stacy added, "who has character to support him through the long haul."

As we talked, more ideas started pouring in: "Someone who values my opinion, a guy who truly listens, eventual physical attraction." "I would love it if he were at ease with people, conversational, spontaneous, and creative." Each one had specific things she was looking for in the "man of her dreams."

How do you act when you are interested in a guy? "I admit," Laura said, "I get nervous and giggle a lot when he's around. Then I'm too eager to talk to him." "I'm too friendly," Amy said. "I always jump when a guy I like calls. Even if he called at the last minute, I would cancel my plans to go out with him."

"I would never cancel my plans to go out with a guy," Stacy

countered. "My activities are my priority, and besides there is something to be said about maintaining some mystery about my life." "Unfortunately, I lose sleep if I'm interested in a guy," Christine said. "I'm very easy to please and I often end up disappointed."

The theme for the movie When Harry Met Sally *is that men and women can't be friends. Do you think single men and women can be "just friends"?* "Absolutely," Stacy started. "I have a ton of guy friends." "Not all guys would agree with you," We told her.

"Well, it can be hard," Jenny said, "But I do think that men and women can be friends."

"My best friend is a guy," Debbie explained. "We've never had an attraction either way."

"Friendship with a man is a rare and precious thing, but somebody usually ends up being attracted to the other person," one of the women said. Then another replied, "When I have clearly communicated that I'm not interested in dating, I can have a great friendship with a man."

What do you love about dating? "I enjoy getting to know people," said Debbie. "And I love going out to eat." "I like the creativity of dating," said Stacy. "I'd rather go on fun and different dates instead of extravagant ones." "Honestly," Christine told us, "I like dating because I'm made to feel special for the evening."

What do you hate about dating? The women's answers came rapidly: "small talk, stress, sexual pressure." "I feel guilty if I don't like the person," Jenny said. "And I hate having to say 'no' to a second date."

After you date somebody and know it's not going to work out, how do you end the relationship? "I think you should be honest right up front," Amy said. "If you don't see the relationship going anywhere, you should be straight up." "Tell him that you want to end the relationship when he can get away quickly," Debbie said. "Saying you don't want to date any more right before you go to dinner or on a long drive puts both you and him in an awkward position."

They all nodded in agreement, even though they admitted that was easier said than done. "What generally happens is that I just let a dating relationship fizzle out," Christine said. "Instead of being honest, I just act uninterested and hope he gets the hint."

What is the "ideal" guy/girl relationship? "I like casual dating relationships," Stacy said. "I'd rather not have the labels of boyfriend and girlfriend, because I like being able to date more than one person."

"The ideal is when you can guard your emotions," Amy said, "and become best friends before you date." "I like a more serious relationship," Jenny said. "I want him to plan special dates. Cherish me."

How does prayer work in your dating life? All the women had different ideas of what prayer looked like in their dating life. "I like praying on dates," Stacy explained, "but I don't like when a guy tries to impress me with his spirituality."

"I pray for direction in my dating relationships," Jenny said. "I have started praying that God would protect me and prevent an unhealthy relationship." "I pray that I am in God's will so I don't lose a friendship with a man I'm dating," said Amy.

How honest do you want a guy to be in your relationship? "Bluntly honest," one of the girls blurted out. "No, no, no— don't tell me you like me right up-front," Stacy told us. "Be completely honest after awhile, but it would scare me if a guy told me up-front he liked me."

"I want him to be tactful," Laura said. "Timing is so important in communication, but it is not fair to expect too much." "I don't need to know everything a man is thinking or what bothers him," Christine said. "I like big picture honesty, not knowing all the little feelings that change." "In some ways I want to know if a man likes me, but yet I like the mystery of not knowing everything he's thinking," Jenny said.

Would you ask a guy out? "No, not a guy I liked," Amy said. *A guy you don't like?* "Well, I'd ask a guy friend to spend time together, but not someone I was interested in."

"Never again," Debbie said. "I asked a guy out once, and it backfired."

"No way, call me old-fashioned," Stacy said. "I'm not convinced that guys like to be asked out. He might be flattered, but he wouldn't take me seriously."

What is an absolute turn off to you? "Several months ago," Christine quickly began, "I went on a date with a man who I thought had a lot of potential. We had a lot in common and spent the whole evening talking about our interests. But when he dropped me off, I knew it would never work. I live on a dark street, and he said good-bye and then left before I got in the house. I had to fumble around to find my keys in the dark and then my way to the door. I didn't go out with him again."

After Christine's story, the comments poured in: "A guy who honks when he picks me up for a date." " Disrespect of mother or family." "Doesn't listen or ask questions." "Calls me someone else's name." "Tries to impress me with money or success." "Lack of initiative in his personal life." "If he can't take care of his own life," Stacy said. "How can he take care of me?"

Do you want to be married someday? "Yes, definitely," Jenny said. "I don't know when, but I want to have a family and share my life with someone. It is awesome that God makes two people one."

"I think I would, but I really want to be open to not getting married," Amy told us. "Society thinks you're not a complete person until you are married, but I want to be complete before I'm married, because it expands your potential."

"Marriage is hard work," Laura said. "I don't know many single people who have tough lives, but married people have tough relationships with each other and their kids. But I want to get married, because it's going to be worth the hard work."

"If I don't get married that's okay, but I would like to have a soul mate to share my life with," Christine said. "I don't know if I want to have kids, but I want to have a marriage like my parents did. They helped and encouraged each other through life's bumps."

"I'm passionate in my relationships and give myself deeply," Debbie said. "This burns you when you are single, because dating relationships are not permanent. I would like a man to invest in and share my life with. I want to be there by his side and expand his potential like I hope he does for me."

"Divorce and death are two of my biggest fears. I would rather not get married than to have that happen, because my dream is to have a permanent relationship with my husband."

So many of our parents are divorced, and even some of our married friends are separating after only a few years of marriage. What are you doing to safeguard your relationships so you don't end in divorce as well? "Praying hard for the man whom I will marry to make sure he's the right one," said Debbie. "I can't prevent divorce," Laura explained, "but I'm looking for a man with character so he is less likely to leave me."

"Prayer is huge, combining trust in God with wisdom," Jenny said. "Listening to warnings from my friends and family; because love is blind I tend to see what I want to see."

"Looking at character is key—how is he treating me? What are his goals? Is he a selfish person? How does he treat other people?" Stacy said.

"I'm trying to become a better person myself," Amy concluded, "because it's not always the guy who destroys the relationship. I want my unrealistic expectations and demands to be transformed by Christ."

The pizza was almost gone. It was a weeknight, so we completed our questions even though we could have asked many more. What do you think about these questions and answers? Do you agree? Disagree? We wish you could have joined in on our discussion so we could have heard your viewpoint as well.

We were impressed with this group of godly single women. They were confident in what they believed, and while each of them expressed the desire to be married someday, none of them had put their lives on hold. While guys were certainly a fun topic of conversation, there were so many different topics we could have covered.

But now we were curious to know what the guys thought. What were they looking for in a woman? It wasn't until two weeks later that we finally found out.

GUY TALK

Just like the women we had interviewed, a group of quality single men lounged around the living room eating pizza and drinking sodas. We told them we wanted their input on women. And we found women one of their favorite subjects to talk about. It was slow getting the guys to talk, but once they started, we frantically wrote their answers, trying to keep up with them. Here's what they told us.

What are you looking for in a woman? "I want to be with someone I can trust," Jeff started. "Someone who is honest with me."

"Honest over time," David interrupted. "Honesty is important to me too, but I don't want her to tell me everything she is thinking when I first meet her."

"I'd like to be with a woman I feel comfortable with," Mark told us. "Someone I can be myself around."

"I definitely want to be with someone I'm physically attracted to," Jeff continued as all the guys nodded their heads. "I love a pretty smile."

"I'm looking for someone who isn't afraid to think on her own," Shawn said. "A woman whose traits offset my weaknesses."

The guys took a moment to think, and then Keith started the ball rolling again. "I would like to be with a woman who isn't just a Christian by name but a lady who truly puts the Lord first in her life. Someone who challenges me spiritually."

The answers started coming in more rapidly: "A woman with the gift of hospitality, healthy, not materialistic, encouraging, compassionate, has dreams and vision, determined, spontaneous, and adventurous."

"I want to be with someone who believes in me," David

explained. "I can do anything if she believes in me." All the guys nodded in agreement.

"I want a woman," Jeff said, "who needs me but isn't clingy." *What do you mean by "clingy"?* All the guys jumped on that. "'Clingy' is someone who is desperate, doesn't trust me, is constantly calling me and asking me questions, makes me grovel, over analyzes, plays mind games, and questions any time we spend apart."

How important is physical attractiveness to you? "Very important," Shawn started. "You don't see personality first, so attractiveness is what catches my eye."

"Men are more visual than women," Jeff explained, "so attractiveness is very important to us." "You absolutely have to be attracted to her," Mark agreed. "I'd like to be with a woman who is cute but unassuming about her looks."

What do you consider attractive? At first the answers were similar: "Pretty eyes, pretty smile, a woman who takes care of herself, someone who is physically fit." Then the responses started to vary quite a bit. "I like short and petite women," one of the guys said. "I like tall women," another guy said. "And I like women who have a natural cuteness about them instead of a polished beauty." "The international look is appealing to me," said another. Long hair, short hair, the natural look, classic look, sporty look, red hair, dark hair, blonde hair. Our hands started to hurt from scribbling down all the responses. "To a large extent," Keith explained, "beauty comes from the inside and the way she responds to me."

What we soon discovered was that each man's idea of "attractive" was very different. There was no cut-and-dried way to look. Each man had distinct things he liked, and we were encouraged to hear that what they liked wasn't necessarily what Hollywood would define as attractive.

Our women's group had told us, "A woman becomes attracted to the man she falls in love with, but a man falls in love with the woman he is attracted to." We saw firsthand that this was true.

How does a woman know if you're interested in her? "It's always a dance until I know if she is or isn't interested," Mark said. "But I will eventually tell her I'm interested in getting to know her more." "I will ask her to do something and let her know I want to spend more time with her," Keith told us. "I want to develop a rapport before I let her know I'm interested." Then Jeff explained, "I approach a woman I like in a way that shows I'm confident in who I am and am not afraid of her. I tell her I would like to take her out." "It takes time for me," David added. "I am subtly involved with her life for a while before I let her know I'm interested."

If a woman is interested in you, how do you want her to let you know? "I always assume that a woman is not interested in me," Keith said. "If she shows too much interest," Jeff said, "it makes her appear desperate, so she's got to be subtle about it."

How is a woman supposed to do that? "Well, she can coyly joke with me," he explained. "And if she spends time with me, that's a good sign, but if she calls me, that would be a flag."

"I like feedback later in a relationship that her interest is growing," Mark said. "But not at the beginning of a relationship."

Can guys and girls just be friends? "How can the sexual element not come into it?" David asked as the guys nodded their heads. "The sexual point always crosses your mind, but after you think about it and decide there will never be a dating relationship, you can become friends." "I have friends who are girls, but there is always that element of 'I wonder if . . . ,'" Jeff said.

The guys said they all casually ask their girl friends to "hang out" with them on a non-dating level. "Either you decide or she decides you will never date," Shawn continued. "And then you can develop a relationship based on just being friends."

What is the purpose of dating? "To see if she's the person I would like to marry," Shawn told us candidly. "I don't assume that every woman I date is the woman I'm going to marry," Jeff said. "But I like dating because you get to know somebody on a different level. You get to develop a deeper friendship."

The guys agreed that if a girl isn't interested in a dating relationship, they would prefer she would say no to a date than go out with them. While hearing no is never easy, they would rather have her be honest than make excuses.

"I always assume a woman will say no when I ask her for a date," David said. "I don't want to set myself up for a fall, so if she says no, life isn't over."

Do you really want a woman to be honest with you? "I want her to say what she really feels instead of me having to drag it out," David started. "I don't want her to expect me to read her mind."

"I want her to tell me what she's thinking straight up," Jeff said. "I want her to be up-front with me. For example, if she isn't interested, I hope she will just tell me that. And I don't want to hear the 'I just want to be friends' line unless she really means it."

"Some women feel compelled to tell you about their every thought and emotion," Mark told us. "I want her to be entirely honest when we have an important discussion, but I don't need to constantly know everything she is thinking."

What is a "high maintenance" woman? "Someone who is

emotionally dependent," Jeff started. "She is externally focused on social and material things," Mark said. "She is competitive with everyone, even her friends." "She lacks confidence in herself," Shawn added.

What does a self-confident woman look like? "She carries herself well," Shawn continued. "She's assertive but not overbearing." "She's confident enough in herself that she can affirm others," David said. "When we have a conversation, she looks at me without being distracted by other stuff." "She has great communication skills," Mark added. "And she is comfortable with who she is."

Do you want to get married? "Yes, but honestly, it scares me to death—I want to be able to be myself in marriage," Keith said. "Yes," David agreed, "to be complete. I think there's a part of life I haven't seen, and marriage will open up a whole new world of living."

"Yes, I really want to share myself with someone who knows me," Jeff said. Shawn continued, "There's a part of me that wants to be married. I would also love to have kids someday." "I'd like to get married too," Keith said. "I enjoy experiences more when I can share them with somebody. The more you get to share, the more your capacity for enjoying life grows."

If you could tell single women one thing, what would you tell them? "Catch me while you can!" Jeff said as the guys laughed. Then they added: "Be real and open." "Be honest." "Have a close relationship with God." "Determine which opportunities in life you want to pursue, and then pursue them." "I would encourage you to be women of purpose and goals," David said. "Be intentional in what you want to do."

The men we interviewed were godly and successful and

interested in single women. It encouraged us to see how they were each seeking God about their dating relationships. And it was also encouraging to know there are quality Christian men who are available—at least we found quite a crew in Colorado Springs!

 COFFEE TALK

1. What is your ideal guy/girl relationship?
2. What do you love about the dating process? What do you hate about it?
3. What are you looking for in a man? How does it compare to what these men are looking for in a woman?
4. How does every man's different idea of attractiveness change your perspective?
5. What are you doing to safeguard your relationships?
6. Are you doing anything specific in your life to become a more insightful woman? What?

- Two -

THE SECURE WOMAN
Waiting for a Godly Man

TRUST IN THE LORD WITH ALL YOUR HEART AND LEAN NOT ON YOUR
OWN UNDERSTANDING; IN ALL YOUR WAYS ACKNOWLEDGE HIM,
AND HE WILL MAKE YOUR PATHS STRAIGHT.
PROVERBS 3:5–6

It was supposed to be the best date of my life! For weeks I (Melanie) prepared: buying a pink formal, exercising, restyling my hair. My senior prom would be the highlight of my high school years. My date, Darren, surprised me by getting us a limousine, and I felt like a princess when our car arrived. He wore a tux with a tie and cummerbund that matched my dress and brought me a beautiful rose corsage. We looked as though we were ready for Cinderella's ball.

We ate dinner at an exquisite country club, and the first few hours were magical. But as our evening progressed, things didn't turn out exactly as I planned.

The problem? Darren liked my best friend! And to make matters worse, we were double-dating with her. As the night progressed, his attention slowly turned toward Sonya. I could see it happening but tried to ignore the obvious so I could continue to enjoy what was supposed to be the most perfect night of my life. At our last stop, however, it was hard to continue denying the attraction between my date and my best friend. I went inside to use the bathroom at our friend's home, and when I came out, I saw our car driving off. Not a good boost of self-esteem for a high school senior! Thankfully, I was able to get a ride home, but my prom date came to an abrupt end before dawn.

While the anticipation of dating and often the date itself can be fantastic, dating can also be a boring ritual or a confidence buster. All of us have had both good and bad dates. With information we've garnered from our own experiences and those of our single friends, we hope to help you enjoy the highs of dating relationships, avoid the horrible lows, and become a secure woman in spite of who you are or are not dating.

IN SEARCH OF . . .

Many of us want to date, but it's not so easy to find a guy whose company you actually like. "How can I find a good guy?" one of my girlfriends exclaimed in frustration. "How do I really know that he cares about me?" Great question! Isn't that what we all want? An incredible man who loves us for who we are. But how can we find him?

When Tosha and I asked single Christian women what they were looking for in a man, their dreams matched and exceeded what we could recommend: integrity, character, honesty, responsibility, humor, and a genuine relationship with God. While in college, I made a list of qualities I was looking for in a future husband, and I've been praying for these qualities ever since. My prayer list includes: spiritual leader, fun-loving, respectful, trustworthy, a good listener, enjoys outdoors, and likes to travel. These things are important to me.

What is important to you? What do you want in a date and in a husband? Do you want a man who's charming or responsible or funny or analytical? Whatever it is, we recommend that you write it down. Then, next time you get swept off your feet, pull out your list of important qualities and compare the man you are currently dating with the man you want to date. And what an incredible feeling when the man you like matches what you are looking for!

By wisely observing a date, you can discover if he is the kind of man you want to date long term. Ask yourself some simple questions: What is his focus? Is he more concerned about himself or about you? Does he listen to you or does he do most of the talking? Does he ask you specific questions about your life? If he is not interested in what you say or think, this is a warning sign that he is more interested in himself.

Does he remember what is important to you? Is he considerate of your time and interests, or does he want you to be at his beck and call? How does he treat other people—his parents, his friends, and the waitress at the restaurant? Is his walk with God sincere? Do his actions match his words? By actively watching, you can tell if he is the kind of person you want to spend your time dating.

Chuck Snyder, author of *Men: Some Assembly Required,* told me that by the third month of dating someone you will know whether he is the kind of guy you want to be with. He said that by this time guys will begin letting down their guard and their true colors will show. However, by asking yourself the right questions, you can often tell well before three months if he's a godly man with high standards and full of character.

Are there any quality Christian single men left in this world to date? We've heard women moan and despair over the years that these men don't exist. Be encouraged! There are godly, quality men who are not married. We've attended the weddings of many of these women who complained about the lack of quality single men. In God's perfect timing, He brought men of character into their lives.

I THINK IT'S HIM! (NOW WHAT DO I DO?)

You meet an attractive Christian guy who seems to have good character, a good job, and actually lives on his own. He loves to water ski (your favorite sport), play piano (your favorite instrument), and cook lasagna (your favorite food). He dreams of building a lake house and having a family. This is your man! You know the two of you will be perfect together. Now what do you do?

Our answer: practically nothing. If he is a successful, attractive guy, chances are that women are swooning around him for his attention. While these women flatter a guy, they do not tend to attract him. The kind of guy you want is an initiator. You want him to call to see if you are busy that weekend, instead of you calling him to see if he wants to go out on a "group activity." You want him to think you are the most amazing woman in the whole world, not just one of the many he could date. Is that your dream? To have a wonderful man think you are wonderful? It's possible!

While we certainly don't condone the physical relationship of Rose and Jack in the movie *Titanic,* Rose was a good example of a woman who was willing to be pursued. Jack picked her out of all the passengers and decided he liked her. He thought she was an incredible woman, and he worked hard to get her. The movie ended tragically, but Jack still told Rose he wouldn't have missed that voyage for anything. For him, it was as precious as life itself to have pursued Rose—and caught her attention! What a good reminder for single women: when a man is really interested in you, he will be the one to make the effort to be near you. You don't have to chase him.

BUT SHOULDN'T I DO SOMETHING?

No matter how hard we try, we can't make anyone, especially a man, like us. However, there are a few things we can do to attract our dream guy.

Look Your Best

The truth is, most guys, Christian or not, are initially attracted to a woman because of her physical appearance. We cringe and say, "That's not fair! He should like me for who I am on the inside!" True, he should. The fact remains, though, that while a woman finds herself attracted to the man she falls in love with, a man falls in love with the woman he is attracted to. We don't recommend spending hours in front of a mirror and becoming a woman who is only concerned about appearance. However, because initial attraction is important for a man, we do suggest that you exercise, eat healthy, dress attractively, and take care to look your best.

Queen Esther was a beautiful woman. In spite of her natural beauty, Esther still spent a year being pampered before she went before the king. Esther 2:12, 17 says, "Before a girl's turn came to go in to King Xerxes, she had to complete twelve months of beauty treatments prescribed for the women, six months with oil of myrrh and six with perfumes and cosmetics. . . . Now the king was attracted to Esther more than to any of the other women, and she won his favor and approval more than any of the other virgins. So he set a royal crown on her head and made her queen."

Take care of your appearance so that you'll become royalty in your man's eyes.

Be Confident

Do you like who you are? Are you confident in your beliefs, opinions, and ideas? Watch out! Guys love being around women who know what they want out of life. Don't be afraid to share your opinion with the man you are dating. If he likes you, he will truly enjoy listening to your ideas. But also keep in mind that sharing your thoughts doesn't mean you have to spell out your entire belief system on the first date or voice your strong opinion on every topic. This can overwhelm a man you've just met. But always be prepared to graciously share your opinion and answer questions articulately without squirming in fear that he may not agree with you.

Another part of confidence is being secure in yourself so that you can rejoice when the man in your life succeeds and encourage him when he is going through tough times. While men often appear to be ultraconfident, they crave the support of a woman who believes in them. Help the man you are dating succeed at his dreams. Encourage his success and cheer on his goals. Be a secure woman who can encourage and support those around you to do their very best.

Seek God

What is your priority? Is it finding a man who will love you or working on developing a closer relationship with God who loves you more than any man ever could? A man who loves God will be seeking a godly woman with the same desires. A godly man will be attracted to your search to know God through daily life experiences.

Seek God with all of your heart. Search your Bible for answers to your questions and learn to talk to God about what is happening in your life. "Pray without ceasing" (1 Thes. 5:17 NASB) by continually communicating with God. What an incredible privilege to be in a first-person relationship with the almighty God!

As a result of your relationship with God, you portray attractive qualities that a godly man will be seeking. "The fruit of the Spirit is love, joy, peace, patience, kindness, goodness, faithfulness, gentleness and self-control" (Gal. 5:22-23). Strive to be kind, joyful, patient, and gentle in all of your relationships, including your dating relationships. A godly man will respect and honor and cherish a woman who displays these characteristics.

Be Independent

Dependent women are sometimes initially attractive to a man because he feels like he is meeting a need in his girlfriend's life. However, extreme dependency soon wears thin and exhausts a man who doesn't understand why the woman he's dating can't think or act without his direction. Independence is a characteristic that quality men find intriguing. *What is she thinking? Why doesn't she "need" me? Does she or doesn't she like me?* he'll ponder. The mystery begins.

By saying *independence,* we are not implying that a woman should insist on paying for her own meals or opening her doors. But clinging to a man to boost your self-esteem or expecting him to meet all your needs is the foundation for an unhealthy relationship. As your relationship grows, you should begin a slow process of mutual dependency. This is a privilege that should be guarded and respected. But by maintaining your own opinions, dreams, and ideas, you will create an exciting relationship that you both will enjoy.

Be Involved

What do you love to do? Do you enjoy snow skiing or back-packing or teaching Sunday School? Do you like to write or sing or play the guitar? Whatever you enjoy, we encourage you to become involved. We've had single women tell us they are putting their lives on hold until they meet their future husband. They don't want anything to interfere with what could happen in the future, so they sit at home week after week and just wait. Life is too short to wait when you don't know what month or year—or if—you will be getting married. Pursue what interests you, and when you meet your future mate, he will be extremely attracted to the fact that you are involved with activities and ministry that you enjoy.

Just as a guy who is sitting at home waiting for a woman to come to him isn't attractive, neither is a woman doing the same thing. One of my favorite movie lines is in the film *Little Women*, when Marmee tells her daughters, "There is nothing more intriguing to a man than the sight of a woman enjoying herself." We agree! Become intriguing by becoming involved. If you enjoy life, others will enjoy being with you.

SHOULD I REALLY PRAY ABOUT MR. RIGHT?

Do you ever feel guilty when you talk to God about dating? Does it seem as if He has so many major projects that He couldn't possibly be concerned about Mr. Right asking you out? We've felt that way too. The fact is, though, He wants to be involved in every aspect of our lives. As single women, dating is one of the biggest aspects. The Bible talks about God knowing how many strands of hair we have on our head (and for those of us who shed hourly, this is quite a task!). He wants to be a part of even

TREASURE CHEST

You like a guy a lot! I mean a lot a lot. You've told a few girl-friends, but you've been smart and not told too many people, because you don't want him to hear something through the notorious grapevine. You are trying to guard your heart, but your heart seems to be bursting with things you want to say to him. Emotionally you are turned upside down. You know you shouldn't pursue him, but what do you do?

We suggest that you start a simple treasure chest. This can be a white envelope spray-painted in glitter, a small velvet box, or a uniquely designed case. It should be buried away from curi-ous guests' eyes or unwanted discovery so it's just between you and God.

In your treasure chest, you can write personal notes to the man you are interested in, telling him your feelings. Or you can write notes to yourself about certain things he did or char-acter qualities you admire in him. To make it personal, you might write your notes in gold ink on linen paper. You may design a beautiful paper for your notes or put them on sta-tionary. Whatever is special to you.

The key is to put your feelings on the paper and not tell them to a man who has not yet developed an interest in you. This will give you freedom, as well as help you remember your feelings later, if and when you have a relationship with him.

Once you write down your treasures, put them in the box and leave them there. Don't read them over and over or dwell on your love letters; in essence hide them as you would jewels in a treasure chest, only to dig them out at the perfect time. If the man you are enamored with someday becomes your husband, what a special moment it will be when you present him with the notes in your treasure chest. If this man is not your future husband, you have saved yourself the embarrassment of drowning him with your feelings only to have him reject your heart's pleas. Your feelings are safe in your treasure chest on an emotional island. You can dig up the chest when the time is right, and at that time, it will truly be a treasure.

the most intimate details of our life.

Instead of feeling guilty about praying for or about a certain guy, we recommend that you pray overtime about this. And if you really like him, don't stop praying. God loves His daughters and wants to protect us from danger and heartbreak. If we are serving Him, He also wants the best for our lives. As I look back on my life, I am so incredibly thankful that God protected me from marrying some of the men I've dated. At the time, they were handsome, charming, and fun, but ten years later they are not leading godly lives. Some of them are divorced. Some are not so handsome or charming anymore because they have chosen alcohol and drugs as their life staples. Only God knows what is going to happen. Be willing to surrender your ideas, and trust God for His best.

Sometimes our hearts tell us one thing while our heads tell us another. Tosha told me once that I needed to pray about a certain man in my life. My heart was giving me all sorts of gushy feelings about him while my head was flashing red and yellow warning signs. As I started praying for direction, God slowly took those feelings away, and I am grateful He did. I could finally see 20/20 instead of being hindered by my blurry feelings and desires. Tell God what you want, but also ask Him for wisdom and direction. Sometimes what we want isn't always best for us. Trust in His answer.

 ## COFFEE TALK

1. What qualities are you looking for in a man?
2. What qualities are you trying to improve in your life?
3. What can you do to become more secure as the woman God made you?

RESOURCES

Elliot, Elisabeth. *Passion and Purity: Learning to Bring Your Love Life under Christ's Control.* Grand Rapids: Fleming H. Revell Co., 1984.

Jones, Debby, and Jackie Kendall. *Lady in Waiting.* Shippensburg, PA: Treasure House, 1995.

- *Three* -

THE WISE WOMAN
Solving the Mysteries of Dating

CHOOSE MY INSTRUCTION INSTEAD OF SILVER, KNOWLEDGE RATHER
THAN CHOICE GOLD, FOR WISDOM IS MORE PRECIOUS THAN RUBIES,
AND NOTHING YOU DESIRE CAN COMPARE WITH HER.
PROVERBS 8:10–11

What is "cool" (or not) in a dating relationship? Do you pay for your dinner? What do you talk about? What kind of gift do you get a guy you're dating? What if you've only been dating a month? When is it okay to invite him to dinner? Should you give him a call?

We don't claim to have the perfect answers for common dating questions, but we've compiled suggestions from both men and women we know. Combined with our own experiences, we hope to provide some helpful tips on dating etiquette.

SHOULD I PAY MY OWN WAY?
An attractive guy asked Melissa to go to dinner with him while she was in his city on business. It was a busy work week, but they agreed on a time when she could break away for the evening to eat, and get to know each other. She was so looking forward to the date that she bought a new outfit and spent way too much time getting ready. He took her to a beautiful seafood restaurant on the water, and they talked for several hours. As the evening progressed, they found they had more and more in common. Melissa was beginning to think that this guy had potential! That is, until the bill came.

He took one look at the dinner bill, and then passed it to Melissa. Because he had asked her out, she thought he would be paying for it, but he obviously had other ideas. She handed him her credit card, not sure if he expected her to pay for both meals. He tucked his credit card in with hers and they split the cost for their seafood dinners.

Melissa was thankful she had brought her credit card, but the respect she had for this man plummeted. It was their first and last date. And the ongoing question still remains: should a guy pay for the date?

Our answer is definitely yes. If a man asks you to go to dinner or a movie or to any event, he should pay for you. Unless you've been dating for a while and you've decided to treat him, a man who respects you won't put you in the awkward situation of paying for your own meal or ticket.

Our suggestion is that you give him the opportunity to pay, but be prepared in case he winks at you over dessert and then says you owe him $10.59. If the latter happens, he probably isn't the kind of guy who will treat you like a princess.

HELP! IT'S CHRISTMAS!

Buying gifts for men can be agonizing, especially if you've only dated for several weeks or months. We've known girls who have bought extravagant gifts for guys they've only known for several weeks. Instead of bringing the men closer because of the great gifts, these guys felt pressure and ran for their lives. So don't purchase an expensive sweater, jewelry, or a new computer for a guy you're dating casually. Not only will he not know how to respond, but he will know you are extremely interested and any mystery you are trying to maintain will have disappeared. Your motives have been put on banners and flown along the beach for the world to see. So be cautious about the gifts you give. If he is a special person in your life, do give him something small during the holiday season. Just don't overwhelm him with extravagance.

What if it's Christmas and you've just started dating or you're dating casually? Some gift ideas include a subscription to a magazine on one of his hobbies, a baseball cap, a mug with candy, a book, a Swiss Army knife, or a CD of his favorite artist. If you absolutely cannot think of anything appropriate to give him, at least find a nonthreatening Christmas card. The Christmas before we started dating, I (Tosha) gave Kelly (now my husband) a simple card that read, "Enjoy your holiday with your family. With joy, Tosha." Months later I learned that Kelly kept that card on his dresser until he finally asked me out!

What if it's his birthday? You've only been dating twenty-one days, but you know he's interested in you, and you are certainly interested in him. Here are some ideas: wrap some of your famous chocolate chip cookies in a decorated box with a card, make him dinner with a homemade birthday cake, or take him a balloon and a card. If you spend too much money on his birthday, a quality man will feel an obligation to buy you an equally nice present. Make him feel appreciated, not obligated. Let him know he is special without overwhelming him.

After you've been dating awhile, then you can purchase a more elaborate gift for your man. However, a well-thought out, nonthreatening gift is perfect in a new relationship.

BUT HE HASN'T CALLED

We've talked to guys who are outgoing and guys who are shy, guys who know what they want in life and guys who are laid back. We've talked to guys with all sorts of personalities and goals in life, and almost unanimously they've told us two things: (1) they will pursue a woman if they are interested enough, and (2) they aren't interested in women who call them and ask them out.

Of course, several of these men told us they like it when a woman asks them out, but the women they date seriously are the ones they pursued. When a male friend tells you he likes to be asked out, watch his life and see which woman he is more likely to date long term—the one who chased him or the one he had to put in the effort to pursue. Actions do speak louder than words.

If a man you like hasn't called you, he probably is not interested. Ouch, I know. I've (Melanie) had it happen over and over again in my life. A guy asks me out, we go out, I have a blast, but he never calls again. The few times I've made an effort to continue the relationship, it's ended in disaster. Why? Because he wasn't interested, and he felt pressure when I tried to become his "friend." Our recommendation—let him go! You don't want to be with someone who isn't crazy about you; and if he hasn't made the effort to call you, then he may not be a bad guy, he's just not the man for you.

Wait for the best! Keep hoping and praying and waiting for a man who can't wait to be with you. Who loves you so much he wants to call you every day to see how you are. Don't push for something that isn't there. No matter how much effort you exert, you can't make him like you. Spend your time being productive in school work, activities, and ministry, not calling men who aren't interested.

TIME FOR FUN

What if he is interested in you? He calls three or four times a week, and he asks you out almost every weekend. And the best part is that you like him too!

While we don't recommend asking him on a date at the beginning of a relationship, the single men we've talked to have all said they love spontaneity and surprises after they've dated a woman for a while. What are some fun ideas for a surprise?

One time a guy I was seriously dating had to work late. I told him I would bring him some dinner, since he didn't have time to go out. Instead of stopping for fast food, I wanted to make his hectic evening special. I made him sandwiches, a fun dessert, and brought flavored sparkling water. We set up our dinner on a dishcloth-turned-table-cloth, and we dined by candlelight on the floor of his office.

Another time, as a poor college student, I heated bread sticks and pizza sauce for my boyfriend, and we ate a late snack on a campus hill, under a beautiful starlit sky. Spontaneity doesn't have to be expensive. It just has to be creative! What are some fun date ideas? Here are a few we've compiled. We're sure you can think of many more.

• Send him a formal invitation requesting his presence at a certain time and place. Surprise him with his favorite meal served by candlelight.

• Have him set aside a Sunday afternoon and then head to a favorite park or mountain hideaway for a picnic lunch.

• Make pizza and popcorn and watch football with him on a Monday night when his favorite team plays (even if you're not a football fan!).

• Take him on a drive into the mountains or along a country

road, and treat him to a meal in a quaint country restaurant.

• Take him to the zoo on a Saturday afternoon (with animal crackers tucked away for a snack).

• Have a theme night. Rent a movie filmed in Mexico and make a Mexican meal. If you have time and want to be creative, get a piñata, a sombrero, or colorful streamers to add to your decor.

Notice how the majority of these ideas include a meal. While you may enjoy the finer entrees in life, if he's a meat and potatoes kind of guy, make sure your surprises are filled with his kind of food. As our mothers said, "The way to a man's heart is through his stomach." Maybe, maybe not, but we've found that most men do indeed like to eat.

NOW WHAT DO I SAY?

"He's so cute!" I told my coworker Janet about a guy who worked downstairs in my office. Every time I had to run downstairs for a project, he would grin at me, and I thought he was quite handsome. As the days progressed, I found myself "having" to run more and more errands to the bottom floor. Janet became amused at my new role as errand girl, and she called downstairs to a friend of hers, and the two of them conspired to set us up. Before I knew it, I had a call from Todd asking me to go to dinner. Yes! He didn't say a lot when he called, but I knew he had to be nervous, and I overlooked any kind of problems as I anticipated our date.

Well, I quickly realized the problem wasn't that Todd was nervous, but that he refused to talk! He picked me up around six, and we headed to a local Italian place. During the ride, Todd didn't say a word. When I get nervous, my tendency is to talk way too much! I started asking as many questions as I could to get him to speak about anything. I knew it was getting bad when I started talking about his high school activities before we even got to the restaurant. He responded to each of my questions with a yes or no or a one-word answer. I tried to tell an amusing story or comment between each question, but no matter what I said or asked, he refused to start a conversation.

Dinner was a combination of my telling stories or us both looking out into space. I was on edge by the end of the meal, since I had run out of things to talk about. We walked around the nearest mall in silence after dinner, and then he took me home. My roommates were appalled that I was home before nine on a Saturday night. Todd was a nice, good-looking, Christian guy, but I felt sorry for him that he had never learned the art of conversation. A fun date is relaxed, one where you can talk and get to know each other. How do you do that? Here are some of our tips.

What Do You Think About . . . ?

No one wants to be around a person who talks about herself or himself the entire evening. An interesting person is genuinely interested in the people around her. So, ask him questions on topics that he enjoys. A great conversation is much like a compelling tennis game. One person asks a question, and the ball is smoothly hit to the other side. The other player responds to the question with a story or anecdote, and then the tennis ball heads back as she either asks another question or gives him the opportunity to tell a story of his own. Back and forth the stories and questions go, and you have a conversation the players enjoy because they are both sharing and listening.

Be a casual conversation starter. It's a lot like writing; sometimes all you need is a first sentence and the rest of the words flow. On a date, sometimes you just need to start talking and the conversation will flow. Ask him about his job (Why did you decide to become an attorney?), his hometown (I've heard the seafood is incredible in Boston—what is your favorite place to eat?), where he went to school (Did you learn to surf in Florida?), or about the latest in news (Who do you think will win the Oscar?). Listen to his answer, and then tell another story that relates or ask another question. The beauty of conversation is that it's not cut and dried. You can be creative and tell different stories. If the topic runs dry, then ask a new question on a different topic. If he's a good communicator, several questions are all that will be needed for a whole evening of fun conversation.

State Your Name, Rank, and Serial Number

A balanced woman will be able to ask several questions to begin a conversation without overwhelming her date. As I said, when I get nervous, I tend to ask my date a lot of questions. After a while he is exhausted because he's had to think of so many answers, and I'm exhausted from thinking up question after question. While it is important to be able to ask great conversation starters, remember that this is a date, not a job interview. If he isn't making an effort to ask you questions as well, it would be wise for you to stop trying so hard and give him the opportunity to lead the conversation. This may mean several minutes—that will seem like eons—of silence. That's okay! Look at silence as the chance for him to get to know you. This is where I faltered with Todd. I attempted to lead the entire evening with question after question and was tired of thinking when the date ended. If you give him the opportunity to ask some of the questions, you will have the opportunity to get to know each other.

How Could You Possibly Think That?

So you ask a question, and you find out his political views are the antithesis of yours. Or you can't stand his choice of music, furniture, favorite sports team, or house pet. Out of respect for someone you've just met, we recommend that you tell him your opinion without criticizing his. Just as we are diplomatic to girlfriends we have just met, so we should be the same with our dates. Someone who is a good listener can hear other views without compromising her own. Don't feel obligated to tell him everything you think and feel on the first date.

After you have dated for a while, heated debates will probably arise. By this time, though, he respects you enough that he probably won't dash for the door when you state your opinion more emphatically. No matter how long we have been dating, however, we must learn to respect each other even when we disagree. We can learn to state what we think without demeaning what he thinks. Of course, if you differ on major beliefs or opinions, you should consider waiting for someone else. If this is a man you want to spend the rest of your life with, conflict on issues that are important to you will only expand in the years to come.

But My Psychiatrist Says . . .

A first, second, or third date is not the time to unload all of your feelings and emotional trauma on your unsuspecting date. Eventually, if the relationship continues, he will want to know everything about you, good and bad, and it will only make him love you more. But if you tell him all of your problems at the beginning of your relationship, he will run like the wind.

Does this seem unfair? I've been out on first and second dates with men who have felt obligated to tell me all of the problems in their life. I was overwhelmed by the end of the date, feeling as if they were trying to make me like them by feeling sorry for them. We want respect and love, not pity, from a man. Do you want his impression of you after the date to be: "How horrible, all those things she's going through. I hope she is able to find help." Or do you want him thinking, "I'm intrigued! What a fun person to be with. She can see good in even the worst of situations. I want to get to know her more."

We are not saying that you should lie or act like life is perfect. If you are still suffering pain from your parents' divorce, we know that is tough. If he asks you where your parents live, this is a good time to explain they are divorced and live in two separate cities. This is not the time to discuss all the emotional trauma it has caused in your life. Someday, when your relationship forms a strong foundation of love and trust, he will want to know about the pain in your past. Don't scare him off on the first date. Wait awhile until you share the good, bad, and all the ugly in your life.

So, When Do You Want to Get Married?

"Ahhhh," the man goes screaming away when the woman intentionally brings up topics like marriage, kids, or family on the first date. Is this unfair? Right or wrong, it's life. A date should be viewed as a time to get to know somebody on a surface level and then move gradually to a more intimate level. When you go swimming in a lake, generally you start at the shore and work your way slowly into the deeper water. As you get accustomed to the temperature, you begin feeling more comfortable until you forget your hesitations, and you are swimming freely.

Dating is much like this. Topics at the beginning of a relationship should be kept to nonthreatening subjects like your career goals or what your favorite weekend activities are. The fact that you want three kids, a doctor for a husband (your date is a pediatrician), and a house in suburbia should be kept in confidence until much, much later.

What if he brings up marriage on the first date or asks you how many kids you want? Respond honestly and very lightly. "Sure, someday I'd like to get married. Not tomorrow, but I look forward to God's plan." Then change the subject. Don't ask him when he plans to get married. Too much, too soon, even if he brings it up, spells disaster. Getting to know you should take time. And if he is intrigued, he will want to take the time.

A candlelit dinner on a wooden table in Williamsburg. An evening walk on the beach with only the moon and stars to light the way. A night out for pizza or a play at a dinner theater. Whether costly or inexpensive, traditional or creative, dating is a fun and mysterious thing. At times it puts you flying on cloud nine while at other times it plummets you deep below sea level. We hope you enjoy the dating process with few heartbreaks and many fond memories. When you ask God for wisdom and then proceed cautiously with the wisdom He gives, we are convinced that you will enjoy dating, make wonderful guy friends, and eventually meet the man of your dreams.

COFFEE TALK

1. Are you unsuccessfully pursuing men instead of letting men pursue you? What can you do to change this habit?
2. What are some good conversation starter ideas?
3. If you are in a serious dating relationship, what are some unique dates you can plan?

RESOURCES

Fein, Ellen, and Sherrie Schneider. *The Rules*. New York: Warner Books, 1995. Authors' note: While we don't endorse the entire content of this book, we've found its overarching principles to be true.

- *Four* -

THE CHERISHED WOMAN
Breaking Off a Dating Relationship

ABOVE ALL ELSE, GUARD YOUR HEART,
FOR IT IS THE WELLSPRING OF LIFE.
PROVERBS 4:23

The phone rang, and Jessica jumped to grab it before the machine came on. It was Matt on the other line, apologizing for calling her so late. She didn't tell him that she had been waiting for two hours to go on their dinner date. He said he'd be right over, so she wiped the tears from her cheeks and headed to the bathroom to cover her swollen eyes with makeup.

They had been dating for over a year, but their relationship hadn't been much fun the last couple of months. Matt had been so sweet the first three months they were dating. He had brought her flowers, called every night, and taken her out to dinner every week. He had been so attentive, wanting to know everything about her. But now he only called her once or twice a week, and he was often late on their dates after spending his Saturdays with the guys. He said he loved her, but he didn't seem to care anymore.

Jessica thought about the changes in her life over the last year as she got ready for their date. She knew that Matt was a nice guy, but they were very different people. Not only did they have separate values and morals, but he didn't have a relationship with Christ.

Jessica had been a Christian since she was a young girl, but her relationships with Christian men had never panned out. When Matt came along, he seemed strong and kind and fun to be with. And he was also interested in her belief in God. They had many talks about Christianity, but he never wanted to make a commitment. As their dating relationship progressed, he seemed less interested in talking about it anymore.

Jessica battled with the pros and cons of continuing her relationship with him. She liked the security of having a man in her life, but she was in turmoil when Matt was around. Honestly, she didn't even really like spending time with him anymore, but she thought being with him was better than being alone.

The doorbell rang, and Jessica tried to put on a smile for their evening out. Her stomach, though, was in knots as she thought again about whether she should end this relationship. She just wasn't quite ready to say good-bye yet.

WHY SHOULD YOU BREAK UP?

It's hard to end a dating relationship that isn't working. We go back and forth in our minds to justify it. "I hate spending every weekend watching him play baseball, but I want a boyfriend." "He really isn't that bad; he always makes up for yelling at me by bringing me flowers." "I know he's not a Christian, but he's so nice!" "He's only lied a couple of times, mainly to protect me from getting hurt." "I know he loves me, he just doesn't always know how to show it."

If you have to continually justify a dating relationship, it probably isn't a healthy one. But it's so hard when you are dating to see clearly what is right and what is wrong. Having a man in your life is not a good reason to be in a relationship. If you have doubts, it's time to examine the relationship to see if it should continue. You don't want to be so focused on your boyfriend that you miss the plans God has for you.

If the man you are dating doesn't have a relationship with Christ, if you don't have anything in common with him, if he isn't treating you with respect and care, if he's pressuring you to compromise your standards, if he's dishonest, if there isn't any long-term potential, you know the relationship must end. The man you are with for a lifetime should cherish you as a precious gift, and until he comes along, guard the heart God has blessed you with.

Number 1: No Relationship with Christ
The most important and often the hardest reason to break up with a man is if he doesn't have a solid relationship with Jesus Christ. This is very difficult, especially if he has every other wonderful characteristic you've been looking for. But, as Jessica told us, "If you don't find someone who has values and a strong relationship with God, you end up moving away from what you believe. Compromising begins, and eventually you end up being someone you never wanted to become."

Before Jessica met Matt, she was a balanced, godly woman who cherished her relationship with Christ more than anything else in her life. Satan tempted her to sin in areas like jealousy, selfishness, and overspending, but she met every challenge and never strayed from her commitment to God.

When her guard was low, however, a new temptation came into her life, and she developed a relationship with a good-looking man who didn't have any interest in knowing God. "Besides," she thought, "Maybe he'll come to know Christ through our relationship." She had never liked the term "missionary dating," but now she was intimately involved with it. Because she was longing for a man in her life, she ignored the still, small voice speaking to her and fell in love with the wrong guy.

We easily rationalize wrong relationships by amplifying the few positives and ignoring the negatives. These men distract us from our relationships with Christ. Over time, we start spending less time with God and then wonder why we aren't as satisfied with life as we used to be. We know the cause, but we don't want to face it.

Dating a nonbeliever may seem wonderful in the beginning, but as time goes by, the intimacy fades because you don't communicate the same way. Your beliefs and value system are based on biblical principles, but no matter how nice he is, his beliefs and values are different. When you don't have a strong foundation to your relationship, it will shake from the ground up.

2 Corinthians 6:14, 16 says, "Do not be yoked together with unbelievers. For what do righteousness and wickedness have in common? . . . What agreement is there between the temple of God and idols? For we are the temple of the living God." When you become a believer in Christ, you become God's temple, and His gifts, not a man's, are the peace and confidence you should seek. But if you continue to build a relationship with a man who is not a believer, he becomes an idol in your life, and your relationship is contrary to God's will. You are a temple of the living God. An awesome privilege that comes with great responsibility and devotion.

Number 2: No Common Interests
Tom and Megan had been dating for six months when she

began to question their relationship. They met in their church's singles group, and she was flattered when he asked her to go to a hockey game. She didn't like hockey, but she wanted to go out with him.

After several months, Megan realized they didn't have anything in common. He loved sports, dogs, hiking, snow skiing, and country music. She loved theater, cats, shopping, and the symphony. Their conversations were becoming more forced as they tried to think of subjects to discuss. Finally, they agreed to end the relationship. While they were both pursing a relationship with God, they just didn't click. They had different goals in life and were heading in different directions.

In a marriage that lasts forever, you will become frustrated quickly if you don't enjoy each other's interests. Dating is preparation for a lifetime of being with the man you love. If you don't love spending time with him, you are in for a rough marriage.

Dr. Neil Clark Warren, in his book *Finding the Love of Your Life*, discusses the importance of marrying a man who is your friend. He says,

> It's enormously appealing to share life at the deepest levels with someone to whom you are more attracted than anyone else in the world. It is the sense of being in partnership with a person who likes the things you like, thinks the way you think, works as hard to make your marriage succeed as you do, and who, above all else, thoroughly loves you and contributes to your growth and self-esteem. When you find a person like this, your dream of experiencing deep happiness and total fulfillment is well within your grasp.[1]

Are you staying in a dating relationship because you like the attention? Do you continually tell people that "opposites attract"? Are you head over heels for a guy with whom you have nothing in common? Does the thought of spending the rest of your life with him fill you with dread instead of excitement? If so, he is probably having doubts as well, and it may be time to break up.

Number 3: Not Treating You with Respect

Another reason to break up with a man is if he doesn't treat you with respect. If he berates you, demeans you, or takes his anger out on you, run, don't walk, away from this man.

Katie had been looking forward to this Saturday night date for weeks. She and Frank had gone out on several casual dates, but they had never gone out on a "real" date until tonight. He had asked her to go with him to an elegant restaurant and then to a play—her favorite way to spend an evening. As she dressed in her long, velvet gown, visions of romance danced in Katie's head.

Her hopes of romance abruptly disolved, however, the moment Frank arrived to pick her up. Irritated because he was running late, Frank took out his frustration on her. Instead of going to the door, Frank honked his horn until she came down to the car. "This isn't what I pictured," Katie mused as she got in the car. When she sat down, Frank flung a wilted red rose at her, and without another word, they were off on their supposedly romantic date. As Katie looked at her rose, she felt the evening start to wilt like the petals of this flower.

Because they were so late, their dinner reservations had been canceled, and they were forced to eat at a casual diner down the street. Katie felt awkward in her velvet dress, but was even more uncomfortable when Frank spent the entire meal talking about his bad day.

After dinner they finally drove to the theater. Because the parking lot was full, Frank had to parallel park on a side street. Thoughtlessly, he jumped out of the car and headed toward the entrance alone. When he finally realized that Katie wasn't with him, he headed back to the car and found she couldn't get out because bushes lined the curb. Even if she could squeeze out, the car door would get scratched, and her velvet dress would be snagged.

Frank, thoroughly frustrated by this time, told her to crawl over the console and driver's seat. With wounded dignity, Katie followed his directions, but as they walked into the theater, she silently determined this would be not only their first "real" date but also their last.

Have you ever had an experience like Katie's? If so, you can probably look back and laugh at your predicament now. But while you can be amused by an occasional bad date, a lifetime with a disrespectful man who doesn't cherish you can be misery.

The man in your life should be respectful, considerate, and kind. He should display the characteristics of Christ (Gal. 5:22-23), including gentleness, goodness, kindness, and self-control. A godly man will treat you like a precious jewel. In his eyes, you will be the most intriguing and beautiful woman in the world. Of course he may forget to call you occasionally, that's only human, but he should also be so loving and kind that it may make you feel uncomfortable (relish that—don't run away!).

Have you ever seen a woman who is treated so well by her

man that she almost shines? She just can't seem to stop smiling. If you are dating someone who treats you poorly, however, you will never be available when the right man comes along. Our suggestion is to get out! If you let someone walk over you, you have no right to complain about having a miserable relationship.

"Why would someone love me?" single women often think as they battle their own insecurities. "If he was really a catch, he wouldn't be with me." Sometimes we allow ourselves to be treated badly because we don't think we deserve better. How unfortunate! We deceive ourselves and deny ourselves the opportunity to get involved with men who truly care about us. Our self-esteem swoops us so low that we reject the men who want to love us.

If you are in this cycle, you must break free! Get out of a relationship that is dragging you down and making you feel insecure and unloved. Then wait on God to bring you a caring man who will treat you well.

Number 4: Lack of Integrity

Angela had been casually dating Jeff for about two months when she got a phone call from a woman named Teresa who said she was his girlfriend. After talking, Angela realized that Jeff had been taking them out on the same dates, saying the same things, and telling them both he wanted a serious relationship. Fortunately, Angela wasn't in the relationship long enough to become emotionally attached, but Teresa was very much in love with him. They had been dating for about three years, and he had promised her they would be married.

Jeff was out of town when Teresa called Angela. She was supposed to meet him at the airport when he returned, and she did.

As they walked to the baggage claim, she told him about the call from his girlfriend. At first he tried to tell her she was mistaken, but when he realized that she knew the truth, he fumbled for an explanation. Angela told him their relationship was over, and she didn't want to see him again. In spite of his consistent calls and letters over the next year, the relationship was over for her. She couldn't be with a man she didn't trust.

Integrity is one of many qualities you should be searching for in a man. And it is one of the most important. If you can't trust the man you are dating, your relationship will slowly deteriorate. If you stay with him, your feelings of worth will be replaced with insecurity. Questions start forming: "Who's he out with?" "Where is he tonight?" "Why hasn't he called?"

A man of character is an honest man. If he doesn't call, your only concern is that he might be hurt. If he's not with you, you don't have to worry that he's dating someone else behind your back. Proverbs 12:22 says: "The Lord detests lying lips, but he delights in men who are truthful." If God hates lying lips and loves truthful men, shouldn't we do the same? Wait on Him for a man of integrity.

Number 5: Impurity

When Janie met Paul, she thought he was a perfect gentleman. He sent her roses two weeks and then four weeks after their first date and told her constantly that she was the woman for him. He was charming and funny and treated her like she was special at the beginning of their relationship.

Something happened, though, after they had been dating for a month. Paul thought it was time for them to consummate their dating relationship, and he couldn't understand why Janie was "being such a prude." He told her he loved her but then accused her of not loving him because she refused to meet his needs. Janie was on the brink of giving in to the sexual pressure until she realized Paul was more concerned about his needs than her purity. With a broken heart, she had to admit to herself that Paul didn't really love or cherish her.

God has given you the desire to enjoy a sexual relationship with the man you love. However, He has also set up marriage so this incredible love will be a lifelong experience. While you both will probably struggle with your physical relationship before marriage, the man you are dating should love you enough to postpone it until you are married. If your boyfriend is treating you poorly or pressuring you to be physical with him, hold out for a man who loves *you* more than himself. Forever is a very long time to live with someone who makes his desires priority over your well-being.

Number 6: No Long-Term Potential

If you find out that the guy you've been dating has been abusing drugs and dating two other women during your relationship, it will probably be easy to cut the ties with him. But if he's a reasonably nice guy who hasn't done anything to hurt you, it can be difficult to say good-bye.

Shauna had been dating Kurt for more than a year. Whenever her friends asked her about their future, she would tell them that she and Kurt were not serious. She explained that they were just having fun. Kurt, however, had other plans. He was telling his friends that Shauna was the woman he wanted to marry. He wanted to spend the rest of his life committed to her.

When Kurt finally proposed that Christmas, Shauna turned

him down, and he was heartbroken. He had invested a whole year of his life developing a relationship he assumed was headed for marriage. She was just on a yearlong date.

A relationship may not have long-term potential for different reasons. One clear sign that it isn't heading toward marriage is that you don't have common goals and dreams. Maybe he is heading to Los Angeles to pursue his career while you want to stay in your small Vermont town. Or maybe he is determined to have six kids and live in the country while you plan to live in a big city and be a mother of one after you turn thirty. Your future should be discussed in detail prior to making a commitment.

Another sign that a relationship may not be heading for marriage is if there isn't any attraction between you—that little spark of chemistry. Never base a relationship strictly on chemistry, but if it doesn't exist at all, you may be in for a rough honeymoon (not to mention marriage).

After dating a man for several weeks or months, you should know if he's the type of man you'd like to spend the rest of your life with. If he's not, be considerate and end the relationship. The longer you drag it on, the harder and more heartbreaking it will be to end it. Instead of just wanting someone in her life, Shauna should have told Kurt that she wasn't interested in a long-term relationship. If you know he's not the one for you, let him know and then continue to pursue the dreams and goals you've set for yourself as a godly single woman.

HOW DO YOU BREAK UP?

It's been four months, and you know it's just not going to work. Whether you've found out the man you are dating is not a man of character or you just don't enjoy his company, breaking up is a miserable thing. What do you say? Do you let the relationship continue for two more months because you don't know how to tell him? Or do you suddenly not return his phone calls, hoping that he will get the hint and break up with you? Whatever the case, prolonging an inevitable breakup is a miserable experience. You think about it, analyze it, and experience it over and over in your mind until you finally do it.

There are two general breakup scenarios. The first is with a guy who treats you poorly, and the second is with a gentleman whom you know you won't marry.

If the man you are dating demeans or harms you in any way, it is time to get out immediately. No questions asked! This can generally be done over the phone so you don't have to face him in such an uncomfortable situation. If he begs to have you back or tells you he will change, hold fast to your decision. If he's going to change, it's healthier if he does so outside of a dating relationship.

If the man you need to end the relationship with is a nice guy, the situation will be trickier. You don't want to hurt him in any way, because you care about him. I've dated Christian guys who were kind and good to me, but I knew we wouldn't make good partners for life. The last thing I wanted to do was tell the man I was dating the truth. However, I knew if I was not honest with him, we would both be miserable. I would be miserable because I knew he wasn't the right person, and he would be miserable because I wouldn't be putting my all into the relationship and caring about him in the way he deserved.

If you have had questions about your relationship for a long time, he probably has started to realize that something is not right. Choose a time and place to end the relationship where he can quickly be alone to think about what you have said. It is best not to talk to him right before a date or if you have a long car ride ahead of you. Out of consideration for him, make sure he can leave when you are both finished. The "talk" is never a comfortable situation. Please pray for wisdom and the right words.

Be honest and kind as you explain that the relationship is not going to work out. Always be considerate of his feelings and emotions and don't force him to talk if he isn't ready. He probably will need time to digest what you have said. Also the line about "just being friends" may seem like a good option, but he will know that probably doesn't have much possibility for a while. Don't say "let's be friends" unless you really mean it, and don't be offended if he says that he can't do that. Kindness and gentleness are key to not wounding someone for whom you care.

Sharon is in her mid-thirties, and she recently had to end the dating relationship she was in. She said, "It is always good to be straightforward and honest. If you don't have the same feelings or you know your value systems are in huge conflict, just say so. It's better to let the person know the truth without being brutal than continue in a doomed relationship." We wholeheartedly agree.

WHAT IF HE BREAKS UP WITH YOU?

You think he's Mr. Right, and then he abruptly ends your relationship. So many questions may go through your mind: "What's wrong with me? What should I have done differently? How can I get him back? Have I lost my chance?" Whether this is an expected end or comes completely out of the blue, follow several steps when a breakup occurs.

First, stay calm. Whether or not you expect the breakup, this is not the time to cry and tell him how horrible he is. Take a deep breath and tell him you will miss him, but you are going to be okay. Your whole body may feel as though it's about to explode. You may feel anguish and pain seething out of your pores. Don't tell him this! This is the time to let him go.

In *Love Must Be Tough,* Dr. James Dobson says that almost every relationship that is headed for marriage will experience one breakup. He says it is key for the surprised person to remain calm.

> Relationships are constantly being 'tested' by cautious lovers who like to nibble at the bait before swallowing the hook. This testing procedure takes many forms, but it usually involves pulling backward from the other person to see what will happen. It is incredibly important in these instances to appear poised, secure and equally independent. Do not grasp the other person and beg for mercy. Some people remain single throughout life because they cannot resist the temptation to grovel when the test occurs.[2]

Susan had watched Ken from afar on their campus for over a year. She respected his views and relationship with God, and her heart's desire was to get to know him on a deeper level. Finally, one day he noticed her and called to ask her out on a date. She was elated! She had waited so long for this.

They went out to dinner and spent three hours talking. The more she learned about him, the more she wanted to know. She thought the evening couldn't be more perfect, but when he dropped her off, he explained that this one date was the end of their dating relationship. Her emotions plummeted. Susan smiled and calmly said good-bye, but the instant she was safely in her dorm, she burst into tears. This was not the way she expected the evening to end! She spent an hour talking to God, telling Him again her desires, and she gave her relationship with Ken to God.

Over the next two weeks, Ken got concerned. He was used to having women call him to try to pursue a relationship, and Susan didn't call. When he saw her on campus, she calmly said "hello" and kept walking. The truth was that he had an amazing evening with Susan, and it scared him. He wasn't quite sure what to do with his feelings, so he quickly put an end to the relationship before it really started.

A little over two weeks after they said good-bye, Ken called Susan and asked her out again. Over the next two years, he pursued a relationship with her, and she enjoyed being with the man of her dreams. After getting to know her, Ken realized that Susan wasn't just the kind of woman he wanted to date, but she was also the woman he wanted to marry.

If the man you love breaks up with you, let him go. A breakup may be a temporary time of questioning or a permanent end to a relationship. Calling, crying, or pleading won't make him return.

If he doesn't come back, the second step is to ask God to take him out of your heart. If he isn't the man for you, God will do this. Ephesians 3:20 says, "Now to him who is able to do immeasurably more than all we ask or imagine, according to his power that is at work within us." God can do more than we can even imagine—including opening up our eyes when we are involved in a destructive dating relationship and mending our hearts if the man we love breaks up with us.

"It was amazing," Marcy told us. "I was having such a hard time recovering from a broken relationship, and I finally went to God with my anguish. Instead of restoring the relationship, God changed my heart. The desperate longing is gone." Be honest with God. If you don't want to end the relationship, tell Him that, but then sincerely ask that His will be done.

The third step is get involved. Choose a new hobby or pursue an interest that has gone by the wayside since you have been dating. Ask God for a fresh perspective on life. You may have forgotten how much fun it is to plan a tea for friends, hike to the back country, or write a new song. You may want to go back to school or travel to a different country. While this is not a time to run away from your problems, it is the time to refresh yourself and get excited about the life God has given you.

The fourth step is to serve and minister to others. After a breakup, it is so easy to become inwardly focused and engulfed by your own desires. Instead of ministering to others in need, you feel able to concentrate only on your own needs. In Ephesians 4:22-23, Paul said, "Put off your old self, which is being corrupted by its deceitful desires; . . . put on the new self, created to be like God in true righteousness and holiness." As you seek God, ask Him to give you opportunities to help others who are in greater need than you. Maybe you could minister to others by teaching Sunday School, working at the crisis pregnancy center, inviting a single mother and her kids to your home for dinner, or helping clean your elderly neighbor's apartment. If you volunteer, God will open up ways for you to serve.

The last step is to find a girlfriend you can be accountable to. The days you are tempted to call your ex-boyfriend just to ask how he is, call your friend instead. When you don't understand why you are in this situation, have your friend pray with you for wisdom and peace. When you need encouragement and support, ask your friend for help. And then be willing to be this kind of friend when someone close to you faces a breakup as well.

HOW DO YOU RECOVER FROM A ROUGH BREAK UP?

Brent and Leslie had been dating for almost a year when he called her to say he didn't want to see her anymore. She had been contemplating marriage, but he had obviously been contemplating other things. Her heart felt like it had been ripped out and stomped on. She replayed their times together over and over, trying to figure out what she could have done differently. She thought about all the ways she could try to get him back, but two weeks later she found out he was dating one of her best friends. Brent had been the center of her life for so long that the shock of losing him plummeted her into depression.

When the man you care for deeply tells you he doesn't want to be with you anymore, it is easy to slip into depression. You think about life without him, and the future looks miserable. It's okay to spend some time mourning the loss of your relationship. If you thought the world of this man, it may momentarily feel as though your world is destroyed.

After Leslie and Brent broke up, she spent hours pouring her thoughts and feelings into her journal. She also spent much time in contemplation and prayer trying to figure out what went wrong and begging God to bring him back. But God didn't bring Brent back. Instead, He used this time in Leslie's life to renew her commitment to Him. The more time she spent in prayer and reading her Bible, the more she realized how much God loved her and valued her like a precious jewel. It didn't matter what Brent thought about her. What mattered was that God thought she was an amazing woman. He designed her as a special creation. He showed her how special she was to Him.

In the third chapter of Philippians, Paul talks about pressing on in his life even though he isn't perfect. Verse 13 says, "But one thing I do: Forgetting what is behind and straining toward what is ahead." The Apostle Paul wasn't referring to the end of a dating relationship when he wrote this, but the principle applies nevertheless. Instead of putting life on hold to concentrate on the past, this is the time to be striving for what is ahead.

Though she's taking things one day at a time, Leslie is beginning to get excited about her future. When the time is right, Leslie looks forward to a relationship with a man who loves her and cherishes her. But she no longer puts her value and self-worth in what men think about her, because now she is more concerned about what God thinks.

When a breakup occurs stay strong and continue with your life. Don't let feelings of worthlessness take over. Having someone break up with you never feels good, but it is so much better than living life in a wrong or difficult relationship. If a man doesn't love you enough to continue dating, it's okay! You are still an amazing woman who is worthy of love and esteem.

The beauty of being a Christlike woman is that God has given you an incredible reason to pursue life. As you think about your loss, crawl into the lap of the Savior and bask in His warmth and comfort. He loves you more than any man ever could. He wants you to live a life of peace and joy instead of anguish and sorrow. Philippians 4:7 says, "And the peace of God, which transcends all understanding, will guard your hearts and your minds in Christ Jesus." Only God can give us that priceless peace during the turmoil of a breakup.

Paul goes on to say in Philippians 4:8, "Whatever is true, whatever is noble, whatever is right, whatever is pure, whatever is lovely, whatever is admirable—if anything is excellent or praiseworthy—think about such things." Instead of concocting schemes to get your boyfriend back, the months after a breakup are the perfect time to concentrate on your relationship with God, your confidence, independence, and involvement. Instead of continuing to mourn your loss, you can also use your time to exercise, be hospitable, travel, relax, and pursue your dreams.

If he has decided the relationship is over, no number of phone calls, phone messages, or car notes will get him back. This is the time to enjoy your singleness. *Carpe diem.* Seize your day!

The weekend after their dinner date, Matt decided he was too busy to see Jessica. She sat at home for the last time waiting for his call. When he finally called late Saturday night, she let him know that she couldn't date him anymore. He begged her to continue the relationship, but now that she had developed enough courage to tell him her feelings, she wasn't going to back down.

Once she had ended their dating relationship, an incredible peace ran through her. She knew she had done the right thing. As the weeks progressed, her time with God became more frequent and meaningful. He filled up the void in her heart and made her whole.

A year later, Jessica met a Christian man named Seth whom she describes as "amazing" and her "gift from God." Because she ended a bad relationship and waited on God, He blessed her with a man who encourages and treats her like a queen. He cherishes her and tells her every day how special she is to him. Instead of crying before her dates, Jessica can't seem to stop smiling. The engagement ring on her finger is only a small symbol of the incredible things God has done in her life.

Are you in a bad dating relationship? Are you at the beginning stages of a relationship that you know isn't right? We encourage you to take an honest look at the man you are with and the relationship you have. If you aren't glorifying God and encouraging each other, it may be time to pursue other interests that will continue to mold you into a Christlike, balanced, and successful woman.

 ## COFFEE TALK

1. If you are in a dating relationship right now, does your boyfriend respect and cherish you as a precious gift from God? If not, do you need to get out of a bad relationship?

2. The Bible has many examples of good and bad relationships. How do the stories of people like King David and Bathsheba (2 Samuel 11–12), Ruth and Boaz (Ruth 2–4), Jacob and Rachel (Gen. 29), Samson and Delilah (Jud. 16), King Solomon and the Shulammite woman (Song of Songs), and Mary and Joseph (Matt. 1) relate to today's dating scenarios?

3. Is your heart broken from a past relationship? What steps can you take to mend your heart, get involved with other activities and ministry opportunities, and pursue the dreams God has given you?

4. What will you do differently the next time you enter into a dating relationship?

RESOURCES

Dobson, James. *Love Must Be Tough*. Nashville: Word Publishing, 1983.

Warren, Neil Clark. *Finding the Love of Your Life*. Colorado Springs, Colo.: Focus on the Family Publishing, 1992.

---

[1] Neil Clark Warren, *Finding the Love of Your Life* (Colorado Springs: Focus on the Family Publishing, 1992), p. 5

[2] James Dobson, *Love Must Be Tough* (Dallas: Word Publishing, 1983), p. 191.

Relationships

The harsh wind blows the tree limbs against the old house and rushes through the broken window by the front door. Dust scatters over the wooden floors of the empty living room. On the cracked kitchen table, a tin cup sits alone with no one left to fill it, and the yellowed paper on the walls slowly peels away.

Rickety stairs lead to an attic filled with treasures from times past. Musty newspapers cover the floor, and a three-legged armchair sits by the dirty dormer window. Fragile letters, a small library of books, an old journal, and a brown teddy bear with one arm lie silent in the cedar chest tucked by the corner. More than ninety years have gone by since anyone cuddled up with one of the leather-bound books and enjoyed wood burning in the fireplace.

If you pick up the dusty journal and carefully open its parchment pages, you can read funny, exciting, and heartbreaking stories about the people who called this place home. You can read about the grand parties they threw at the turn of the century, the busyness of their daily lives, and even about the silly quarrels had by the brothers and sisters running up and down the now cracked staircase. But then you wipe back a tear when you read about the youngest girl's death after *she fell out of a tree. Outside the hazy window, you can see a tall oak tree with a tombstone beside it, and you know that's where her life came to an end.*

After more than sixty pages, the journal suddenly stops, and the lives of these people end for you. While their lives probably went on, you don't know where they headed. Out farther west maybe to mine gold or buy a ranch? Or did they move to a big city to pursue a life of comfort and wealth? The stately house once filled with laughter and parties now holds only traces of its occupants.

A home, you see, is only as grand as its residents. When the family moved away, this house lost the life it once had.

Our lives are much like this house. The relationships we develop with family and friends encourage us, excite us, and make us grow. But when we ignore the importance of healthy relationships, we slowly become dusty and empty inside.

God has given us family and friends, and we should cherish these special gifts. Every time we meet someone, we have the opportunity to learn something new. The people in our lives help us laugh at the funny things and then cry with us when times get rough. And even more important, God has put us in their lives to help them through the ups and downs as well.

The old house isn't completely hopeless. Someone could put new paper on its walls, fix its cracks and leaks, and fill its rooms with people. You can also mend broken relationships from the past and fill your life with new and exciting relationships.

- *Five* -

THE FRIENDLY WOMAN
Becoming a Good Girlfriend

A GIRLFRIEND LOVES AT ALL TIMES,
AND A SISTER IS BORN FOR ADVERSITY.
PROVERBS 17:17, PARAPHRASE

With a suitcase in each hand, I (Melanie) kicked open the door of my dorm room. It had been an eight-hour drive, but finally I was back at school after spring break. Both my roommates were sitting on their beds waiting for me, and I could tell immediately that something was horribly wrong.

"There was an accident over break," Letha told me. I put my bags down and prepared myself for the worst. "Kevin was killed," she said.

"What?" I said in shock. I had just seen him the day I left for break. This couldn't be real. Minutes passed before I could say anything.

"Where's Tracey?" was the next thing out of my mouth. Kevin's fiancée, one of my best friends—where was she? I ran down the hallway and found her on her bed. We held on to each other tightly and sobbed over the loss of her soulmate.

No one ever expects someone she loves dearly to die in a plane crash. Weeks, months, and now even years later the realization that Kevin is dead still hits me. These were the hardest days of Tracey's life; the man she planned to marry was suddenly gone. And with Kevin's death, many of her plans and dreams for the future disappeared.

Because it was the middle of the semester, Tracey decided to finish out her junior year. I still don't know how she was able to do it, but it helped her to keep her mind busy. In spite of her misery and anguished questions, her faith in God gave her the strength to keep living.

Another source of strength was a group of girlfriends she had cultivated since her freshman year. Tracey had always been a real friend, and during this time of crisis, we would do anything to assist her. We helped her sort through Kevin's things, attended his funeral with her six hours away in Kentucky, and supported her emotionally as much as we knew how. During this time of agony, Tracey had friends who stood by her in the most practical ways possible.

WHAT IS A FRIEND?

Over the course of our lives, we will have many girlfriends. Some of them we meet casually through work or school or church. We say hello and stop to talk briefly about the weather or work or common interests. These friends come and go in our lives; some of them we remember on occasion and wonder, "What ever happened to . . ." And some of them drift out of our lives forever.

We also will have those friends whom we have bonded with over coffee or shopping trips or weekend getaways. We can confide in these women and talk about our emotional ups and downs, guys, God, life, the latest movies. They are our buddies, the friends we enjoy spending time with. Even if one of us moves away, we still call occasionally or e-mail just to keep up with life.

And then we have those few friends who know us so

incredibly well that we can tell them almost anything, and we know they will always be there. They don't care if we are happy or angry or depressed or excited about life. They stick with us through breakups, job transfers, PMS, and bad hair days. They may have known us since grade school, or we may have only met them recently and made an instant connection. Friends for life.

Tracey was a true friend to me during college. She was always there when I needed someone to talk to or go to dinner with or just take an evening walk around campus to de-stress after a long day. We met the first day of our freshman year, and after four years of fun dates, pranks, and April Fool's jokes, we graduated together to pursue our careers. In the midst of all of our fun times, we also had to face the horribly painful time of Kevin's death. Tragedy tests whether our friendships are superficial or deep. Tracey found out that she had built strong friendships because her girlfriends didn't flee when she faced crisis.

Do you have girlfriends who stick by your side through both the fun and the rough times? Are you developing strong friendships by being a true friend yourself? It's easy to be a friend when life is going well, and it's easy to jump ship when life turns sour. Are you in it for the long haul? I wish that I could say that all of my friendships have been as solid as the one Tracey and I shared. Unfortunately, I've had friends who have abandoned me during tough times, and I've also gotten so caught up in my selfish needs at times that I haven't been a true friend either.

Having strong friendships is key to living a successful life as a Christian single. Our girlfriends give us support when we need it, laugh at our jokes (even when we screw up the punch line), and cry with us during our emotional lows. They listen and encourage us through the darkest times.

But even as we desire to have close friends, knowing where to find and develop quality friendships sometimes is difficult. We have a lot of acquaintances and casual friends, but we have no one foundational who will be there through the good and bad that life offers. Let's explore how to be a good friend as well as how to find great girlfriends.

WHY HAVE FRIENDS?

Where do you go when life turns sour? Who will stand by your side even when you aren't smiling? Good friends encourage you when you are down, believe in your dreams, open your eyes to new ideas, motivate you to excellence, and stick like glue when you need them most. They don't run when you suffer a crisis or are having a rough day. While guy friends often come and go as they get married and develop other relationships, girlfriends will be there for a lifetime. We asked some of our single girlfriends what they thought was important in a friendship.

Encouragement
"My friend Jeanetta and I have stuck by each other through the joyful and fun times, and through the yucky times," Lisa explained. "Jeanetta has listened to me extensively in times of emotional crisis, even when it's lasted a really long time. Never does she decide I'm not fun enough anymore and move on. Never does she give up on me and cease listening. She is my friend when I'm at my best and when I'm at my worst. Our friendship is not conditional on how pleasant I am to be around or how high maintenance I become. She helps me process my

thoughts and guides me when appropriate. We help each other see our lives more truthfully and objectively, and we know we can count on each other till death do we part."

Proverbs 17:17 says that a "friend loves at all times." "All times" is difficult, especially when life isn't pleasant, but a real friend will be an encouragement no matter what the time or temperature or events in her own life.

Believe in Your Dreams

"Lark was the epitome of what I would like to have been," Jennifer said. "She was a California native, college cheerleader, not afraid to vocalize her opinion, and bound for a successful career. Yet, for some reason, she claimed to look up to me. She helped me to become the person I am today by being honest with me and not allowing me to sell myself short. When I was interested in an internship in D.C., she was all for it. When I considered attending law school, she drove me to the LSAT test. When I was discouraged about my love life, she always took the time to listen, even if she'd heard the same thing over and over again! She showed me over the years that I needed to believe in myself, go for my dreams, and not be afraid to take that first step. She's the best friend that I've ever had, and I believe I'm the person I am today because of the influence she's had on my life."

Instead of seeing what Jennifer saw in her own life, Lark was a visionary who believed in what Jennifer could become. She encouraged her emotionally and practically to pursue the dreams she wanted.

Open Your Eyes

"I was always feminine," Allison told us, "but definitely a tomboy who spurned makeup and girl magazines. At twenty-seven,

I realized that I had no clue about how to do things like put on foundation or relate to men. I was too focused on my band and career, and I didn't see many guys I wanted to date. On a missions trip, I met Angela, and God ordained that we would be friends. She taught me everything I ever wanted to know about hair, makeup, nails, clothing shopping, how to put outfits together, and how to have self-respect with men instead of running after them."

Angela changed Allison's life in a practical and caring way. She spent time teaching Allison how to become the woman she desired to be. If we take the time to listen to our friends, our eyes can be opened to new ideas and opportunities that we never would have known before. Every friendship is a unique experience to learn a little more about ourselves and life.

Motivate You to Excellence

"When I was a freshman in college," Holly told us, "I began a close friendship with a girl named Angie. As our college years progressed, however, we grew apart in extremely different ways. I was content to call it quits, but she was content only to show me by example what a true Christ-controlled personality is. She went out of her way to help me in whatever I happened to need. But, more importantly, she gave of herself, emotions and all, and did all she knew how to help our friendship. She cared enough about me to make the extra effort. Angie doesn't know how much I respect her and look to her example of how to be a friend when it might not be easy, but when it works together for the greater good."

Friends motivate us to excellence in two ways—through their words and through their example. Proverbs 27:17 says: "As iron sharpens iron, so one man sharpens another." Real friends can tell us the truth, even when it hurts, because we know how much they care about us, and they want the best for our life.

Stick Like Glue

"I have a friend," Laura said, "who is going through a rough time and really needs friends around. Because I have been so blessed in my friendships with other women, I have felt that I need to be a special support to this friend, even when I don't feel like it, and it would be easier to 'do my own thing.' This experience has brought me to a new appreciation of the effort it takes to be a good friend, because a lot of times I just don't feel like it! It's so much easier to do for yourself instead of doing for others."

It is hard to be around friends who are heartbroken after a break-up, upset at the loss of a job promotion, or just feeling a bit lonely. However, a true friend will stand by your side—no matter what.

WHERE CAN WE FIND FRIENDS?

Friendships are invaluable gifts. But where do we find these gifts? After college, I worked at a summer camp for three months and then spent several months as a nanny. This was a lonely time in my life. Fresh out of a university where I was surrounded with close friends, I found myself in an environment where I was the only Christian. And because I didn't feel comfortable participating in the activities of my peers, I was very alone.

In my journal from my early twenties, I begged God to fill the empty void in my life: "God—my heart aches. When I slow down and emerge from stacks of books and piles of paper, I'm just me. And I'm lonely. God—please fill that loneliness. You are all I need! You are God of my insecurities and of who I am, and God of who I'm not. I know You want the best for me. Please heal my heart and fill it with love for others. I need to get my eyes off of me and onto You. Catch my gaze, Lord, and keep it on You!"

Before we begin to seek friends, we need to let God seal the gaping holes in our heart. A girlfriend can encourage and support us, but only God can satisfy every emotional need. Once we give Him our emotional needs, we can begin asking Him to fill our need for close friends.

God gave us the deep desire to have relationships, but often we don't ask Him for girlfriends because we think that request is trivial. God, however, is interested in every detail of our lives, and wanting girlfriends is a need He has placed in our hearts. So ask! If you don't have close friendships or even casual friendships, tell God about it. He wants you to talk to Him.

Jesus says, "Ask and it will be given to you; seek and you will find; knock and the door will be opened to you. For everyone who asks receives; [she] who seeks finds; and to [the woman] who knocks, the door will be opened" (Matt. 7:7-8). While Jesus' example wasn't specifically about friends, it is the perfect diagram to follow for actively seeking friendships. For some women, this is a fun and exciting experience; for others, it is difficult because they fear potential rejection.

Unfortunately, singles groups don't always help in finding friends. As I've moved and joined new churches, attempting to break into the tight-knit cliques of some singles groups has been agonizing. Instead of welcoming me to the group, some women have looked at me as uninvited competition. What a horrible thing to experience in a group of Christians! But this attitude is very real among some single women.

Instead of making me part of an in-group, God gave me the opportunity to befriend several other women who were also new to the church. I was able to develop fun friendships of encouragement, support, and play time as we took weekend trips all over the East Coast.

If you don't find friends in your church, seek friendships at work, in your aerobics class, or at your apartment complex. Many other women out there need relationships in their lives as much as you.

After we have asked and sought, it's time to knock. When we go to a party, there is generally certain protocol we must follow to attend. First we get directions to the party, then we find the house, and then we knock on the door to be let in. If we don't knock, there's no sense in asking and finding, because we haven't gone inside the home to enjoy the festivities. Would we sit in the car all evening and watch our friends go in and out of the event? What fun would that be?

It's the same with finding friends. Once we've asked God and sought out friendships, we need to be active in knocking on the doors. As women, we often want to pursue relationships with guys we like. When the urge comes to call that guy, this is a good opportunity to redirect that urge to phone a girlfriend. Be aggressive in pursuing girlfriends! Have a tea party or coordinate a dinner out. If you are adventurous, find girlfriends who like to hike or camp or travel. If you like to shop, call a girlfriend for a day at the mall and an evening at a coffee shop. Or if you just want to talk, call a girlfriend to see how her day was or even send her an encouraging note.

If we spend our lives sitting and waiting for friends to come to us, we may never form friendships. And if you knock on the door and someone doesn't want to open it to your friendship, consider that door locked and move on. Don't let the fear of rejection stop you from finding that wonderful gift of friendship. It really is the best gift you can give yourself!

HOW TO BE A GOOD FRIEND

Once you've begun making friends, it is essential to learn how to be a good one, or you will quickly burn bridges and your friends will disappear. Learn to be a friend for the long haul. The kind of friend you desire is the kind of friend you need to be.

Listen to Your Friends

One of my girlfriends once told me, "The perfect combination is a friend who provides a listening ear, offers godly counsel, and can make you laugh at yourself." Another friend said, "Taking the time to listen to someone's problems, even if you've heard them twenty times before, is the test of a true friendship. I recommend listening when her heart is breaking and only giving advice if she wants to hear it. Sometimes she just needs someone to confide in, even if the answer may be blatantly clear to the other person."

Listening to others is a selfless art that takes time and practice. It's much easier to be concerned about our own lives than take the time to find out what is happening with others. We've noticed that a good listener is rarely without friends. People tend to flock to her, because they know she will be genuinely interested. So, instead of being caught up in what we are saying, we should ask specific questions: "How did it go with your boss today?" "Is your dad feeling better?" "Did you get your dog back?" "Do you miss home?" Let others know how much you care by being genuinely interested in their lives.

Encourage Your Friends

A smile and a hug are sometimes all that are needed to turn around a trying day. Sometimes a card or a quick call or an e-mail can turn an otherwise dismal afternoon into a pleasant one. It's the most amazing thing to have a friend take the time to encourage us. If you know your friend is going to have a rough day, think of a way you can help make it better. If she is sick, it's the perfect opportunity to take her some chicken soup and orange juice. As single women, we sometimes feel loneliest when we are sick or in emotional turmoil. A good friend will reach out to others when they are in need. And often our own loneliness will start to fade as our perspective turns outward to others instead of concentrating on our own difficulties.

Be Honest with Your Friends

"Better is open rebuke than hidden love. Wounds from a friend can be trusted, but an enemy multiplies kisses" (Prov. 27:5-6). Ouch! How can rebuke and wounds possibly be better than love and kisses? Because of honesty. A good friend is honest, one who can speak the truth in love. She is able to let her friends gently know when she sees disaster ahead because of the decisions they are making. Why does she do this? Because she loves her friends and honestly wants the best for them.

Have you ever had a friend who was sugar sweet to you but said horrible things about you when you were away? These are the enemy's kisses. A friend will tell you up-front what she thinks with the intent that her honesty will help you grow to be a godly and balanced woman. She is serious about holding you accountable for your actions when you stray into dangerous territory, because it would break her heart if something bad ever happened to you. If you are getting ready to sing an off-key solo before your peers or heading off to work with a mismatched suit, she will warn you so you don't appear foolish in front of your other friends. She is willing to risk being honest because she wants to see you succeed.

Be There for Your Friends

When my stepsister got married, my stepmom's best friend from childhood showed up at our house and helped my stepmom clean, sew, cook, and stay sane. Even after forty years of friendship, Janice was there when my stepmom, Lyn, needed her most. Janice had a busy life of her own several states away, but she was right there to help her friend with all the practical work of getting ready for a wedding.

Galatians 5:13 says we should "serve one another in love." Has your friend been studying all week for a final? That would be the perfect time to help her with her laundry. Does she need a ride to the airport to go home for a long weekend? What a fun time to talk and help her avoid the long-term parking fees. Is she working late again tonight? Take a quick dinner to her office. It's being there in small ways that add up to a solid friendship.

Pray for Your Friends

I love the practical parts of the Bible that help us in areas like friendship. In Colossians 1:9-12, Paul writes specifically to his friends in Colosse and says:

We have not stopped praying for you and asking

God to fill you with the knowledge of his will through all spiritual wisdom and understanding. And we pray this in order that you may live a life worthy of the Lord and may please him in every way: bearing fruit in every good work, growing in the knowledge of God, being strengthened with all power according to his glorious might so that you may have great endurance and patience, and joyfully giving thanks to the Father.

What an incredible friend Paul was! He was praying that the Colossians would be wise, patient, joyful, and live a life worthy of the Lord. As Christians, we need to pray for specific needs in our friends' lives. We can encourage them by praying that God will strengthen them and give them a joyful and thankful heart. The best friend is one who will encourage and support while asking God for wisdom, strength, and understanding.

Another way we can build friendships through prayer is to get on our knees when our friends go through tough times. Too often, women flee when we experience a misunderstanding or a difficult situation. Instead of running away, this is the perfect time to run to God for guidance and direction.

Have you ever tried to tear a piece of string? If you tug hard enough, the string would probably break. But, if you try to tear braided string, no amount of pulling would rip it apart. Ecclesiastes 4:12 says: "Though one may be overpowered, two can defend themselves. A cord of three strands is not quickly broken." The beauty of having God at the center of our friendships is that He can braid our separate strands together, strengthening us so we can stand strong during the rough times.

HOW TO KILL A FRIENDSHIP

Instead of cherishing and respecting the friends God has given us, we sometimes let our selfishness and expectations get in the way of His gifts. If we become possessive, competitive, a gossiper, or self-centered, we can easily lose the girlfriends whom we love. One of the most heartbreaking experiences in life is to build a friendship over years only to watch it quickly be demolished by your own actions. If you haven't lost a friend, we want to help you avoid the anguish that a broken friendship can cause.

Possessiveness

Possessiveness will quickly end what might otherwise be a healthy friendship. I'll never forget the night that one of my roommate's friends yelled at her for half an hour on the phone because my roommate wanted to spend the evening with her fiancée. Her friend felt neglected, even though they had eaten lunch together that day. She was an extremely possessive and overbearing person who based her self-esteem on whether or not my roommate had time to be with her. After many tears and frustrating moments, my roommate had to set some ground rules for their friendship.

A woman who is possessive usually has a hard time making friends, and when she does, she wants to cling. As a result, she squeezes the life out of her friendships. It is absolutely key that friends respect each other's independence so their friendship can breathe and grow. If not, it will slowly suffocate.

Betraying Trust

Another way to kill a friendship is to exploit someone's confidence. When a secret is shared and the information travels along the grapevine, the friendship will quickly be over. Nothing compares to the honesty, integrity, and loyalty of a close friend, and nothing devastates more when this trust is abused.

In Matthew 7:6, Jesus says, "Do not give dogs what is sacred; do not throw your pearls to pigs. If you do, they may trample them under their feet, and then turn and tear you to pieces." How horrible to be referred to as a pig or a dog! But in essence, that is what a friend becomes when she reveals secrets that are not hers to tell. The information our friends share with us should be regarded as a precious gem and be protected as such.

Competition

When we start looking at our girlfriends as competitors, we have found another way to slowly strangle the life out of our friendships. Whether we are competing for social status, a job promotion, or the attention of a man, we begin ending the friendship. Friends exist to support and encourage each other, not to demean or criticize or compete.

When we face competition in our friendships, it is best to be honest with each other about where we stand. In college I had a dear friend, Ariel, whom I loved and admired. In our junior year, we met a young man who sparked interest in both of us. My admiration for Ariel grew tremendously the day she told me that she was interested in Bradley, but that she would be happy for me if he was interested in me instead of her. Bradley and I broke up a year later and Ariel got married to another wonderful man soon after, but our friendship didn't waver because we took time to be honest with each other. There were no surprises, and that honesty formed a strong foundation of trust for us.

Not Allowing Differences

Jennifer is one of my best friends, even though we are very different. She loves fishing, cooking, and listening to John Denver. I love two-stepping, writing, and exploring ghost towns. How does our friendship work?

Jenn and I have three important things in common. First, we both have a deep love for God and want to learn and grow spiritually. Second, we both love life. We enjoy trying new things and going on adventures. We have traveled to the Smoky Mountains, Myrtle Beach, New Mexico, and Washington, D.C., together for long weekend getaways. The third reason we have remained friends is that we respect each other's independence. Both of us really like our space. On a Friday night, I may call Jenn and ask if she wants to see a movie. It would not be unusual for her to tell me she wants to spend the night by herself. No problem. I don't get offended or upset, because sometimes I want to be alone as well.

We need to recognize and appreciate the differences in our friends. Just because they might not like all of the same things we do or if they want to spend an evening without us, we need to be kind and let them pursue their interests. The instant we become jealous of their time or try to change their hobbies, we are again on the track of losing a friendship.

Having a friend is a privilege, not a right. When we work at becoming a good friend who respects and cares for others, we form lasting friendships that are a blessing from God.

Whether to have fun, encourage, or be a support in a crisis, girlfriends are key to having a balanced and godly life. I thank God for Tosha and Tracey and my other girlfriends who have been with me through both the good and bad. Do you have girlfriends like that? I honestly don't know what I would do without them!

COFFEE TALK

1. What qualities do you admire in your best friends?
2. What is the importance of having close girlfriends?
3. Can you think of a rough situation in your life that girl-friends helped you through?
4. What can you do to become an even better friend?

RESOURCES

Brestin, Dee, *The Friendships of Women,* Colorado Springs: Chariot Victor Publishing, 1988.

Brestin, Dee, *We Are Sisters,* Colorado Springs: Chariot Victor Publishing, 1994.

Carlson, Dolley, *Gifts from the Heart,* Colorado Springs: Chariot Victor Publishing, 1998.

- Six -

THE RELATIONAL WOMAN
Developing Quality Relationships

A WOMAN WHO HAS FRIENDS MUST SHOW HERSELF FRIENDLY.
PROVERBS 18:24A, PARAPHRASE OF KJV

Jamie took another hors d'oeuvre off the colorful banquet table and then quietly sat down again on her folding chair in the corner. For the entire evening, she had been filling her plastic plate with snacks and eyeing her coworkers huddled in groups to swap stories and laugh at each others' jokes. Her eyes went to the clock again, but it had only been ten minutes since her last glance. The lights and confetti around the room sparkled, but Jamie didn't feel dazzled. In fact, the dismal fog of loneliness surrounded her in spite of the hundred smiling people crowded in the room.

While Jamie withered away in the corner, her office partner, Alexis, was making her rounds through the groups of people. She had been talking the last fifteen minutes with their boss, his wife, and their two girls. The children had their arms around Alexis' legs and giggled as she leaned down and captured both of them in her arms. Alexis had been so busy catching up with her coworkers that she didn't have time to eat. As the company's anniversary celebration slowly crawled by for Jamie, it seemed to fly for Alexis. Jamie sighed as she watched Alexis move from group to group and wished she could be like her. Alexis seemed to like everyone, and they flocked to be around her. "Why don't people like me?" Jamie moaned as she took another bite of her cold food.

80

The truth was, her coworkers didn't dislike Jamie. They just thought she didn't like them. Instead of realizing that she might be shy or insecure, they believed that Jamie was incredibly uptight. She never asked them questions or joined in their conversations. She always sat in the corner and acted as if she didn't like to talk to people, mainly because she was intimidated by them. It may have been a fun party for Alexis, but for Jamie it was pure torture.

All of us wrestle with insecurities of varying degrees. We wonder if certain people like us or if they just tolerate our company. We don't always know if we can relate to people of different ages and backgrounds. For most of us, though, to grow and find fulfillment, we need to have friends who offer us new perspectives. We need to risk reaching out to a variety of people and then reap the wonderful results of making new friends.

WORK FRIENDS

Each of us probably spends forty or so hours every week at our job. Jamie spends her eight hours each day briskly going through stacks of paper; then she rushes home quickly every night. Alexis works just as hard as Jamie, but she also smiles as she walks through the halls and says hello to everyone she passes. While Alexis doesn't spend an hour at the coffee pot with her friends, she does ask the other people in the room how they are doing as she fills her coffee mug. Often they invite her to spend time with them after work, and if she's free, she readily accepts. Most of the people at Jamie and Alexis's office are not Christians, and Alexis loves the opportunity to get to know the unbelievers God has put in her life.

We know that developing friendships at work is sometimes

difficult, but when you work with people forty or more hours a week, it is important to have good relationships. How can you successfully maneuver through the complicated world of office politics and communication? Here are a few tips:

• Be friendly to everyone at work, not just your superiors.

• If you have free time, ask if you can help a coworker with a deadline.

• Don't get involved with gossip; instead, kindly excuse yourself from any conversation that is intended to hurt a coworker. People will respect your concern for others and probably cease to come to you with the latest sour news.

• Lighten up! Laugh at yourself when you make a mistake, and then learn from it.

• Become a sponge when it comes to learning. Ask your coworkers and superiors how to succeed in your field, and get their advice on how you can improve your current position. They should appreciate your enthusiasm to be a better worker.

• Be wary of office dating. Not only can it distract from your work, but if the relationship doesn't work out, you will have to see the former love of your life every day, eight hours a day. This gives a new meaning to the word agony when he begins to date someone else.

Are you friendly to the people you work with, or do they just come with the job? People at Alexis's office flock to her because she is so interested in what is going on in their lives. But Jamie's insecurities keep her from reaching out and developing relationships. Even if you are shy, we encourage you to face and overcome your fears and get to know the people God has put in your life.

CHURCH FRIENDS

While you establish good relationships with your coworkers, you also need to have a life outside your job. Every activity you are involved in will present potential friendships. You will meet people on your volleyball team, in your apartment complex, at your book club, at the gym, and even in the Laundromat. However, some of the most important relationships you develop will be the friends you meet at church.

A special bond develops quickly between people who have a relationship with Jesus Christ. It is easier to relate to others who have the same beliefs because you are on a similar path. You have given your life to follow Christ, and when you meet others who are following Him as well, you can encourage each other on your journeys. Christian friendships should inspire you to keep moving forward when you hit rough spots and hold you to a high standard when you feel temptation dragging you down.

As a single woman, you may consider joining your church singles group to develop relationships. In a quality group, you will be able to meet people close to your age who are also enjoying their single years. We've been involved with a multitude of different singles groups and have come to the conclusion that there are two types. Some are excellent church groups where singles learn, grow, and reach out to the believers and unbelievers in their lives. Other singles groups, though, can breed competition among their members because people are more intent on finding a date or marriage partner than seeking the Lord.

We encourage you to look for a church that will motivate you to minister. A church that encourages you to love and care about people. A church that looks at you as a whole person and teaches you the truths of God's Word. If you find a wonderful man in the process, that's fantastic! But if that's the sole reason you are developing relationships at church, you should reexamine your priorities.

OLDER FRIENDS

In church and at work, you will have the opportunity to meet people of different ages and backgrounds. When you become friends with someone older, you have the privilege of getting a new perspective on life. Older friends have already been where you are and probably have insight and good advice to offer if you are willing to listen. Why not go to lunch with an older coworker and find out her story? What has she seen that you may have only read in history books? What can you learn from her years of experience? How can you encourage her with your enthusiasm for life?

As you develop friends with people of different ages, don't forget to visit the places where people are nearing the end of their lives. Nursing homes, for example, are filled with elderly people who would like a friend. Have you ever spent a Sunday afternoon visiting a retirement home? The courtyards, cafeteria, and bedrooms are filled with people who would cherish a visit from a young friend (if you're reading this book, they would consider you young!). It's such an amazing experience to both learn from people who have lived long lives and encourage them. They have so much wisdom to offer those of us who are younger.

Proverbs 19:20 says, "Listen to advice and accept instruction, and in the end you will be wise." If you are open to listening to the advice from those who are older than you, your mind will be stretched and you will gain insight and wisdom.

YOUNGER FRIENDS

Do you have friends who are ten, fifteen, maybe even twenty years younger than you? Children can be so much fun! I (Melanie) love baby-sitting my friends' children. We have a blast singing, playing, and reading a mound of stories. It's such a joy to be a kid for a couple of hours and enjoy the simple things in life like a caterpillar or a coloring book or even the ducks on a pond.

It's often easy to get so caught up with more mature friends that we neglect developing relationships with little ones. Have you ever walked into your church and had a two year old run up to you saying your name and begging to be held? Children want to be with adults they like, and it feels so good when they want to be playing with you.

Younger friends in their teen years can also add some spice to your life. If you've lost touch with the current culture, you will quickly learn the latest music, styles, fads, and fashions. Just as your older friends can give you wisdom and insight, so you have the opportunity to pass on your insight to those who are younger than you. Share with them stories from your own adolescence and the bits of life knowledge you've gained. As you give a little of your life to a younger friend, you could reap the benefit of a lifelong friendship.

GUY FRIENDS

One of the greatest challenges of being a single woman is knowing how to relate to guy friends. We love being with certain guys who have no attraction to us beyond that of being a great buddy. We go to dinner, movies, and the mall and then spend hours getting and giving advice over coffee.

Our male friends give us a perspective that no girlfriend ever could. It's not a secret that guys usually think a little different than us, and it's important for us to have a man's point of view. It adds a whole different dimension to our lives.

Guy friendships can also be more complicated than our other relationships, because, as Harry put it in *When Harry Met Sally*, "the sex part always get in the way." If you fall in love with a guy friend and he falls in love with you, your long-term relationship is off to a great start. However, if you fall in love with a guy friend and he isn't in love with you (or vice versa), your friendship is going to experience some rocky times.

The truth is that some of your guy friends will fade away as you both develop new relationships. Other guy friends may remain your buddies for a lifetime as you befriend the love of their life. And one special guy friend just may be blessed with having you as the love of his life.

MARRIED FRIENDS

The longer we are single, the more bridesmaid dresses we get to hang in the back of our closets. Another friend joins that distinguished group of married people, and we think we may never see her again. Instead of being happy for her, we often become afraid that all we're going to have left of her friendship is an unusable dress.

But just because your friend says "I do" doesn't mean she's saying "good-bye." Marriage changes friendships, but it certainly doesn't eliminate them. Your newly married friend will probably want to spend most of her free time with her new spouse, as she should; however, it doesn't mean she wants your friendship to end.

The first year of marriage is a scary time as the bride tries to figure out her new life. It may seem like she's cut off her best friends, but the truth probably is that she's trying to understand how to relate to people in her new role as a wife. Don't cut her off! Call her to find out how she's doing and if she would like to get together. Maybe you can ask her for lunch or coffee or invite her and her husband over for dinner. We've heard many complaints from newly married women that their single friends seemed to abandon them after the wedding. We hope you run toward your friend and not the other way.

The whole scenario changes, of course, if one of your best guy friends gets married. His new wife will probably not be happy if you call him on a regular basis or ask him to go out for coffee. If you want to remain his friend, the best thing to do is befriend his wife! Get to know her even better than you know him, and you will have two wonderful friends.

NON-CHRISTIAN FRIENDS

As you develop friendships with all kinds of people, make sure that you are also building relationships with people who don't know Christ as their Savior.

As Christians, we are called to love people and point them to Christ. Yet sometimes this is difficult when we have a nice, sterile "Christian bubble" around us. There have been times in my (Tosha's) life when I didn't even know a nonbeliever. I worked with believers. I went to church with people confessing a relationship with Christ. All my older friends, younger friends, guy friends, girlfriends, and married friends were Christians.

But then I began to realize that pointing someone to Christ can start with a simple friendship. And opportunities surrounded me, just as they surround you. It is an act of obedience to God for each of us to seize the day in these relationships.

Ask God to burden your heart for a specific person. Then start building into her life. Spend time with her, sincerely getting to know her as an individual. Listen to her story, hear about her struggles, and encourage her. When the time comes, tell her your own story, but don't gloss over the tough parts. As you are sincere, honest, and transparent, she will see what it looks like to have a relationship with God in the real world.

Your new friend may choose not to come to Christ. While that decision will be painful for you, it should not mean you end your friendship. Rather, continue being a true friend to her as long as she is willing to continue the relationship. You never know what might develop.

On the other hand, you may have the joy of leading your friend to the Lord. What an awesome privilege: having a friendship that impacts her life, as well as yours, for eternity!

A godly, balanced woman has lots of friends who offer her new perspectives on life. She risks reaching out to a variety of people, and, as a result, reaps the wonderful results of new friends. She grows by being a part of their lives, and her friends grow as they get to know her.

While Jamie still struggles with relationships, she has decided to step out of her corner and talk to the people who make her nervous. She watches Alexis closely to see how she relates to people and tries to learn.

Alexis has mastered this art of making friends. She has married friends, church friends, guy friends, work friends, and both older and younger friends. The truth is that she just loves people—no matter what their age or interests. As a result, these people love Alexis too.

 # COFFEE TALK

1. Do you relate more with Jamie or with Alexis?
2. What types of people do you feel comfortable with and what types make you nervous?
3. What can you do to expand your base of friends?
4. How can you reach out to help a younger or older friend?
5. How did Christ interact with unbelievers and how can we follow His example? Consider passages such as Mark 2:13–17, John 4:5–42, and John 8:1–11.

- *Seven* -

THE CONSIDERATE WOMAN
Living with Roommates

BETTER IS A ROOMMATE NEARBY THAN A SISTER FAR AWAY.
PROVERBS 27:10, PARAPHRASE

The front door to my townhouse was wide open when I (Melanie) arrived home. It was 11 P.M., and I approached the door slowly. The lights were on, but no sign of my roommate, Betsy. I called her name twice, and finally she replied that she was upstairs.

Absurd visions of what had taken place ran through my mind, and I rushed upstairs to make sure she was okay. "Don't you smell smoke?" she asked when I arrived in her bedroom. I sniffed the air, and it was definitely smoke. No fire at either of the neighbors, and I wasn't about to mess around with a potential electrical fire. I picked up the phone and dialed 911.

In less than five minutes, sirens were heard at the end of our street, and a fire engine with flashing lights pulled up in front of our little home. Four firemen in full gear climbed down from the truck and rushed into our home. I pointed upstairs, and the four of them went into action, scouring our house for potential flames.

After an examination of walls, outlets, and appliances, we were told that we definitely did not have a fire. It seemed, one of the firemen told us with a straight face, that a bug had been caught in Betsy's halogen lamp. The poor bug had died quickly, but he would be remembered forever for the smell he caused.

We thanked the firemen for coming to rescue us and expected the evening to come to a close. However, it seemed our four new friends liked the idea of hanging out in a townhome better than going back to stagnate in the fire station.

All four of them congregated in our kitchen and lectured Betsy and me on the dangers of halogen lamps and gas heat and informed us about the electrical makeup of our dryer. They checked out all potential fire hazards in our home and then reminded us that we had dirty dishes in the sink. I promised to clean the house before I invited them over again!

After a half hour lecture and conversation, we weren't sure if we should be offering them cookies and milk or asking them to leave. Finally, the four men decided it was time to go back on call for a real fire. But we were told that if we ever had a fire, even a hint of smoke, to call them again. Betsy and I erupted into giggles the moment we said good-bye and closed our door. We thought we had new friends for life.

My father, always looking out for his oldest daughter, later asked if I got any of the firemen's phone numbers. "Of course, Dad," I told him, "911."

WHY HAVE A ROOMMATE?

In the past eleven years, I have lived with almost thirty roommates. As the oldest child, I never had a big sister to look up to, and God brought a myriad of big sisters into my life to mentor me through my late teens and early twenties. Some of the girls I have roomed with were key in befriending me, educating me, and assisting me in becoming a godly, balanced woman. Others were examples of what kind of roommate I did not want to be.

Why have a roommate? Isn't it easier to live on your own?

RENT OR BUY?

As a single woman, you have to make a tough choice when it comes to renting or owning. Since 25 to 50 percent of your income probably pays for where you live, you want to make wise decisions in determining whether to have a lease or a mortgage.

The benefits of renting. Renting gives you the opportunity to get acquainted with a new city while deciding if you are going to make it your home. You only make a small deposit (usually one month's rent) and your monthly rent. Renters have the flexibility to get out of a lease quickly if they need to move, and the upkeep of an apartment usually consists of a quick call to the maintenance man. Rentals also may have attractive amenities like a swimming pool, washer and dryer, or tennis courts.

The downside of renting. You have no rights to the property. You may live in the same place for three years, but you will never get refunded the money that you paid into it. While you don't have to worry about repairs, you may not be able to paint or make any significant changes to the property because it's not your own.

The benefits of buying. Owning a home gives you the flexibility to paint, plant flowers, and make whatever cosmetic changes you want to the house. If you want to start a vegetable garden in the backyard, you can because the property is yours. Owning a home is generally a good investment. Your monthly payments build equity that can result in a profit when you sell the house, and you have a healthy tax break that you don't get when you're renting.

The downside of buying. With home ownership the house

is entirely yours—all the cracks, leaks, touch-up painting, and appliance breakdowns are your responsibility. A house requires upkeep and maintenance that you don't have to think about when you're renting. Owning a house will also lock you into a certain area for awhile (or until you sell it), so it is not a good plan to purchase a home if you are planning a move in the near future.

Having a female roommate can be important to a single woman, because it gives her an opportunity to learn, someone to help financially, a person to be accountable to, an element of safety, and a friendship that could potentially last a lifetime.

Every person I have lived with has provided an education for me—whether her characteristics were positive or negative. Fortunately, most of my lessons proved to be positive. Deann taught me how to delegate household chores. Kristen showed me the importance of daily exercise. Connie taught me how to clean. Sherri was a constant example of how to be professional on the job but lots of fun at home. Allison encouraged me to start jogging—just for ten minutes and build up to thirty. Betsy supported me when I needed to get out of a bad dating relationship. Ariel and Letha made me take study breaks to go have some playtime in college. And I'll never forget Tracey's strength and reliance on God when her fiancée was killed. If you've had roommates, you can probably make a list of the things you've learned from them. Every once in awhile it's a good idea to review that list and remember the lessons.

By listening, watching, and learning, every roommate can have a positive effect on your life.

Having a roommate is also a great financial investment strategy. Because saving money should be a priority in a single woman's life, having a roommate can give you the opportunity to put the extra money you would use to pay rent into investments or a savings account. After living by myself for nine months and not having any money left over for savings, I decided that living with someone would be the smart financial decision. The $250 I saved each month went into my bank account instead of my landlord's.

Accountability is another key reason to have a roommate. When living on your own, it's easy to relax standards and values because there is no one else around to be concerned. A wise roommate can act as a sounding board and adviser when tough questions and decisions arise.

Some roommates hold each other accountable spiritually, checking to make sure they've had their "God times." Other roommates give each other the freedom to hold them accountable sexually. "Did you go past your limits on your date tonight?" they might ask. Still other roommates use the accountability factor to help each other stick with their diets and exercise routines. A half-empty container of ice cream would spark an investigation into who splurged too much on her diet! Whatever way you implement it, accountability can help you and your roommates become better people.

Safety is another extremely good reason to have a roommate. I never slept well when I lived on my own, and I still don't get a good night's rest when my roommate is out of town. My mind consistently battles with God's protection on one side and criminal intent on the other. A lieutenant at our local police department told us, "There is always safety in numbers."

SAFETY TIPS

- *Establish safety rules for your household.*
- *Let your roommates know where you are and when you'll be back—watch out for each other!*
- *Put a pole in your sliding glass door track, and keep all your windows locked when you're not at home.*
- *Always use the peephole before you open the door. If you don't know the person, either don't answer the door or ask through the door if you can help them.*
- *Communicate with your roommates if a maintenance man or service person is coming. Ask for identification before you let workers in your house.*
- *Keep a fire extinguisher and baking soda in your kitchen.*
- *Check and recheck your fire alarm.*
- *Leave one light on if you are all gone for the evening.*
- *Install a telephone in your bedroom or keep your cordless phone in your room at night.*
- *Keep a flashlight near your bed.*
- *If you list your telephone number, use your first initial instead of your first name.*
- *Obey your safety instincts. If you sense a problem, don't let someone in your home.*

He encouraged singles to live in groups if possible.

He went on to explain that sometimes having a roommate can create a false sense of security. He said that all the residents in a home should be aware of their environment and work together to create a safe household. Whether you live in an apartment, townhome, or house, you and your roommates should have secure deadbolt locks, fire extinguishers, working alarms, and a telephone in each bedroom in case an emergency occurs. As with Betsy and me and our halogen lamp, it is always smarter to call 911 in a potential emergency than to wait until the crisis has already occurred. By talking with your roommates about safety, you can create a home that is prepared in case of an emergency.

When I (Tosha) was in college, I lived with five friends in an old, isolated house on a mountain. We dubbed it "the green house." Out in the middle of the woods, we didn't have very many passersby. However, help was not readily available either. With so many people in and out of our house, doors were constantly left unlocked and windows open. When I would come home late by myself, I could only hope and pray that no one malicious was waiting inside.

Finally, we had a much-needed roommate talk about the obligation each of us had to bolt doors, lock windows, and leave night-lights on. This talk should have occurred before we moved in together; fortunately, it took place before something horrible happened. By making safety a priority, you and your roommates can prevent an emergency in your home.

The final reason for having roommates is to develop strong friendships. When you live with someone for several months or years, she becomes your family. As with any relative, you either learn to love or resent her company.

Sherri was my (Melanie's) roommate in Virginia Beach for three years, and we spent hours laughing, talking, and enjoying life together. She convinced me to spend a week in Orlando with her several years ago, and we have gone on vacation every year since including weeks in Cancun and Breckenridge. Five years ahead of me in life, Sherri has been my adviser, mentor, and big sister as well as friend. Life is sometimes lonely for single women, but with roommates you have the opportunity to have close friendships that can last long after you stop living together.

CHOOSING A ROOMMATE

Eight hours at work and then four more hours of night school trying to get her degree—Belinda had an extremely long day. All she wanted to do when she finished her homework at midnight was fall asleep in preparation for another grueling day. She had three roommates at the time and lived in a four-bedroom house. Two of the women had become close friends, but the third, well, let's just say there were a few small personality conflicts and one major conflict that came in the form of her cockatoo. He was a temperamental creature, and when he wasn't happy, the entire household was compelled to hear about it.

That night the cockatoo was not happy. The minute Belinda's head connected with her pillow the screeching began. Screeching at decibels she never knew a bird could reach. I twisted and turned, and the screeching got louder. No amount of sheep counting or loading up of pillows over her ears would make the highpitched sound disappear. Usually a calm person, Belinda's reserve broke. Fortunately (or unfortunately), the bird's owner was not home that night, but her other roommates heard her yell from the top floor, "I'm going to have bird stew for breakfast!" and return to her room making detailed plans on how to find other accommodations.

At that moment, Belinda realized the extreme importance of carefully selecting who you choose to share your home with. While having a roommate can be an exciting and growing experience, it can also turn into a nightmare if you move in with someone who conflicts with your personality or moral values—or in Belinda's case, pet selection.

Before asking someone to room with you or moving into someone else's home, take time to get to know the person or people you will live with. Have a meal together or meet with them in their home and discuss each others' expectations. Ask questions: How do you divide chores? Do you split food or does each person buy her own? How often do you clean your house? How do you pay bills? How often do you have guests? And how long do these guests typically stay?

If you are a social person, you will feel trapped if your roommate doesn't like to have people over. If you are a night person, you may be irritated when your roommate turns out to be a morning person and cleans the house with her stereo blasting before 8 A.M. Make sure to discuss potential differences in personality and style as well as how you will resolve those if you decide to live together.

No matter what your or your potential roommate's personality or expectations, you should look for several critical characteristics, including: flexibility, responsibility, high moral standards, cleanliness, and integrity. Within each of these characteristics lies a multitude of questions—questions that should be discussed openly and frankly prior to your roommate relationship.

Having a roommate can be devastating if you don't choose with caution, but by getting to know your future roommate in advance, you can increase your chances of making room-mating a growing and fun experience.

FINDING A PLACE TO RENT

Finding the right roommate should make your life a little less stressful, but finding the place that meets your needs is equally important. Here are a few tips:

• *Make a wish list.* What is important to you? Low rent? A safe, quiet neighborhood? Something close to work? Dishwasher? Washer and dryer? Air-conditioning? No smoking? Garage? Swimming pool? A place that allows pets? Determine what is essential and what you can live without, and then don't compromise on your essentials. This will help narrow your search and find a place that's perfect for you.

• *Start searching.* Check work and church bulletin boards, roommate-finding services, classified ads, the internet, and even a realtor. Some helpful internet sites are www.rent.net, www.aptguides.com, www.aptline.com, and www.rentcheck.com.

• *Ask direct questions.* Before signing on the dotted line, make sure you have answers to all of your questions. For example: Is there a deposit, and if so, how much is it and is it refundable? What do I have to do to get my deposit back? How long is the lease? Is there a penalty if I need to break the lease? What are the utility costs? Who is responsible for maintaining the property? What is the turnaround time for maintenance needs? Don't sign anything you haven't read thoroughly or are unable to comply with.

BEING A GOOD ROOMMATE

My twenty-eighth birthday was emotionally tough. It was an odd milestone in my single womanhood. Even though two years had passed since I had roomed with Sherri and Connie, a large package from them arrived at my office the Friday before my birthday. I saved my present until Sunday and then opened it to find a beautiful Victoria's Secret terry cloth robe and a variety of lotions and bath spray. It was so good to know they cared enough about me to send a special gift!

Not only is finding the right roommate important, but learning how to be a good roommate is also key. Although Sherri and Connie are no longer my roommates, their thoughtfulness while I lived with them—and even after I moved out—exemplified to me how to be a good friend. When you become a quality roommate, you'll make your home a pleasant and fun place to live for your roommates and guests.

Creativity, responsibility, and flexibility are important qualities to develop on the road to becoming a good roommate. The sky is the limit when it comes to being creative at home. I once had a roommate who left the house before I did in the morning, and every couple of days she would leave me an encouraging note or Scripture on the kitchen counter. My day would always start with an appreciative smile.

Think of things you would enjoy receiving from a roommate, then do some of those fun things for the women you live with. Bring them flowers, cook a special dinner, celebrate their birthdays with a surprise party, or attend a recital, performance, or an event they are part of. Being a creative roommate doesn't have to be complicated, but your roommates will always remember your kindness and encouragement.

Responsibility is another essential quality to becoming a good roommate. Having a spotless house was never critical to me as it was to many of my roommates. Receiving phone messages, however, was at the top of my importance list.

Every woman has her own definition of responsibility. A responsible roommate pays her half of the bills and rent on time, takes phone messages, cleans the house, respects her roommate's privacy, and cleans up after her guests. She is considerate of her roommate and encourages suggestions for improvements. Understanding each other's definition of responsibility creates an atmosphere that is positive and fun as each woman works to honor and respect her roommates.

The last key quality for being a good roommate is flexibility. Sometimes your roommate will forget to change a light bulb or take that phone message or tell you her college friend may show up for the weekend. When this happens on a sporadic basis, it is often better to grin and bear the weekend guest than criticize your roommate for the surprise. Learning to respect and enjoy each other instead of being critical and demanding creates a fun home environment. Work hard at being easy to live with. The characteristics that you form in your home will shape every area of your life.

MANAGING YOUR HOME

It wasn't until I decided to live on my own that I discovered the extensive duties of cleaning and managing a house weren't easy tasks. I had been blessed with hardworking roommates who took up my slack while I was in grad school. Vacuuming, dusting, mopping, and putting away dishes were foreign to me, and I got a crash course the instant I moved into my own apartment after graduation. I learned my lessons quickly and was able to implement my practical education when I became a roommate again.

Communication is the key factor in working together to keep a home in order. When roommates take the time to discuss what is important to them, the level of respect for each other is expanded.

After learning what is important, the responsibilities in the house can be delegated different ways. Each person can be responsible for specific duties, or the duties can rotate each week. An easy way to rotate these duties is to have them listed on an erasable board so the names can be changed easily at the beginning of every week.

Roommates should also determine what tasks they are willing to pay to have someone else do, like mowing the grass or cleaning the carpet. No matter how the general household tasks are divided, each woman should be responsible for her portion of the duties as well as cleaning up after she cooks or entertains guests.

Paying the rent, utility, cable, and other bills is also a critical responsibility in managing a home. All the bills should be kept in a designated location, divided equally among the roommates, and then paid on time. A late payment reflects poorly on all the occupants of a household. Also, one person should be designated as the contact with the landlord if major problems or maintenance difficulties arise. This lessens the confusion of several people calling the landlord about the same problem.

Managing a home is exciting and challenging. With good communication and responsible attitudes, each roommate can come home at night to a relaxed environment and clean house.

Fresh out of college, I lived in a townhouse with Deann and Kristen. Two months after moving in with them, they both became engaged. In nine months they were both married, and I was looking for a new residence.

After seven years and many married roommates later, I'm convinced that living with me must be the incentive for these women to find husbands! However, as I change roommates on an annual basis, I'm thankful for every living situation I've had. I've learned new things, been encouraged, and formed solid friendships for years to come. And how else would I have learned the importance of letting the phone ring at least twice before I answer it, the necessity of owning an espresso machine, the art of watching TV while running in place, or the hidden dangers of dialing 911?

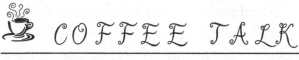

COFFEE TALK

1. What have you learned from the roommates you have lived with?
2. What are the advantages and disadvantages of having a roommate?
3. Have you established rules of safety for your home? Do you need additional rules?
4. Are you a good roommate? What can you do to be a better one?

- Eight -

THE FAMILY WOMAN
Improving Family Relationships

LISTEN, MY DAUGHTERS, TO A FATHER'S INSTRUCTION;
PAY ATTENTION AND GAIN UNDERSTANDING.
PROVERBS 4:1, PARAPHRASE

At Christmastime, my grandmother's front window is always filled with brightly colored lights and white electric candles. A beautiful arrangement of red bows and greenery is strung along the bedroom window, and fresh white snow covers the expansive lawn and the oak tree by the house.

Every Christmas my sister and I (Melanie) fill our arms with presents and walk up the cracking cement stairs to the front door of my grandma's house. The wreath I made several years ago is always displayed proudly on the door, but we never have time to look at it because one of my aunts opens the door before we even knock. There are lots of hugs and kisses, and the smell of baking ham permeates the air. The Christmas tree is intricately decorated with lights and ornaments holding memories from years past. A kaleidoscope of colorful ribbons and red foils and green matte paper filled with wonderful surprises is tucked under the tree.

When I was younger, I couldn't wait to unwrap the carefully chosen gifts that had my name on them. When I was five, I hoped for a new baby doll or a book I could almost read by myself. By the time I was ten, I wanted Ballerina Barbie with all of her accessories or a small baking set on which I could create my

104

own desserts. During my junior high and high school years, all I wanted was the latest clothing to wear when I returned to class.

Presents were so important during those growing-up years, but now when I go to Grandma's, I don't run to look under the Christmas tree. It is more important for me to hug the people who brought me the presents. My cousins and I usually end up eating all of Grandma's cookies and playing an intense game of hearts before the day is over. I love talking to my aunts and uncles and then going down to the basement to remember those golden days of growing up. I used to sit downstairs for hours on a bean bag chair and read or play tiddlywinks with my brother and sister. Now we occasionally go to the basement to grab a soda, but we no longer use it as our playroom. Our games these days are more advanced and require a card table in the living room instead of a cement floor.

Life seems to change so quickly. My parents divorced when I was twelve, and then my grandpa died when I was eighteen. As the years have passed, we have said good-bye to other loved family members and welcomed new spouses and babies to our small family. Every Christmas is just a little bit different, but I love that it is one of the most constant things in my life. There are no big surprises at Grandma's. I always feel secure and welcome, and it makes me look forward to going home.

FAMILY PAST
As we grow older, we change jobs, living arrangements, friends, and churches. Some of our closest friends may move away or the job we thought we'd be in forever suddenly ends. Change is inevitable, but one of the few constants God has given us is our family.

Our parents, grandparents, aunts, and uncles have known us since the beginning of our lives. They remember when we took our first steps and said our first words. They can recall our first days of school, third-grade Easter pageants, and those lengthy piano recitals. They may even remember our first boyfriends, our winning volleyball seasons, and our senior prom dates. They were the ones snapping photographs and talking proudly about "our girl," so excited to be part of our lives.

The people we grew up with helped mold us into the women we are today—for good or bad. While many of our childhood memories are positive, some of us also have painful, haunting memories. But no matter how our lives have played out or if we live nearby or far away from our families, their influence still affects us. How we utilize what they've given us is up to us.

Relish the Past

As I read through my childhood journals, I'm reminded of happy growing-up days. I remember the time that my dad, my sister, my brother, and I were driving down a country road singing "Father Abraham" at the top of our lungs. When the chorus commanded us to "turn around," my father stopped the car, and all four of us jumped out onto the pavement and "turned ourselves around." These were happy times with my family that I cherish.

I also recall fun with my extended family. I used to beg my parents to take me to my cousin Katy's house to play. Her home had been part of the underground railroad in the 1800s, and the dark basement, cubbyholes, and cupola gave our creative minds hours of adventure. We still love to talk about the mysteries we would create and then solve in our preteen years.

It's easy to dwell on the negatives in our lives, but how much we miss when we allow them to crowd out the positives! These happy memories help us grow as well as form some of the personality traits we have today. My dad's dedication to creating a fun environment, for example, has made me appreciate life. Katy's and my many childhood adventures have led me to want to discover uncharted territory.

When you look back on your childhood, what memories first come to mind? Are they the negative ones or the positive? We're not advocating that you gloss over or deny the negative, but if there's good, we want you to hold onto it. Remember it, enjoy it, relish it. Thank God for it, and ask Him to show you how it has impacted your life for good.

Forgive the Past
While I have lots of good memories from growing up, there were a lot of hard times as well when my parents separated. According to the statistics, about half of us grew up in single parent homes.

Parents play a key role in our lives no matter how old we are. If you had a bad relationship with your father when you were growing up or your mother abandoned you to live with another man, your self-esteem can be severely impaired. If you don't know why you are always attracted to men who treat you poorly or you don't feel secure enough to build a relationship, it could very well stem from the relationship you had with one of your parents.

When we look at the past and face tough situations with our family, it is easy to become bitter and let this bitterness fester as we grow older. The little seed grows into a huge bush of thorns that scars our hearts deep inside. Some of us deal daily with rough memories from our past. The thought of forgiving those who have wronged us sometimes seems impossible. Yet we continue to long for the healing that only God can give.

If you are struggling to forgive someone in your family, we encourage you not to go through the process alone. First and foremost, ask God for His help. Express the depth of your hurt to Him, and realize that you are powerless to get beyond the pain without Him. The bigger the hurt, the more you will need Him to enable you to forgive. Then, confide in a Christian friend or mentor whom you trust and ask her to help you. She will be there to hug you while you cry as well as offer a balanced and scriptural perspective. Your friend can hold you accountable so that you won't slip back into negative thought patterns or actions, and she can encourage you to keep pursuing healing.

Also, when dealing with the years of pain caused by a family member, it is often helpful to start a forgiveness journal. This can be a blank book or just some loose-leaf notebook pages. As offense after offense comes to mind, write the specifics in your journal. In the privacy of your relationship with God, record all the hurtful details, such as "she said this" or "he did this." Then ask God to help you forgive, detail after detail, offense after offense. As more things come to mind over time, repeat this process until all the specific instances of pain you can remember are out of your head and written in your journal.

In the forgiveness process, you may also want to look for specialized resources at your local Christian bookstore. Sometimes it is helpful to write a letter of forgiveness to the offender, even if you decide not to mail it. You may also consider joining a support group or seeking professional help to deal with the issues. Don't give up on your search for healing no matter how long it takes.

And remember, just because you forgive a family member does not mean that you allow this person to continue hurting you. Obviously, every situation is different, and there are some relationships you should keep working on. However, in other situations, such as abuse or neglect, you must move yourself to safety even as you go through the forgiveness process. Please set appropriate boundaries to protect yourself. Forgiveness does not mean that you have to welcome the abusive person back into your life. Forgiveness means that you release him from his debt to you and go on with your own life.

A harsh past does not have to control our lives today. Jesus Christ is an incredible healer of hearts. He lovingly mended my heart when I asked, and He can mend yours as you face the past.

FAMILY PRESENT

For some women, the thought of going home elicits fond memories, and they are excited about seeing relatives and reliving part of their childhood. For others, going home brings pressure, strife, and the dread of uncomfortable questions. Some of us live hundreds of miles away from home, while others are just down the road. Every situation is different, yet every one of us faces striking similarities when we go home.

Every year when I go home, I have to deal with a multitude of emotions. I'm excited to see my dad, stepmom, sister, and other relatives. I love to relax and spend time playing games and catching up. It is also a disappointing time, as I wrestle with the emotions and challenges of being from a broken home. Probably most of us have a mix of emotions when it comes to going home.

How can we make the most out of spending time with our families? By listening, learning, and respecting our relatives while warding off situations that leave us feeling lonely and depressed. Here are a few more specific ideas.

Create Treasures

Do you sit across from your aunts and uncles every holiday and wish you were spending it with your girlfriends on the beach? Do you swallow back a yawn as everyone talks about their jobs or their year in school? Maybe it's time for you to spice up family holidays by asking questions about your older relatives' past adventures and life lessons.

Our families offer a wealth of stories and wisdom. My father's ancestors were Moravians, and they came to America several hundred years ago to escape religious persecution. On my mother's side, my aunt told me that all the women were strong and independent. Recently I learned that my great-grandmother ran a grocery store back when women weren't supposed to work outside the home.

These stories and words of wisdom define who we are today. Unfortunately, they're easily forgotten. So why not write these stories and personal memories in a "family treasure chest" book? Create a scrapbook filled with family lore—ask your relatives to give you any old letters and photographs they might have.

Or you could create a computer file filled with family history and then pass out an updated version every Christmas. Instead of dreading your great-great-uncle's talks about the Depression again, listen closely and write down his colorful recollections.

You could also interview your different relatives on video-tape. This makes for both a fun memory and a great Christmas gift. By being creative, you can start enjoying your family history and your relatives' words of wisdom.

> ## QUESTIONS TO ASK YOUR RELATIVES
> *Who gave you your name and why? What are your earliest memories? What are your favorite memories? What was your family like when you were a child? What were your dreams? What traditions did your family have? What was your first job? Did you go to college? How would you describe your school years? How did you come to know Christ? What were your single years like? How did you meet your husband or wife?*

Listen to Wisdom

We were eating brunch at the Village Inn. I was a twenty-six-year-old single, and my father had flown in to check up on his daughter. Dad and I were talking about my plans, and I informed him that I was going to cash in my 401K plan to help with a down payment on a house. My dad listened intently, and when I had finished spelling out my plan, he looked at me and said, "This is the point in the conversation where you say, 'Dad, what do you think about this?'"

I grinned and asked my dad for his opinion, knowing that I really didn't have much of a choice. He outlined for me the problems with cashing in my retirement plan and told me that I would lose a large portion of the money to taxes and penalty fees. By the end of our brunch, I decided that I would save for the down payment and leave my 401K to grow on its own.

As I've grown older, I've realized more and more that my

parents are indeed much smarter than I thought they were when I was a teen. My dad is king when it comes to loving and encouraging his family, organizing his life, saving money, and investing for the future. My stepmom, Lyn, is queen of cooking, creative decorating, and planning fun family parties. When I have questions about insurance or a new recipe, my dad and Lyn get a call. I've come to appreciate the fact that I can learn a lot from them in so many different areas.

What have you learned from your parents and other family members? Whether it's financial, practical, or relationship questions, your relatives are probably filled with knowledge from lessons they learned when they were in their twenties and thirties. Maybe they share this advice freely, but if they don't, we hope you ask. As independent single women, we should always be open to learning from others. And who better to ask than the group who should love and care for us—our family?

Strengthening Relationships

The hair pulling and scratching and the infamous "I'm telling!" Do you have brothers or sisters? Whenever I see two little kids fighting at a sandbox or the McDonalds playground, I recall fighting and arguing with my sister, Christy, and my brother, David. I was the oldest, so I tended to be the tormentor. I would poke, blow on, and stare at my sister until she got so irritated she didn't know what to do. My brother always went straight to Mom when I would pick on him, and I would have to pay the penalty. Yet, the memory of spankings and sitting for long hours in my room must have grown quickly dim, because in a matter of hours I would be tormenting them again.

But twenty years later, my brother and sister are two of my

dearest friends. They know me better than any of my high school or college friends, and they still love me for some strange reason. Because of this closeness, we are also able to be honest with each other. They can tell me if they don't like someone I am dating or if I say something hurtful. I may be upset initially at their comments, but once I get past my pride, I know they are usually right.

Do you have someone in your life who is honest with you even when it hurts? Your siblings and other relatives know you so well and are often able to see past what you are blinded to. If you have a good relationship with them, ask them about guys, your career, strained family relationships, etc. You may be surprised at their advice.

Field Tough Questions

"So, when are you getting married?" Ah, the dreaded questions. They always seem to come up at family reunions. Someone always asks, "Are you dating anyone?" "How's Andy (your last boyfriend with whom you had a rough breakup six months ago)?" "Any marriage prospects?" Over and over the questions

STAYING IN TOUCH

How do you stay in touch when you are in Boston and your family is in San Jose? Here are some ideas: Picture albums or a website filled with photos of your new home, car, and work place. "I love you" calls. Care packages to relatives in college. Newsletter routed via mail or e-mail. Videotape of your favorite places and new friends. Ideas like these can keep you feeling near even when you're far apart.

are asked, and over and over again you have to respond, "No, I'm not dating anyone." "I don't know how Andy is; I haven't seen him for six months." "Nope, not even close to being married." Before the day is over, you want to plant yourself in the corner of the room and pray you don't have to sing the "singles blues" to anyone else.

Does every family get-together have to end with you feeling as though you need to find a man ASAP? Instead of slipping into depression, this is a great opportunity to show how God has worked in your life and molded you into a godly, balanced woman. When the questions start, this is the perfect time to laugh and say, "Dating? I hardly have time to go out with my girlfriends! Did I tell you about what was happening in my church (or in my career, hobby, or travel experiences)?" Having a man does not prove that you are a successful woman. Talk about the other things going on in your life, and then make sure to ask your family a lot of questions as well. By conversing on topics that are important to you, you should be able to avoid answering questions that leave you feeling lonely.

Blend Unique Families

Because so many parents are divorced, many of us have been through visitation and court appearances, and some of us have lived with stepparents, stepbrothers, and stepsisters. We may love our stepfamilies, or we may have a deep bitterness toward them. Often we wonder if we should feel guilty for caring for our stepfamilies, and sometimes a parent breeds this guilt by degrading the opposite stepparent. We are stuck in the middle of one of the most awkward situations a little or big kid has to face.

After my parents divorced, I wasn't able to spend much time

with my father. In fact, I was a sophomore in college before we really started getting to know each other. I remember him coming to visit me at my university, and I was so proud to be walking around campus with my dad.

As I got to know my father, I also spent time with my stepfamily. In spite of all the challenges we've faced, God mended hearts and molded us together into our own little family.

We are not going to pretend that every stepfamily situation can work out smoothly. There are too many uncontrollable factors, too many areas that we aren't responsible for that can still cause pain long after childhood ends.

However, with the grace of God, we can love even those family members who have wronged us. One of my favorite passages when I'm hurting is Psalm 34:17-18, which says, "The righteous cry out, and the Lord hears them; he delivers them from all their troubles. The Lord is close to the brokenhearted and saves those who are crushed in spirit."

If your heart has been broken, God can mend it. He can heal those wounds created by a torn or broken family and even build friendships from a tough situation.

FAMILY FUTURE

My family has added new members through marriage and birth, and we keep growing in closeness as well. We have so much to look forward to as a family as we watch each others' lives expand and grow.

Living at Home

What happens when you've grown up, but you are still living at home? Many single women opt to stay at home to save money and have security. But this choice has unique challenges as well.

Eva, a twenty-four-year-old engineer, decided to move back in with her parents after college. While this arrangement worked for the short-term, she and her parents both started feeling bitter after five years of living together. She was upset because they still had a curfew for her and wanted to know where she was when she wasn't home. They screened her calls and wanted information about every man who phoned. Her parents didn't understand her need for independence, because, after all, she was their child and was still living at home.

While certain situations require women to live with their parents, we recommend that single women move out on their own by the time they either turn twenty-one or complete college. By finding a roommate and then taking the leap to start your own home, you will grow as a single woman and learn how to live as an independent person. This will not only give you security and confidence, but you will never again fear "being alone." You will learn to enjoy decorating your home, using your money for what you think is important, pursuing your

TAKING CARE OF YOUR PARENTS

At some point in your life (and some of you may be facing this now) the tables may turn, and you may be taking care of your parents. To find out what professional and volunteer elder care services are in your parents' town, contact the National Eldercare locator number at (800) 677-1116. For a variety of services and information, look up AARP's (American Association of Retired Persons) website at www.aarp.org.

personal interests, and traveling when you get the urge.

When Eva finally took the leap to rent an apartment with several girlfriends, her relationship with her parents improved. They now respect her as an adult, and she respects their advice without the pressure of feeling that she must implement their every suggestion. While she was able to save money living at her parents' house, she enjoys the freedom of living in her own place.

Saying Good-bye

It's hard to say good-bye to a child you have raised for eighteen years. Unfortunately, a happy relationship during your growing up years doesn't always guarantee a happy adult relationship with your parents. Some parents have a difficult time with the transition of you becoming an independent single woman.

However, it is important for you to become an independent adult between the ages of eighteen and twenty-one. You need to begin living life on your own. You will never fully grow up until you are able to utilize the information you were raised with and learn to make decisions by yourself. But even though you are no longer a child who must obey her parents, you are an adult who should respect them.

"'Honor your father and mother'—which is the first commandment with a promise—'that it may go well with you and that you may enjoy long life on the earth'" (Eph. 6:2-3). You may not always agree with your parents, but a godly woman respects and loves them anyway, because God has asked her to do so.

Planning Family Fun

Just because we have grown up doesn't mean we have to put an end to participating in family fun. Jackie's family, for example, spends a week every summer at a cottage on Lake Michigan.

They water ski, picnic, and catch up on their time apart. Sara's parents host their family every Christmas at their second home in the mountains. They love hiking and popping corn in their wood-burning fireplace. Monique's family stays up all night on their get-togethers playing "Midnight Monopoly."

What does your family enjoy doing together? Maybe you can suggest a picnic in the park or a ski trip next time you are home. Or why not take your mom or dad or grandmother out on a "date"? Take them out for dessert or coffee, a game of tennis, or plan a hike at your local state park. Be proactive in finding out what they enjoy doing, and then plan a special day just for them.

Create Your Legacy

My senior-year history teacher had all of his students interview an older person and write a biography on his or her life to present in class. I had the privilege of interviewing my grandpa. We talked about the years when he grew up and how he lived during the Depression. We talked about World War II and where he was when he heard that Japan had bombed Pearl Harbor. He told me how he had met my grandma and why he wanted to marry her.

A year after I interviewed him, my grandfather died of cancer. Eight years after his death, I typed my high school report on parchment paper and laminated Grandpa's story. At Christmas, I wrapped it up and gave it to Grandma. I have never seen my grandmother cry like she did that day. It was very special for her to have another memory of her husband.

Create a legacy by filling your family treasure chest with photos and keepsakes and a notebook filled with memories. Remember your grandparents' stories so you can someday tell them to your own children. Stop and appreciate what your great-aunts and uncles went through during the Great Depression and World War II. Learn about life when it was simpler and family was more important because you had to rely on each other.

This year I'll be spending Christmas Day surrounded by my cousins and aunts and uncles at my grandma's house. We'll eat a brunch of ham and eggs and then sit around the brightly lit Christmas tree. We'll open gifts as we catch up on the news of our lives. Christmas hasn't changed much since I was little. Although the family faces have changed slightly and the gifts are different, I know what to look forward to every December 25.

When are you going to spend time with your family again? It doesn't matter if it is a special holiday or this coming weekend; the important thing is to cultivate your family relationships by spending time with them and creating a legacy that you will cherish for a lifetime.

COFFEE TALK

1. What are some of your favorite memories from your childhood?
2. Have you forgiven the people who hurt you in the past? If not, what is the first step you can take toward forgiveness?
3. What kind of relationship do you currently have with your family? How can you proactively improve relationships?
4. If you are still living at home, how does your independence affect your relationship with your parents? How can you

improve your relationship with them while seeking to be more independent?

RESOURCES

Brestin, Dee, and Lori Beckler, *My Daughter, My Daughter,* Colorado Springs: Chariot Victor Publishing, 1999.

Cloud, Henry, and John Townsend. *The Mom Factor.* Grand Rapids: Zondervan Publishing House, 1996. Authors' note: This is a great resource to find out how your mother has impacted your life.

Conway, Jim. *Adult Children of Legal or Emotional Divorce.* Downers Grove, Ill.: InterVarsity Press, 1990.

Friel, John, and Linda. *Adult Children: The Secrets of Dysfunctional Families.* Deerfield Beach, Fla: Health Communications, 1988.

Reflections from a Mother's Heart. Nashville: Word Publishing, Countryman, 1995.

Sandvig, Karen J. *Adult Children of Divorce: Haunting Problems and Healthy Solutions.* Dallas: Word Publishing, 1990.

Wright, H. Norman. *Always Daddy's Girl.* Ventura, Calif: Regal Books, 1989. Authors' note: This is a great resource to find out how your father has impacted your life.

Wellness

··

Breathless from exertion and exhilaration, the three girlfriends took a break from their hike. The steep, rugged mountain trail they were climbing had leveled out on a huge boulder, providing an opportunity to rest and enjoy the incredible scenery and a bubbling mountain stream.

In the distance the women could see other boulders, similar to their own place of respite. Beyond those, even farther in the distance, the mountains opened up to reveal the hills where their city lay.

Transfixed by the beauty, the women were silent, each absorbed in her own thoughts as she considered her reasons for taking this challenge.

The well-conditioned leader had exerted little energy getting to this point. She looked at the jutting boulder across the valley and wondered how to find a trail to it. Greater challenges remained to be conquered, but her current challenge was to get her friends to the trail's summit.

Her roommate resting nearby took a big swig of water. Tough did not even begin to describe how she felt about this trail, but she was not about to quit. For motivation, she reminded herself of all the calories she was burning.

The third woman enjoyed the exercise, but she came along mostly for the scenery. The visual rewards were worth the difficulty of the trail.

When their eyes were full and their hearts ceased pounding, the women resumed their journey. One foot in front of the other, they made their way up to the quiet reservoir on the mountaintop.

A lifestyle of wellness is a lot like the challenge those women encountered on their mountain climb. For some, a steep mountain trail is just an everyday hike; they've done this before, and they'll do it again. For others, physical exertion is a worthwhile anomaly in their lifestyles. Still other women enjoy physical challenges because of the fun along the way.

Wherever you are in your personal trek to wellness, we challenge you to reach new heights in health, beauty, and sensuality. It always takes willpower to go against gravity, to push upward into the elevation, to go further than you have before. But the sense of accomplishment and health you feel along the way is worth the pain of climbing.

Ready for a challenge?

- Nine -
THE HEALTHY WOMAN
Living Well

IF YOU FIND HONEY, EAT JUST ENOUGH—TOO MUCH OF IT,
AND YOU WILL GET SICK.
PROVERBS 25:16, PARAPHRASE

Feeling good is something that I (Tosha) often take for granted. It's not that I'm not grateful, for I know my health is a gift from God. However, many times I forget how valuable that gift is. That is, until I get sick.

Ohhhh! I moaned to myself as I struggled from bed in the early hours of a Monday morning. Clutching my stomach, I shuffled to the bathroom then felt the wall to find the light switch. When I flipped on the switch, the light showed my reflection on the mirror. *I look awful,* I thought, *and I feel even worse!*

I suppose that no time is a good time to feel bad. Yet today was a particularly bad time to get sick. I needed to get to work early, I had a book deadline to meet, and I had appointments scheduled the whole day. As I considered the prospects for the week, I was not comforted to remember that I had scheduled little time to rest.

As I miserably held my head over the toilet and swabbed my brow with a wet washcloth, I wondered where I got this bug. I couldn't remember coming in contact with somebody sick, but, then, neither could I remember doing anything to take care of myself. For the last month, I had rushed from one appointment to another and pushed myself to meet one deadline after another.

In the midst of this busyness, I had not taken care of myself. It was fast food meals . . . or no meals. Candy bars for energy and cold sodas for the road. No healthy food. Not enough sleep. No extra supplements of vitamins and minerals. As I crouched on the bathroom floor, exhausted but unable to sleep, I longed for the pain to go away and morning to come. I had a lot of time to think about how I could have stayed well, prevented this sickness, and been peacefully sleeping in my bed.

That was an awful morning, one that reminded me how much I like to feel good. You have probably had some times like that yourself. Did you ever think, though, that perhaps a few days of feeling bad are actually healthy reminders for us to take care of our bodies? Although not all sickness and health problems can be avoided, a great many can be prevented through a lifestyle of wellness, which begins with eating healthy, hydrating, detoxing, sleeping, supplementing, and preventing. Feeling great starts with what's inside.

EATING

On a brisk summer night in the Colorado mountains, a group of friends and I were at a beautiful campground for a one-night, "girls only" camp out. As the sun began to set behind the mountains and the shadows began to fall, we circled the warm fire, laughing, talking, and cooking our dinners.

It's always interesting to watch women watch each other, especially when it comes to food. Even by the light of a campfire, the glances and looks we tend to give each other are quite obvious. High-fat items are often viewed with disapproval, while low-fat items—even if they don't taste as good as their more fattening equivalents—are met with approval. As slender Anna started to grill her hefty Polish sausage, I saw a few pairs of eyes furtively look at her. When Stephanie got out her Healthy Choice can of soup, she made sure to point out to her observers that it was low-fat. When I got out my hot dogs (which I only eat when I camp), Tiffany asked if I had bought the new no-fat variety. And as the rest of us sipped on our caffeine-free diet sodas, several women looked critically at Melanie getting out her caffeine-and-sugar-packed Coke.

It was just an informal camping trip, but we still found a way to bring our comparison sticks along with our tent poles. Our conversation for the first hour and a half of dinner was all about food, calories, and fat. High-fat, low-fat, guilty, not guilty. By the time we were finished politely berating ourselves and each other for eating what we did, nobody seemed too thrilled about the prospect of making s'mores. And what's a camp out without a traditional s'more?

As I drove down the mountain the next day, I reviewed the prior evening. It had been great fun, combining all the incredible elements of good friends, fresh air, bubbling creek water, and relaxing campfire flames. It was unfortunate, though, that we had put a damper on the evening by making each other feel like gluttons when all we did was eat a couple hot dogs and roast a few marshmallows.

Now, I do believe that feeling great on the inside starts with what we eat. But our overall lifestyles of healthy eating, not just one night's dinner, determine our wellness. My simplistic view of eating is a plus and minus system: I get a plus every time I eat something healthy and a minus every time I eat something unhealthy or less than good for me. At the end of the day, if I have a lot more pluses than minuses, then I'm doing great. If I have more minuses than pluses, though, then the next day I need to average that out with more pluses. An occasional hot dog on a camping trip, a piece of Snickers pie on a special holiday, or a cheeseburger at a picnic is not going to spoil my wellness or make me gain weight—*if* my overall diet is dominated by pluses. Those occasional treats create balance for me when my diet follows nutritional standards.

EACH DAY WE SHOULD EAT . . .
* *Starches and grains: six to eleven 1/2-cup or 1-slice servings*
* *Vegetables and fruits: five to nine 1/2-cup servings*
* *Dairy: two to three 1-cup or 1-ounce servings*
* *Meat: two to three 3-ounce servings (each the size of a deck of cards)*
* *Fat: around 40 grams or 20 to 30 percent of total daily calories*
* *Sugar: the less refined sugar, the better*
* *Sodium: one teaspoon or 2,400 milligrams*

You have probably seen the food pyramid that has the starches and grains at the wide bottom of the triangle, the veggies and fruits next to the bottom, the proportionately fewer dairy and meat products toward the top, and the fats and sugars at the tip of the triangle. In reality, this is often a hard standard to follow. It's easier to eat a Poptart as you drive to work than to make blueberry pancakes and find time to sit down and eat. It's much simpler to buy a ninety-nine-cent burger at the drive-through than to bring a tuna sandwich with you for lunch. And at dinner, downing a bag of low-fat popcorn with a diet soda or boiling a bag of ramen noodles is more convenient and less time-consuming than preparing a well-rounded meal to eat alone.

Still, despite the inconvenience of eating well-rounded meals as an on-the-go single, it is vital that you have a healthy diet. So we suggest that before you go grocery shopping, think through a list of nutritional possibilities for two weeks.

> ### HEALTHY IDEAS!
> • *Breakfast: yogurt, whole wheat toast, low-fat granola cereal, oatmeal, fruit, grits*
> • *Lunch: homemade soup, garden salad, chopped chicken sandwich, fresh mozzarella and tomatoes, fruit*
> • *Dinner: lasagna, spaghetti, fajitas, baked potato with broccoli, homemade pizza, Crock-Pot chicken, stir-fry*
> • *Snacks: power shakes, fruit, muffins, carrot slices, popcorn, natural fruit popsicles, cheese slices, rice cakes, sherbet*

After you have decided what sounds appetizing, write out a shopping list. Then, when you have about three hours, take this list to the store. For the first hour, shop wisely, selecting just what you need, using your coupons and buying what's on sale. Shopping with your list in hand will help you avoid picking up the chips and cookies and less nutritious items usually located on the ends of the aisles. Be sure to buy some plastic wrap, plastic bags, and foil if you don't have any at home.

Once you get home with your groceries, take the time to prepare the food items for the next two weeks. For example, prepare the lasagna and freeze individual portions. Fry the meat for the fajitas, and make the chicken salad. Marinate some chicken to stick in the Crock-Pot. Put one cup of oatmeal in a covered bowl, along with some brown sugar, so it's ready to heat up with water in the office microwave. Wash the fruit and vegetables, and shave the carrots. Make the muffins, and store them in individual bags. The more you do to prepare your food during this concentrated time, the more convenient it will be later. Then, after a long day of work, you can come home and defrost a healthy, already-made meal for dinner. Or on your way out the door in the morning, you can grab a bag of muffins to eat while you go.

Feeling great starts with eating right. As you eat healthy on a regular basis, you should find that you have more energy, less body fat, and a clearer complexion. And if pluses dominate your personal nutritional survey, then an occasional hot dog and s'more will be a treat you can enjoy!

SUPPLEMENTING

When I was a teenager living in Florida, white spots started appearing all over my tanned skin one summer. At first, I didn't pay any attention to them, figuring that they would go away in a few days. But when more and more spots kept forming, I finally showed my mother. Concerned, she took me to a dermatologist. He told us two things: I had some sort of pigmentation problem (which I cannot remember the name for), and I would be cured by eating carrots.

We went home feeling pretty foolish. My family had huge gardens growing every type of produce you can imagine. We ate fruit and vegetables with every meal and then some. But, of all things, I was not eating enough carrots. Sure enough, after eating several carrots a day for a week, my spots went away.

Even if you are doing your best to eat a well-balanced diet, you may still have a nutritional deficiency. Before you run to the health food store to buy vitamins, though, we suggest that first of all you do some research about benefits of whole foods. Your problem may be corrected as simply as mine was, by just eating more of a certain food.

Unfortunately, just because you eat lots of fruits and vegetables does not mean that you don't need extra vitamins and minerals. If you think that you should take supplements, do some additional research. Go to your local library and spend some time studying the pros and cons of different vitamins, minerals, herbs, and natural food supplements. Or buy a resource book such as *Prescription for Nutritional Healing* (see resource list). It gives detailed explanations about vitamins, minerals, herbs, and nutritional supplements, and it describes which ones to use for different physical problems. You may find that some of your health issues are preventable or curable by using information from a guide such as this. However, make sure that you check with a health professional before solely relying on a medical self-help book. And always, if you have any doubts, questions, or lingering problems, schedule an appointment with your personal doctor.

Once you understand and feel comfortable with the information, then go shopping at the health food store. Purchase what you have learned to be the essential vitamins, minerals, herbs, and food supplements. We suggest that you purchase all-natural varieties rather than ones that are synthetically or chemically made. Read the labels and ask questions of the clerks so you make the best choice. But do take caution: don't go overboard. Too many good-intentioned people waste a lot of money stockpiling vitamins and minerals, only to have four dozen unused bottles take up permanent shelf space at home. Be wise about what you purchase as well as how much you purchase. Also, some vitamins are toxic in large doses—too much of a good thing can not only be counterproductive but sometimes dangerous. So know what you are taking as well as the proper dosage.

By supplementing your diet with necessary vitamins, herbs, and minerals, you will take another important step toward a lifestyle of feeling great.

HYDRATING

I wish I could move the clock forward! I thought, swallowing the final drops of water from my ever-available water bottle. Eight hours a day I worked a desk job in downtown Dallas, and every hour I prided myself on drinking as much water as possible. This afternoon I would be leaving early to go on a mission trip to a small town in south Texas. In anticipation, I refilled my water bottle with Dallas tap water at the drinking fountain and stuck the bottle in my take-home bag.

Ten days later, after drinking cup after cup of country well water in that hot, dry town, I returned to work in Dallas with my trusty water bottle in hand. I made my daily trip to the water fountain and pressed the button to fill my bottle. As the water gushed into the bottle, an unusual odor struck my nose. Sniffing the opening of the bottle, I realized that it was my *water* that smelled. Daring to put it to my lips, I was repelled by the chlorine taste. Not until I went somewhere where they did not use a lot of chemicals in the water did I realize how gross city water tasted. Disgusted by the water fountain, I let my water bottle sit empty at my desk, deciding it was better to dehydrate than drink chemicals. However, this was not a good idea either, since my goal was all-around wellness.

Eight 8-ounce cups of water per day is the goal in a lifestyle of wellness. It is a lofty goal, but it has some incredible benefits. Which of us would not want to have clearer skin and more energy? Which of us would not want to take an easy route to enhance weight loss and avoid sluggishness? Muscle tone, constipation relief, and waste removal are more benefits from drinking enough water.

> *Drink your water cold! Some evidence suggests that your body will burn calories as it brings the water to body temperature.*

If you are drinking eight 8-ounce cups of water daily, good for you! You could probably tell us a story or two about the benefits you are enjoying. Few of us reach that goal, though, for reasons like: *It tastes bad! It tastes dull! I can't remember to drink it! I'd rather have a soda! Doesn't my tea count?* Whatever your reason(s) for not drinking enough water, here are some ideas to make God's best drink easier to swallow.

If tap water tastes awful to you:

• Consider purchasing a water filter. Because no single water filtration system will solve every water problem, it is important to find out what the particular water problems are where you live. Call your local health department and ask their recommendations about what water filters would be best for you.

• Buy bottled water at the grocery store. You can choose between mineral water, purified/distilled water, sparkling water, or spring water. Bottled water is not necessarily safer than what comes out of your faucet, but it might taste a lot better to you, depending on the amount of salts and minerals naturally occurring at each water source. (Be sure that you brush your teeth with fluoride toothpaste so that you'll get the necessary fluoride, which bottled water doesn't provide.)

If you can't remember to drink your two quarts of water each day:

• Keep a water bottle with you wherever you go. Stick it in the car when you drive to work, keep it with you at work, take it along with you when you run errands. You are more likely to drink water if it's with you.

• Make a hydration plan. Sarah drinks two glasses in the morning, two more around lunch, two in the afternoon, one at dinner, and one more before going to bed. Julie takes a break at the office every two hours, when she goes to the bathroom and refills her 16-ounce water bottle. Before she even leaves work for the day, she has had her quota of 120 ounces. If the water supply at work tastes terrible, take along filtered water from home or store some bottled water at your work station.

• Drink for ten seconds from every water fountain you pass.

If you would just rather have a soda or coffee:

• Give your body a break! Your digestive system must flush wastes from your diet constantly. If you drink a Diet Coke instead of water, it must also filter out carbonated water, caramel color, aspartame, phosphoric acid, potassium benzoate, natural flavors, citric acid, and caffeine. Get the point? Instead of making your body filter all your drinks, too, put something pure into it to help wash out the impurities. Also, caffeine actually dehydrates your system, making your body work harder to stay hydrated.

• Take twenty-eight days to develop a taste for water. Don't allow yourself to drink sodas, coffees, teas, or anything else but water for a month. It will take some getting used to, but over time your cravings for less pure things will go away. It works!

• Make special drinks a treat rather than a necessity. My sister loves to drink Crystal Light with her meals, but she drinks water at her desk all day. A friend of mine loves to drink a hot cup of Celestial Seasonings herbal tea every morning, but after that she drinks water for the rest of the day.

• Keep some lemons and limes handy. Restaurants serve these in your water glass, so why not use them at home? Next time you go to the store, buy a lemon, cut it in wedges, and refrigerate them until needed. Just be careful to drink with a straw, because citrus can damage the enamel on your teeth due to its acid content.

Drinking water is a necessity for wellness. So, drink your water! In fact, go get a glass of it right now—I did!

DETOXING

Even when we strive to eat a balanced diet, take vitamins, and drink enough water, toxins can still build up in our bodies. Medicine, pesticides, pollution, and overindulgences strain our systems, causing headaches, diarrhea, illnesses, diseases, or emotional problems. First, skipping medicine prescribed by your doctor is not a good idea. We shouldn't just quit eating fruits and vegetables from the grocery store either. An extreme measure would be to avoid environmental pollution by moving to another area, but chances are that your new city will have some pollution too. You can control your overindulgences, but even that is not a foolproof method of avoiding toxins. These nasties are a fact of modern life.

You can rid your body of toxins, though. Detoxification is the process of allowing your body to rest, heal, and rebuild. Also known as fasting, detoxification will give your organs a rest, strengthen your immune system, and purify your body. You will experience an increase in your energy level, since your body won't have to use so much energy to digest food. Other added benefits can include sweeter breath, clearer eyes, and weight loss.

There are different approaches to fasting. Some health professionals recommend that you only drink water and juice during a fast. Another approach for detoxification is to give the body nutrients, such as protein, complex carbohydrates, and essential fats. For fasts such as these, it is important that you detox under the supervision of a health professional.

A less strenuous but still helpful form of fasting is mentioned in the Old Testament. When Daniel and his friends were taken captive, they were placed in the king's house. Of all the places where they could have landed during their captivity, they hit the gold mine! Instead of slaving out in the fields, mining in the quarries, or working in commoners' houses, they got to live in the luxury of a palace.

Rich food and wine were abundant, and even for the captives, every meal was a banquet. As appealing as that food might have been, though, Daniel and his friends purposed in their hearts to not defile themselves with food that had been offered to idols and that violated the dietary restrictions God had established. So they made a special request of the chief official. "Please test your servants for ten days," they asked, "Give us nothing but vegetables to eat and water to drink. Then compare our appearance with that of the young men who eat the royal food" (Dan. 1:12-13). The official agreed to allow the four friends to try their fast.

You can almost imagine the looks they received when they sat down at meals. While everybody else gorged on rich foods and fermented drinks, Daniel and his friends ate plain vegetables. "They might as well be working out in the fields, if that is what they want to eat!" you can imagine their fellow slaves joking. All jokes ended, however, when at the end of ten days, Daniel and his friends "looked healthier and better nourished than any of the young men who ate the royal food" (v. 15).

While the Bible did not include this story primarily to establish a dietary precedent, it does provide a nutritional illustration worth observing. When Daniel and his friends ate "live" foods, such as vegetables and fruits, they were noticeably healthier than their companions.

With this example in mind, you may want to try a ten-day cleansing fast eating only organic vegetables and fruits. If your budget won't allow organic produce, soak your fruits and vegetables in a mixture of white vinegar and water to help remove outside pesticides. We encourage you to do some additional reading and talk to your doctor about detoxification. Find out how often and which forms would be good for your body. By detoxing on a regular basis, like once every three months or twice a year, your digestive system will be cleansed and purified. And you will not only feel great, you will look great too.

SLEEPING

How many sheep have you counted lately?

Carol has counted quite a few. Every night she gets in bed and lies there for several hours before finally falling asleep. She and her fiancé just broke their engagement, and she is trying to decide where to go from here.

Monica just graduated from college and is going through a national job search. At the end of this month, her apartment lease will be up. She will either have to re-sign the lease, find another place to live, or be on the road to a new job. The stress of not knowing her future keeps her awake well into the night.

Maria is working her way up the ladder at the television station. Although she excels at her job and gets great reviews, she is paying a price because she must work the night producer shift at the station. Working at night and sleeping during the day throws off her internal clock. On the weekends she tries to go to church and spend time with friends, but it is just too difficult because she is so tired.

Sleep problems have been called a hidden nightmare in our culture. Carol's, Monica's, and Maria's stories are just a few of the millions that could be told. What is your sleep story? Do you stay awake for unending hours at night? Do you rely on over-the-counter sleeping pills to get some rest? When was the last time you had a good night's sleep?

Worry, stress, and busyness are major contributors to insomnia. Being overweight, suffering depression, smoking, drinking alcohol, or consuming sugar and caffeine can also keep you awake at night. Whatever the cause of your sleep loss, here are some suggestions to get great ZZZ's.

• Ask God for help. When David could not sleep, he looked to God in the darkness, praying, "On my bed I remember you; I think of you through the watches of the night, because you are my help" (Ps. 63:6-7a). During one particularly unrestful period of my own life, I followed David's example by meditating on this verse: "It is vain for you to rise up early, To sit up late, To eat the bread of sorrows; For so He gives His beloved sleep" (Ps. 127:2 NKJV). Since God does not slumber or sleep (Ps. 121:3-4), He will help us whenever we call on Him—even if that is in the middle of the night.

• Do your devotions. If you have not spent time with God for the day but are lying there wide awake, use this as an opportunity to read your Bible and pray. God is pleased and honored when we seek Him, no matter what time of day it is.

• Journal. Instead of lying awake in bed, get up and start journaling. Write in detail what is bothering you. When you are finished (or exhausted), close your journal and mentally leave your problems tucked in the pages. Crawl back in bed with the mind-set that your worries and problems are no longer in bed with you.

• Make a list. You may want to keep a pad of paper and pen next to your bed. Then, next time you're wide awake thinking about all that must be done, write everything down without turning on the light. This will help you get the details out of your mind without completely waking up your senses.

• Unwind. A bubble bath, candlelight, and classical music are great ways to unwind from a hectic day. If you are having trouble falling asleep, make relaxation an evening ritual.

• Don't just lie there. If you still haven't fallen asleep after being in bed for twenty minutes or longer, get up. Go empty the dishwasher, write a letter, read a book, do some laundry, or watch television until you finally feel sleepy.

• Drink some warm milk or herb tea. Celestial Seasonings has a tea actually called "Sleepytime." I'd say it's worth a try, just don't add any sugar.

• Have a consistent sleep schedule. If you wake up every

weekday early for work but sleep in on the weekends until noon, you are setting yourself up for sleep problems. By being fairly consistent about when you go to bed and when you awaken, your body will not have to compensate and readjust.

• Consider purchasing better bedding. I seldom had a good night's rest until I finally purchased a good mattress set. It was expensive for my budget, but it made all the difference in the quality of my sleep. Feeling rested has been worth every penny!

• Check out your local health food store. Find out what natural remedies they have for insomnia.

If, after trying all these things, you still cannot sleep, we rec-

TO ALL NIGHT OWLS AND PARTY ANIMALS

Sleep may be neither a problem nor a priority in your life right now. You reason that you're young and healthy enough to push your system to the limits. So, you give your body about four hours of rest a night, somewhere in-between your late late night activities and early morning work or classes. While doing this on an irregular basis might not harm you, this pattern could have major consequences if it becomes your routine. Regular lack of sleep causes serious stress on your body, and stress is a common factor behind multiple illnesses and diseases. Among other problems, regular lack of sleep can seriously harm your immune and nervous systems. When you're sleepy, it's difficult to concentrate and dangerous to drive. According to the National Institutes of Health, "Getting too little sleep creates a 'sleep debt,' which is much like being overdrawn at a bank. Eventually, your body will demand that the debt be repaid." [1] *Beware of depriving your body of the amount of rest you need, for it can have more serious ramifications than just being bleary-eyed in the morning. Begin to establish good sleep patterns tonight.*

ommend you contact your doctor. Prolonged lack of sleep could be a sign of a different problem, which you will want to get help for. A good night's rest is the foundation for feeling great.

PREVENTING

"You can do more for your health than your doctor can," proclaims the introduction to *Take Care of Yourself,* a self-care medical book. With all the natural foods, exercise facilities, and supplements available, that statement has never been more true, especially in prevention. As the old adage goes, "An ounce of prevention is worth a pound of cure."

An ounce of prevention certainly includes eating right, supplementing, hydrating, and detoxing. Other preventative measures, though, are also worth taking. If you are doing some of these already, then good for you! You are well on your way to preventing future health problems and living a life of wellness. But here are a few reminders.

Protect Your Skin

Magazine ads feature models with dark, savage tans. Television shows feature dozens of sun-bronzed beauties. Roadside billboards, movies, and television commercials all nonverbally tout society's image of what is attractive: tan is in; pale is out.

If you were born with naturally brown or dark skin, then you are fortunate to escape the pressure of needing a tan. However, if you are light-skinned, you have probably felt, at one time or another, that you must have a tan to look good. Unfortunately, evidence shows that any tanning of the skin is a sign of permanent skin damage.

Instead of spending hours baking in the sun, try using a skin-bronzing cream for a natural looking tan. If you absolutely must have a "real" tan in order to feel good about your appearance, at least protect your skin as much as possible by using sunscreen with a minimum sun protection factor (SPF) of 15. Or, do something radical: just be yourself—whatever skin color God made you.

Don't Smoke

When my grandmother Eleanor was in her twenties, she smoked because it was glamorous. Many people smoked, but few realized the health risks. Unfortunately, what started out as glamorous soon became a deadly addiction. Years later, when it was proven that smoking causes cancer and a multitude of other problems, Eleanor couldn't quit. It was not until her husband died of lung cancer that my grandmother quit cold turkey. She has not smoked since, and I'm sure she has lived longer than she would have if she had held onto the deadly habit.

If you smoke, we encourage you to quit while you are still young. Find a way to stop using your own initiative, group accountability, medical treatment, or the readily available nicotine patches. For more information or help, call the Office on Smoking and Health Centers for Disease Control at 1-800-CDC-1311, the American Cancer Society at 1-800-ACS-2345, or the National Cancer Institute at 1-800-4-CANCER.

Secondhand smoke can also be extremely dangerous to your health. According to the American Cancer Society, more than four thousand people die every year due to secondhand smoke, and those at highest risk are the ones who involuntarily inhale twenty or more cigarettes a day. If you are regularly breathing others' fumes, take charge of your health by changing your environment. Move in with a new roommate, if neccessary. Ask to switch to a work station farther away from the coffee/cigarette break room at work, have your friends or family members smoke outside your home, and stay away from restaurants and bars that are filled with smoke. Don't wait until smoking takes away your wellness.

Take Care of Your Teeth and Gums
Normally, I don't bargain with God. However, I regularly bargain with God when I'm sitting in the dental chair for my semi-annual checkups. "God, if You will just help me not have a cavity this time, I promise that I will floss every day for the rest of my life *plus* work at the soup kitchen every night for the next two years!"

I hate dental exams and cleanings; and I especially hate getting a filling. However, whether I like it or not, the American Dental Association recommends two visits to the dentist every year.

So, in a lifestyle of wellness, prevent dental problems by scheduling regular checkups. Brush after eating sweets, or avoid eating sweets when you can't get to a toothbrush soon. If it's too much of a pain to floss every night, make it a habit to floss every other night. Or, use a water pick to clean your teeth. A little prevention is a lot better than having to bargain with God once you get in the dental chair!

Do Breast Exams

I know, I know—this is a yucky one to discuss. A lot of women avoid it with common excuses like, "*I'm* not going to get breast cancer, because it's not in my family!" or, "*I* won't get breast cancer because I have small breasts!" or "I'm too young to worry about that!" However, breast cancer is in the top five leading causes of death among women. That makes these excuses about breast self-exams (BSE's) and clinical breast exams (CBE's) potentially lethal.

As a trainer in the health industry, my sister has all sorts of plastic models and mannequins to help people learn how to take care of their health. Her displays are all impressive, but one of her exhibits stunned me. Inside one small clear bag was a kernel of corn, a marble, and a golf ball. The kernel represented the size of a breast tumor that can be detected during a routine

---

A SHOWER BSE

While you are in the shower, use your soapy fingers to examine your breasts. Starting where your underarm joins your breast, firmly examine your breast by slowly circling from the outer edge in toward your nipple. Repeat on the opposite breast. If you notice any abnormalities in your breasts, such as a change in texture or skin color, skin dimpling, a retracted nipple, any unusual discharge, or a lump, contact your doctor immediately.

---

mammogram. The marble represented the size of lumps usually found by women who do regular BSE's. However, for women who do infrequent breast exams, the average tumors are usually the size of a golf ball before being found. I don't know about you, but if I'm going to have a problem, I'd like it to be found while it is kernel-sized!

The American Cancer Society recommends that women between the ages of twenty and thirty-nine have a CBE once every three years and do a BSE once a month. You should do your BSE one week after your period ends, when your breasts no longer feel tender or swollen. If your menstrual cycles are irregular, you should do a BSE on the same day of each month. You can do a BSE when you are lying in bed, standing in front of a mirror, or taking a shower. As you monitor changes in your own body, you will be taking a huge preventative measure for your health.

Have Regular Pap Smears
"So, how did your Pap smear go today?" That just isn't a question likely to be discussed by two girlfriends over lunch. Trust me, I know this preventative measure is not pleasant to discuss, even with your best friend. As a single celibate woman, it's easy to talk yourself out of going to the gynecologist for that yearly visit, especially since you don't need to get any birth control prescriptions. However, a Pap test is the best to way to detect cancer in your cervix or vagina. The American Cancer Society recommends that most women have Pap tests and pelvic exams every year, but your doctor may recommend that you have this done less frequently. Whether your doctor recommends that you

have a Pap test and pelvic exam done every twelve, twenty-four, or thirty-six months, discipline yourself to take this preventative measure.

At your gynecological appointment, a health-care professional will examine your cervix and gently scrape cells from just inside the opening of your vagina. If you are a virgin, don't hesitate to request that they use the smallest instruments possible. And while it will be somewhat uncomfortable, it should not be painful. Just close your eyes and relax by thinking about the most fun vacation you have ever taken. The procedure will be over just like that! After your exam is completed, reward yourself for taking this preventative step by getting a healthy juice drink on your way home. As you are enjoying it, congratulate yourself for being so brave, and remind yourself that you won't have to endure this procedure again for a while.

Like most people, I have to learn the hard way. When I was sick during the early hours of that Monday morning, I had determined to do whatever it took to get well—and stay well. Unfortunately, my resolve stayed strong only long enough to get me well. After getting better, I went back to doing what I always did.

I forgot to take my vitamins. I didn't get enough sleep. I inhaled more sodas than water and ate more fast food than healthy meals. Before long, I got sick again. And again. And again. I was miserable for several months.

Finally, I felt bad long enough to know that this was not the way I wanted to spend my life. It was time to change how I took care of the body God had given me. I jump-started a lifestyle of wellness by eating healthy, hydrating, detoxing, sleeping, and supplementing. These helped my body feel great from the inside out. Chances are, they'll do the same for you.

 COFFEE TALK

1. Do pluses or minuses dominate your eating habits? Why? Does this need to change, and if so, how?
2. What preventative measures are you regularly doing, and which ones do you need to be doing?
3. What is your most compelling motivation for being proactive about maintaining all-around wellness?

RESOURCES

Balch, James F., M.D., and Phyllis A. Balch, C.N.C. *Prescription for Nutritional Healing*. Garden City Park, N.Y.: Avery Publishing Group, 1990.

Family Medical Reference Library. By the editors of Consumer Guide. Lincolnwood, Ill.: Publications International, 1993 and 1997. Authors' note: This set includes *Family Health & Medical Guide, Home Remedies Health*, and *Prescription Drugs*.

Kennedy, Maureen. *All Your Health Questions Answered Naturally*. Mountain View, Calif.: MKS, 1998.

Vickery, Donald M., M.D., and James F. Fries, M.D. *Take Care of Yourself*. 5th ed. Reading, Pa.: Addison-Wesley Publishing, 1994.

---

[1] *http://www.ninds.nih.gov/patients/Disorder/SLEEP/brain-basics-sleep.htm,* 9/20/99

- *Ten* -
THE ATTRACTIVE WOMAN
Looking Well

You are taking care of your body, and you feel great. Eating healthy has become a lifestyle for you, and your water bottle has become a daily ritual. You are getting enough sleep, you've detoxed recently, and you are supplementing your diet with vitamins and minerals. You're feeling really good about your lifestyle of wellness.

You feel great, but how do you look? How do you want to look?

Attractive women come in all shapes and sizes, forms and packages. Because each of us is a designer original, our different qualities, styles, and tastes portray unique kinds of beauty. Every woman, as she takes care of herself, has this beautiful aspect about her. You are doing your best to live a lifestyle of inner wellness; now let's look at some areas of outer wellness.

TAKING CARE OF YOUR SKIN

Never had a zit? Then you are a blessed woman, indeed! However, the majority of us have moaned about acne on more occasions than we'd like to count. There's nothing like having blemishes on your face to make you feel unattractive.

If you desire to look attractive, you have a lot of company. Most women want to look nice. God made us with this longing, and He even validated it by giving a prescription for how to be beautiful. "This is the way the holy women of the past who put their hope in God used to make themselves beautiful," Scripture says when describing traits of inner beauty (1 Peter 3:5). A godly woman with a pretty attitude will also be an attractive woman. Of course, our biblical perspective of beauty must also take into account all of Scripture. Even as we desire to look our best, we should be careful not to be consumed by our looks, for the Bible also teaches the "Beauty is vain" (Prov. 31:30 KJV.) This is yet another are where we can be challenged to pursue balance in our lives.

When I (Tosha) was a teenager, I longed for the day when I would go to college and leave my acne behind. Unfortunately, college days arrived and so did new outbreaks of acne. Although they were less extreme than those during high school, they still embarrassed me on a few dates and in a few pictures.

Now I'm out of school and, thankfully, acne seldom comes into my life. That may be due to age, or it may just be that I take care of my skin better now, thanks in part to my sister Shannon's advice. She encouraged me to get on a good facial cleansing system by telling me her story. She had never wanted to spend the money to buy facial cleansing products, but then, one day, this thought hit her: *Why wouldn't I?* Not able to think of any good reasons (except money) she carefully budgeted and saved enough to buy a quality makeup remover, cleanser, and astringent. By incorporating these into her daily regimen, she has achieved a clearer complexion than ever before. This helped me too.

Unfortunately, even with a good cleansing regimen, occasional acne breakouts still plague both Melanie and me. For these we have found help from an item called "tea tree oil," which can be found at any health food store. By dabbing a little of this natural antiseptic on the problem areas, acne usually disappears within a day or two. Sometimes more extreme blemishes require tea tree oil for a week. Benzoil peroxide products also help, but these need to be balanced with a good moisturizer.

If you have tried to get rid of your blemishes using ointments, soaps, and tea tree oil, all to no avail, you may want to check your diet. Eliminate potential causes from your diet one at a time, for a month at a time. Common suspects include sodas, chocolate, sugar, or greasy foods such as chips or pepperoni pizza. If you find that when you delete chocolate from your diet, you don't have as many zits, then you will have to decide whether those chocolate candy bars, cookies, or milkshakes are worth the price. Whatever you eliminate from your diet, be sure to keep drinking lots of water.

If the problem areas still persist in spots like your forehead or cheeks, go to an experienced beautician for a new hairdo that cleverly hides those areas. While cover-up makeup can work for some, just the right hairstyle may be your secret. On the other hand, sometimes the oil from your hair is the problem. In that case, have your beautician help you find a style to keep bangs out of your face.

Taking care of your skin includes more than just getting rid of or disguising zits, though. Use a good moisturizer every day to protect and enhance the quality of your skin. This does not mean that you have to buy an expensive lotion at the department store; you may be able to find a generic brand at a drugstore that does exactly what you need. Look for moisturizers containing antioxidants, SPF 15 sunscreen, and nutrients. Choose one that is hypoallergenic.

At night, reapply moisturizer or a gel, such as aloe vera, to your face, and then cream your hands, feet, and other rough areas. If your skin problems are persistent, go to a dermatologist for professional help. Take care of your skin, and it will take care of you.

EXERCISING

My freshman year in college, I (Melanie) enjoyed the doughnuts and French fries in the cafeteria more than the salads and fruits. After four years of eating high-fat foods, I had gained an extra twenty pounds that made me feel sluggish and made my clothes too tight. After a year of haphazard exercising and faulty dieting, I finally decided to lose my college weight. A staunch diet of low-fat foods helped me take off the weight within several months, but my legs and stomach were still flabby.

After I unsuccessfully tried several different types of exercise, my friend Allison encouraged me to start jobbing to turn my flab into muscle. When I explained that I didn't have the stamina, she told me to start running slowly for just ten minutes at a time and then work up to fifteen and then thirty minutes. I decided to take her advice. I counted every minute my first few sessions until I reached ten. But then something happened: I was jogging twelve minutes and then eighteen and finally up to thirty. Not only did this feat give me a sense of accomplishment, it quickly toned my legs and stomach. I now try to do aerobic exercise several times a week, and it makes me feel great!

Unfortunately, some Christian women don't give—or apply—advice like Allison did. When I (Tosha) was younger, one of my leaders actually did a devotional about not exercising. She read from the King James Version, "For bodily exercise profiteth little, but godliness is profitable unto all things" (1 Tim. 4:8a), then proceeded to explain why we didn't need to worry about exercising. Judging by her inactivity and girth, I think this woman really took her interpretation to heart!

A better translation of this verse shows the comparison involved: "Physical training is of some value, but godliness has value for all things, holding promise for both the present life and the life to come" (NIV). Physical exercise has value for this life; spiritual exercise has value for both this life and eternity. Obviously, the importance of being a godly person supersedes being a physically fit person. However, physical fitness still has plenty of merit including giving us more daily energy and potentially lengthening our lifespan.

As a godly, balanced single woman, you are already seeking to exercise spiritually. But are you exercising physically?

Experts say that we should exercise three times a week to maintain our physical wellness. Following that advice has been my New Year's resolution quite a few times! But I always seemed to get bored and break my resolution by the beginning of February.

Exercise does not require an expensive health club membership, a stationary bike, or your own weight equipment—although those things are nice. Exercise does not necessarily mean that you have to go jogging for an hour three times a week, even though that is a great idea if you enjoy it. Exercise can be anything that raises your heart rate and/or works on your muscles. How about trying some of these:

• Go for a long, brisk walk with a friend.

• Do your housework at triple speed (pushing the vacuum burns calories!).

• Socialize by doing rather than dining (instead of eating ice cream, play volleyball).

• Go dancing, or learn how (this is a great way to exercise, socialize, and have fun—all at the same time!).

• Do aerobics while you watch the news.

• Play hard (a grown-up game of tag is still a lot of fun).

• Go hiking.

• Park your car in the farthest parking spot at the mall (during the day, of course).

• Ride your bike.

• Learn a new sport.

• Swim laps at your apartment complex pool.

• Take the stairs instead of the elevator at work.

• Go for a prayer walk (exercising both physically and spiritually).

Exercise should be whatever you enjoy. If the thought of aerobics sends chills up your spine, then try some of the other activities that interest you. Shanna, a physical fitness trainer, told me that doing different types of exercise is helpful for two reasons. It helps keep you from getting bored, plus it enables you to work out different muscle groups. Whatever you do, remember that exercise need not be a boring or a misery-invoking process. Make it something fun that you look forward to. Encourage your friends or roommate to exercise with you so that you can hold each other accountable and reap the benefits together.

DIETING

I will never forget returning to college for the fall and passing my friend Lori without even recognizing her. We had become friends during our sophomore year when we were in the same discipleship group. The two of us had a lot of things in common: our personalities, our likes and dislikes, our hobbies. The only major difference between us was the way we took care of our bodies: I had done my best to avoid the "freshman fifteen" and the "sophomore sixteen" by passing on the tempting high-fat foods in the cafeteria and exercising; but Lori had spent a lot of late nights studying and staying awake by eating cookies, munching on chips, and drinking soda. As a result, she carried a lot of extra weight and was, in general, not too happy about her figure. She went home for the summer determined to do something about it.

She got back to college having reaped the benefits of an eating plan that worked. A shapely figure, a new hairdo, and a glowing smile portrayed a confidence that I had not seen before. When we passed each other in the dorm parking lot, she said my name several times until I finally recognized her voice and realized who she was.

"Lori! You look great!" I exclaimed, as I hugged her newly healthy frame. It's always good to see friends whom you haven't spent time with for a while, but it's even better when you see that they have accomplished something and are really happy. Lori's smile said it all, but I was still curious about exactly what had happened.

Later, she told me she had gone home and lived by herself for the summer. Determined to do something about her weight and complexion, she purchased healthy food only. No Oreos or rocky road ice cream in her house. No chip bags or, her nemesis, chocolate sitting in her cabinets. Rather, fresh vegetables and fruit had slimmed her figure; low-fat carbohydrates had given her energy to exercise; and lots of water had cleared her complexion. Without joining Weight Watchers or going on the Slim-fast diet, Lori lost many unnecessary pounds. And she looked beautiful.

I've never forgotten Lori's story, because it made a huge impression on me. Lori went home with *will*power—"I will eat healthy food like salads and fruits" as well as *won't* power—"I won't veg in front of the TV rather than exercise." As a result, her appearance changed dramatically for the better.

Regardless of whether you have twenty pounds to lose, twenty pounds to gain, the "perfect" figure, or something in between, the "will and won't" diet applies to every one of us who wants to be healthy, fit, and beautiful. It goes something like this for me (when I'm obeying it):

I *will* exercise today, even though I'd rather read this book. I *will* eat a spinach salad for lunch, even though a big bagel loaded with lots of cream cheese sounds better. I *will* cook a well-rounded meal for dinner tonight, although I hate to mess with the dishes. I *will* fill my cup at the water fountain rather than getting another soda. I *will* eat my five fruits and veggies today before I allow myself to eat dessert (and by then, hopefully, I'll be full and won't want dessert).

I *won't* buy a high-fat snack out of the machine but *will* eat the apple I brought to work with me. I *won't* have seconds on dessert, though it looks awfully tempting. I *won't* drink caffeine for a regular pick-me-up, even though that may be okay every once in awhile. I *won't* skip exercising today. I *won't* eat

EATING DISORDERS

If you have an eating disorder, our life is probably a series of daily, conscious decisions to either overeat and purge or not eat at all. In a society that judges fat as the unpardonable sin, you are doing everything to avoid that judgment. Magazine models are stick thin and movie idols flaunt their figures with just threads of clothing. And while it's politically incorrect to tell jokes about a person's sexuality or race, a good fat joke will make everybody laugh—almost. With this sort of stigma, it is no wonder that you struggle with an eating disorder in your desperate attempt to be thin. Compulsive overeating, bulimia, and anorexia nervosa destroy countless lives every year. You may have just started down this road, or you may have journeyed quite far down to the dangerous end of it.

Wherever you are on your journey, we encourage you that the "will and won't" diet can work for you too. However, we know that knowledge and diet plans alone will not prevent you from continuing to harm yourself. So, please, for your wellness, seek professional help. You can start by looking up www.remuda-ranch.com on the web. This Christian counseling and referral center is specifically geared to help people with eating disorders and should guide you to the help and resources you need.

fast food again tonight.

Your "will and won't" diet will probably vary from mine. However, the basics will be similar. It all boils down to making a series of daily, conscious decisions about a balanced diet—and then sticking with those good decisions.

Sometimes those good decisions become hard to follow. When eating gets out of balance and becomes more of a compulsion than a necessity, then it has become an addiction. The Bible uses a different word for addictions: idolatry. I think the Apostle Peter must have had overeating, along with other things, in mind when he wrote the following words: "For we have spent enough of our past lifetime in doing the will of the Gentiles—when we walked in lewdness, lusts, drunkenness, revelries, drinking parties, and abominable idolatries. In regard to these . . . they will give an account" (1 Peter 4:3-5 NKJV).

Do you find yourself lusting after food? Are you worshiping at the altar of a snack machine, buying little daily idols called candy bars? If you're home alone, do your feet automatically take you to the refrigerator? When you're at a party, do the tables of food often beckon you to overindulge? If so, it becomes a matter of obedience to God to bring your eating habits under His control. Nothing, not even the desire for a candy bar, should control us more than He does.

Even though she followed an incredible diet during college, Lori's struggle with food and dieting still goes on. However, she is willing to persevere because of her dedication to God. Recently she wrote me: "I am still struggling with my eating, but I am   discovering that it really is a matter of obedience to God. Slowly, I am handing this addiction over to Him. It is really easy to sacrifice food when it is not something you particularly care for, but it is a lot harder when the food is something you really like. Being obedient to God in this area of my life is difficult, but I am thankful for the experience." The "will" part of Lori's diet plan is to honor God more than she desires food; the "won't" part is to control her food addictions by avoiding what is harmful. As her friend, I can attest that she's doing great.

Regardless of your current body shape, we highly recommend the "will and won't" diet club. Women around the country are having great success with this diet plan. It doesn't cost any more than your regular grocery bill, and you don't have to attend any group meetings or pay membership fees. For the sake of your overall wellness and beauty, we encourage you to give it a try.

ADDRESSING PMS AND MENSTRUAL PROBLEMS

All night long Susan had tossed and turned with cramps, signaling the start of yet another painful monthly cycle. When her alarm sounded at 6:30 A.M., she knocked it off the dresser as she tried to make it cease screeching. With that mission accomplished, she called in sick and fell back into an unrestful sleep.

By mid-morning, Susan woke up again, still feeling horrible. As she got out of bed and shuffled to the bathroom, she reasoned, *Maybe if I take a shower, I'll at least look better.* The hot shower diminished the pain a bit, but it didn't do much else for her. She wrapped herself in a towel and climbed out of the tub. Gazing at her reflection in the mirror, she decided it was time for a change in her appearance. She didn't feel very beautiful and reasoned that a pair of scissors would help.

Thirty minutes later, her waist-length hair was scattered all over the floor. Her optimism was shattered when her great idea for a new "do" did not work. Sobbing, Susan crumbled to the floor. *What have I done?* she cried. She felt awful, and now she just knew she looked that way too. For the next forty-eight hours, Susan didn't leave her apartment as she reeled with the dramatic and wide-ranging effects of her menstrual cycle and menstruation.

The symptoms of PMS are as varied as the women who experience them. Many women have emotional upsets, such as mood swings, high anxiety, and irritability. Some women, like Susan, feel compelled to do things they normally would not try. Other women experience physical problems like incessant cravings, exhaustion, headaches, bloating, cramping, and severe pain. All of these symptoms worsen depending on age, stress levels, nutritional habits, sexual activity, and former pregnancies.

Regardless of the severity of your PMS or menstruation, God is concerned about this area of your life. The Bible tells about a woman who bled for twelve long years. The constant pain, embarrassment, and ostracism she endured finally drove her to extreme measures. *If I can just touch Jesus' clothing,* she thought, *I know I will be healed* (Matt. 9:21). This faith motivated her to go to Jesus. Not feeling worthy to take up His time, she slipped behind Him and quietly touched His garment. Jesus immediately and caringly noticed her. He turned to her and said, "Take heart, daughter. Your faith has healed you" (v. 22). Right then, her twelve years of struggling with a very private issue came to an end.

As this woman did, every woman can go to God about the female problems she is enduring. As you approach Him for help, the first thing He will surely do is encourage you. "Daughter, take heart," He will whisper to your soul. He'll remind you that you are not alone in this and that He cares.

God may not choose to heal you, as He did that woman. Without a doubt, though, He will help you, possibly by enabling you to find your own solution to soothe your body and spirit. You may want to start with these ideas: Keep track of your symptoms and their severity, then ask your doctor's advice.

Check the health food store for natural herbal remedies, such as raspberry-leaf tea, crampbark tea, borage oil, evening primrose oil, or Dong Quai. Maintain a healthy diet by eating more fruits and vegetables. Don't give in to your cravings; eliminate salt, caffeine, sugar, dairy products, and, yes, even chocolate! Take long, hot baths or use a heating pad to ease cramps. Get out of the house and go for a walk. Avoid making any major decisions while you are experiencing PMS.

By asking God for help and taking care of yourself during your monthly cycle, you will look beautiful all month long, even if you don't feel so great. This beauty will be evident not only in your appearance but also in your attitude and demeanor.

DRESSING APPROPRIATELY

You've done everything you can to lead a lifestyle of wellness. You feel great, and you look beautiful.

However, what is the image that you now present? When people see you coming, what do they notice first? How do you show off the beauty of your wellness?

Sarah is one of the most attractive girls I have ever met. Her story is something like my friend Lori's, except that she didn't just gain weight in college, she had it since childhood. She learned to hide the pounds behind baggy clothes and long skirts, but she never did feel good about herself. Finally, one year during her early twenties, Sarah made the New Year's resolution to get in shape, and she stuck with her resolve. Ten months later she had practically recreated herself, and she looked great.

With her new figure, though, Sarah acquired a new attitude. She deliberately purchased clothing designed to provocatively show off her body. She filled her closets with low-cut shirts, skin-tight jeans, mini-miniskirts, and short shorts. Wearing these, she was able to turn men's heads in her direction like she never had before. And Sarah loved the attention.

In contrast to Sarah, I have another friend who did just the opposite. Julie has a sweet face, soulful eyes, and cute figure. She always looked nice, and she had a bevy of friends. One day, Julie decided that she wasn't going to wear her nice clothing, iron her clothes, or fix her hair and makeup anymore. When she told me of her decision, I asked for her reasoning, figuring she must be pressed for time. Julie's answer surprised me. Depressed because of a recent breakup, she told me that she was going to look this way to see which of her friends really liked her. Instead of looking nice, she intended to deliberately look less than her best.

Two friends. Two opposite perspectives on appearance. Sarah dressed provocatively; Julie quit taking care of herself.

Neither of these extremes is biblical. A beautiful, godly woman should have balance in her appearance, being neither provocative nor frumpy. Paul wrote, "Women should dress themselves modestly and decently in suitable clothing" (1 Tim. 2:9 NRSV). *Modestly* and *decently* are the key words here.

No matter how great your figure is, if you dress to draw undue attention to yourself, you are not dressing modestly. And no matter what you want to prove to your friends, if you don't present yourself appropriately, then you are not dressing decently.

We realize that modesty standards are a cultural thing. It was not too many years ago in America that it was indecent for a woman to show her ankles. And in other parts of the world, some tribal women don't even wear blouses to cover their breasts. We can't imagine dressing in either of these ways, but we do have standards to heed as Christians.

I asked some respectable, godly guy friends their thoughts about modesty and decency. They agreed wholeheartedly that these are important issues for Christian women, and they offered some intriguing insights.

To them, modesty indicates personal and spiritual maturity, as well as self-confidence. A woman who is modest, and at the same time attractive and friendly, portrays a sense of balance. This is impressive to a godly man.

On the other hand, a woman who dresses immodestly is communicating that she wants to play a game, a "ritual dance of the flesh" as one man termed it. In this dance, the immodest woman will reveal to a man her "assets" in exchange for his attention. This is a win-win situation in the world's eyes, but it is a lose-lose situation for Christians because this dance is only skin-deep. Neither participant ever gets to really know who the other person is on the inside. Instead, on the woman's part, her lack of modesty portrays neediness, insecurity, and a "high maintenance" personality.

You may have grown up in a home where you never learned modesty. I have one friend whose father made her return to the store whatever school clothes she purchased that he did not consider sexy. Now, as an adult single woman who is a new Christian, she is almost clueless about which of her clothes are too provocative.

My guy friends had several suggestions for modest dressing. They included: avoid wearing short skirts, short shorts, loose or low necklines, and extremely tight-fitting clothing. The guys noted, though, that women's body types and personalities make specific guidelines difficult to establish. Some women can wear fairly low-cut blouses and be modest because of their, well, you know, lack of upper body. Other women could try on that same shirt and make onlookers blush. Two girlfriends can go to the same store and try on the same dress, yet look totally different because of their personalities. The outgoing friend looks seductive, while her reserved friend looks just great in it.

With all our physical and personality differences in mind, a general rule the guys suggested is this: Dress remembering that Jesus is with you. Christ obviously knows the reasons and motives for why you dress the way you do, whether you are dressing immodestly to draw attention or dressing frumpishly because you are depressed. As a godly, balanced woman, dress to please Him first and foremost not only by being modest but also by taking care of yourself.

Also, dress to make a statement about your personal worth. Your physical body contains some things of great value: your soul and spirit. While you wouldn't dream of selling your soul, what about your body? If you value yourself (and you should), don't dress as though you can be bought cheaply. One guy friend told us, "You don't want to advertise goods that aren't for sale, and you don't want to attract the type of men who are buying!" How you dress can be a commercial to some men about how easy you are. If what you wear leaves little to the imagination, then observers are going to be imagining you in situations that you don't want to be in as a godly woman. By dressing appropriately, you will show others how valuable you consider yourself.

So, do what you can to look nice. Take care of yourself. Look pretty. Be beautiful. Always remember, though, that modesty and decency are "musts" in the wardrobes of godly women.

Throughout history women have tried to make themselves

beautiful. Makeup was invented long before Maybelline and Cover Girl got their trademarks. Nice clothes were in vogue well before there was electricity to light runways for models. Hair styling was popular centuries before the perm was created. Since the beginning of time, women have longed to be attractive.

The godly woman is no exception. Because she knows she is a designer original, she cares for her body with a lifestyle of wellness. She cares not only for her inner beauty but for her outer appearance as well. We encourage you to keep doing this so you will not only feel great but look great too.

 # COFFEE TALK

1. What does the Bible say about a woman's desire to be attractive? Use a concordance and look up some references with key words such as beauty and appearance.
2. Out of all the exercises listed, which ones do you enjoy the most? Which are you doing? If you aren't exercising, when will you start and what will you do?
3. How do PMS and menstruation affect you? If they are a problem, how can God help you with this?
4. What motivates you to dress the way you do? Does your style please the Lord?

RESOURCES

Begoun, Paula. *Don't Go to the Cosmetics Counter without Me.* 3d ed. Tukwila, Wash.: Beginning Press, 1996.

Evans, Debra. *Beauty and the Best.* Colorado Springs: Focus on the Family Publishing, 1993.

- Eleven -
THE SENSUAL WOMAN
Pampering Yourself

SHE MAKES COVERINGS FOR HER BED;
SHE IS CLOTHED IN FINE LINEN AND PURPLE.
PROVERBS 31:22

During a sunset stroll one evening, Melanie and I were casually discussing friends, relationships, and whatever else happened to come to mind. Between our observations about the shifting clouds and heavenly hues, Melanie casually mentioned her single roommate from grad school. "Sherri is one of the most sensual people I know," Melanie described her.

I about stopped in my tracks. *Sensual* certainly wasn't an adjective that I would want used to describe me! "Is she a Christian?" I blurted, after swallowing hard. "Definitely," Melanie answered without hesitation.

In the split second before Melanie finished explaining about Sherri, a trial took place in my mind. In my life history, the word *sensuality* had always been used with a negative connotation. To me, being a sensual woman meant not having modesty or discretion. Images of Sherri, dressed in a miniskirt, painted with heavy makeup, and indiscriminately flirting, came into my head. Before ten words were spoken in her defense, Sherri was judged and condemned in my mind.

The split second passed, though, and Melanie—oblivious to my mental courtroom—continued describing her friend. "Sherri loves Southwestern decor, clean sheets, classical concerts, fine

163

dining, peach-scented lotion, and foot massages."

I could not have been more shocked. *Southwestern decor has something to do with sensuality?* I mused.

"To Sherri," Melanie kept going, "sensuality means not just using but enjoying all the senses God has given her. I've never met anybody with a perspective quite like that before, but I think she's right."

Despite Melanie's positive explanation, I wasn't going to be too quick to change the judgment I had passed on Sherri. I had to go home and check the dictionary first.

WHAT IS SENSUALITY?

Pulling out my handy dictionary, I found that sensuality has several definitions. This is what I read:

> 1: relating to or consisting in the gratification of the senses or the indulgence of appetite: fleshly 2: sensory 3a: devoted to or preoccupied with the senses or appetites b: voluptuous c: deficient in moral, spiritual, or intellectual interests: worldly; esp: irreligious syn see carnal, sensuous [1]

The latter definitions weren't appealing, in my opinion. In fact, they reminded me of the description in Ephesians 4:19: "Having lost all sensitivity, they have given themselves over to sensuality so as to indulge in every kind of impurity, with a continual lust for more." Not a favorable picture! So, my initial negative reaction to someone being described as sensual was, to some extent, justified.

However, I realized that another definition of sensuality refers to the neutral word *sensory.* Nerve impulses from the sense organs convey messages to the nerve centers, giving sensations. So, in positive contrast to the other definitions, one meaning of *sensuality* has to do with the five senses.

After reading the definitions, I realized that my judgment of Sherri was unfair. Sherri enjoyed living out the positive definition of sensuality, whereas I did my best to avoid the negative definitions. Sherri's example challenged me to stop and think. I started rearranging my view of what it means to be a sensual Christian woman.

Certainly God gave us our senses to help, protect, and guide us. But didn't He also give us our five senses to enjoy? Scripture is full of references to our senses, such as, "Oh, taste and see that the Lord is good" (Ps. 34:8 NKJV), surely alluding to both our spiritual as well as physical taste buds. God Himself enjoys sweet smells; remember the woman who ministered to Jesus in His final days by anointing His feet with "very costly fragrant oil" (Matt. 26:7 NKJV).

Without a doubt, God wants us to enjoy the senses He has given us. But do we? Sure, we use our senses every day, and sometimes we taste a delicious bite or hear an enjoyable song. However, in your busy, stressful world as a single woman, how often do you *deliberately* add enjoyment of your five senses to your schedule?

ENJOYING OUR SENSUALITY

Ah! I thought. *There's nothing better than a nice, hot bath!* I splashed some bubbles just to accentuate my thoughts. My tub was just an ordinary ceramic tub, but candles set around the edge illuminated the water and made shadows dance on the ceiling. The hot water, the warm flickering glow, and the fragrant bubbles relaxed and refreshed me.

A few years ago, I didn't often allow myself this luxury because I considered myself too busy to enjoy something so time-consuming. The only reason, in fact, that I was taking a bath now was out of medical necessity. I had pushed my body beyond its limits, and stress along with carpal tunnel syndrome was taking its toll. Medicine and chiropractic treatments were of some value, but my doctors told me the only thing that would really help was to relax.

So relax I did. My nice hot bath that evening was followed by a bath the next evening, and the next, and the next. And soon my nerve and muscle problems began to go down the drain with the bath water.

What about you? Have you ever looked at your schedule and felt so overwhelmed that you could collapse? Is your dayplanner filled with people to call, deadlines to meet, and projects to accomplish so that you're running from the time you get up until the time you fall exhausted into bed? Is it laughable to suggest that you should take time to enjoy your senses?

If so, you're not alone. Melanie and I are right there with you. Probably many of your friends are too. So I have a suggestion. Pull out your planner. Get a red pen and a yellow highlighter, then look at next week's schedule. This will be hard, but you can do it. Make an appointment with yourself! Write it in red and highlight it in yellow. Schedule a few hours just for you, since nobody else can. This could be the most important meeting of your week.

But what do you do during your appointment? Be creative! There are thousands of great ideas for luxuriating in the five senses God has given you.

Some quick starters for enjoying your senses include taking a long, hot bubble bath with scented candles and classical music. Or you could lie by a fireplace and watch the flames. Relax by a window on a rainy day or stroll through a pretty park.

You could also try some things you used to do as a kid, like frolic in the sprinklers. Roll in the grass or identify shapes in the clouds. Play in the mud or just tromp through some mud puddles. Build a snow igloo—then eat lunch inside! Climb a tree and wave at passersby. We adults usually feel too mature and responsible to do things like this anymore. But weren't they such fun when we were kids? Make sure you include time in your schedule to do whatever is enjoyable to you.

THE SENSUALITY OF TASTE

After having a baby, I decided that the sense of taste must be the first that we really experience. My infant daughter, Anastasha, wants nothing more than to put everything she can find into her mouth! It matters not whether it's food or toys, a napkin or a book—Anastasha wants to get her lips around it.

Now, I'm certainly not advocating following Anastasha's example, or else we'd all be overeating and indulging in things not palatable. However, there are some great ways that we can enjoy our sense of taste.

Invite some friends over and spend the evening cooking gourmet food. Try out some unique recipes, especially the ones that call for special spices and herbs. Then sit down and enjoy the delicacies you've created.

Do something special for your own private mealtime. Find a tall-stemmed glass that is especially pretty—the beauty of the glass will add sensual pleasure to the taste of the drink.

Then have some sun tea or sparkling cider, or whatever other drink you enjoy, along with your meal. Relish the sips you take between bites.

For a fat-free sensual delight, buy a pint of strawberries and eat them whole. Or cut up the berries on your favorite frozen yogurt or angel food cake.

When it's cold outside, see how many warm drink combinations you can make. Try mixing your coffee with spices, chocolates, or flavorings, with whipped cream on top. Heat your favorite juice in the microwave—orange juice warmed with a little tea is really good. Make some Russian Tea out of spices and Tang. The more warm combinations you create, the better.

Then, when the sun begins to warm things up outside, start creating some cool drink combinations. Fruit slushes and virgin daiquiris are easily made in the blender. So are what I call "power shakes": yogurt, slightly frozen, and then blended with dried milk and whatever fruit you have in the kitchen. A sensual—and healthy—delight. Or create your own flavors of sun tea, then sip a glass in the shade.

When you get in the mood to bake, make something different than traditional chocolate chip cookies. Bake coconut macaroons, petit fours, pecan pralines. Make a pretty raspberry torte instead of just a cake mix. Yes, it will be a lot more effort to find a recipe, get the ingredients, and figure out how to make it. But, just for the sake of tasting something different, go for it!

If you're like me when you go out for dinner, your car automatically drives to one of your favorite top three restaurants. And my top three favorites are good ol' American food. But to enjoy the sensuality of our taste buds, we should try a variety of restaurants, including ones with international cuisine. I've heard that Indian food is delicious, but I've never been brave enough to try it. So Melanie and I have spotted an Indian restaurant close to our church, and we're going for lunch there soon!

A whole world of different foods, drinks, spices, and edible creations is out there to discover. Be a sensual woman and enjoy your taste buds.

THE SENSUALITY OF SMELL

When I was in graduate school, my life was busy. Very busy. I worked full time, attended school full time, tried to keep up with my homework, and ministered to teenagers. I scarcely had time to eat and study, much less to relax.

During my busy days, I would scurry from one point on the campus to another. Like the rabbit in *Alice in Wonderland,* my theme song was, "I'm late, I'm late, for a very important date. No time to say hello; good-bye, I'm late, I'm late, I'm late." Meals were devoured, conversations were brief, and work consumed my schedule.

Along the sidewalks of the seminary, though, were some beautiful distractions. For the first year of my busy life there, I ignored them. But then one day an old saying came to mind: Take time to smell the roses. As I contemplated the truth of that cliché, it dawned on me that life is made up of more than degrees, accomplishments, and schedules. Life is best enjoyed when it's made up of simple things, like fragrant roses. That day I made a personal resolution: never again would I consider myself too busy to stop and smell the roses.

Since then it has become somewhat of a hobby to sniff every pretty flower I see. No matter if it's a flowering weed in my yard, a manicured rose in a garden, or a flower arrangement on a banquet table, I make sure that I get a good whiff. In my opinion, God made flowers smell good for just one reason—our enjoyment. So enjoy them I do.

What about you? When was the last time you really thought about the pleasure of using your nose? People who have lost their sense of smell sorely miss it. So let's enjoy what God has given us.

Have you visited a bakery lately and relished the smell of freshly baked bread? How about baking some yeast bread at home? That will delight the taste buds too.

Do you have any scented candles? I have some but seldom light them, because I'm too conservative to burn them up. Are you like me? Always waiting for a special occasion to make the room smell really good? Well, I'm going to grab my candle and light it right now. How about you?

Making a eucalyptus swag is a fun way to enjoy the sense of smell in your home. You can buy bunches of eucalyptus at almost any craft store. Make a fan-like arrangement, secure it with wire, and decorate it with a big bow. Voila! You have an instant, and very fragrant, decoration for your home.

Next time you eat an orange, save the rinds. Simmer them, along with a few cloves, in water on the stove. Your home will smell wonderful. Or try simmering some pine cones or cinnamon sticks. They smell great too.

When you're at the grocery store, treat yourself to the most fragrant potted flower that you can find in the plant department. Baby carnations, hyacinths, and Easter lilies are just a few of the many aromatic delights.

Peach-scented lotion and berry-scented massage oil are extra pleasing to the nose. Don't just use them when you're going out; take pleasure from them when you're home alone.

God gave you your sense of smell to enjoy. So, to borrow an old saying: Stop and smell the roses.

THE SENSUALITY OF HEARING

The saxophone at a jazz concert. The whispers of a little child. The trees rustling in the wind. The buzzing of a bee.

Ears to hear are something that we so often take for granted. At least, I do. But how different life would be if we could not hear. What if everything was silent—no music, no voices, no laughter? If it were taken away, we would realize how very important the sense of hearing is.

Spring is arriving where I live, and with it the birds. It's still cold outside, but yesterday I threw open the windows for a little while just to listen to their harmony. They were chirping and singing so cheerfully that I couldn't help but smile at their enthusiasm. Have you taken the time to listen to some singing birds lately?

In a world of many sounds, few are better than the sound of water. A mountain creek, a city fountain, and ocean waves must be among life's most relaxing things. If you are fortunate enough to live near a beach, take an afternoon just to listen. If there's a nearby creek, go listen to it bubble. If you're stuck in the city, find a fountain in a park—or at least some kids splashing in a pool.

Popcorn popping, a clock ticking, a church bell ringing— deliberately stop what you are doing and listen. Enjoy your sense of hearing by turning the normal audio of life into stereo!

Check out some CDs or tapes from your local library, or borrow some from a friend, and listen to music styles that are new for you. It can be a great cultural experience to listen to music popular in other countries.

God gave us our hearing for many reasons, including helping us communicate and warning us of danger. But I believe He also gave us hearing for our enjoyment. So let's luxuriate in the surround sound.

THE SENSUALITY OF SIGHT

Just recently a friend told me that she concentrates on observing God's "love gifts." She deliberately tries to see God's special touch on each day, whether it be frost that delicately covers the trees, beautiful roadside flowers of spring, or billowy clouds. These things are easily missed as we scurry about. However, by consciously looking for God's little blessings, our eyes will find delight.

Have you ever gotten up early to watch a sunrise, then made sure to watch the sunset on the same day? If you have never done that, roll out of bed early this weekend and try a wonderful new experience. If you live on a coast, we envy your ability to watch the colorful sunrise or sunset over a glorious body of water. These incredible colors are God's love gifts to us.

Plant some seeds in a sunny window during the spring, and watch them grow. I enjoy planting marigold seeds and observing their growth from tiny seedlings to colorful flowers.

Drive out into farm country and see the farm animals. Besides being interesting to watch, animals are great entertainment—if you're willing to find the enjoyment in the commonplace.

Have you ever been to a ballet? That is a unique visual treat. If you can't afford a ticket to a high-price production, call a children's dance studio and find out when the next recital is.

Read a romantic novel. (We highly recommend the classic *Jane Eyre*, by Charlotte Brontë.) Watch an old movie, and observe the characters in the background. Notice the delight of children playing—and laugh with them!

Concentrate on the delicate features of a flower, the shadows of a tree, or the intensity of the sky. Watch the dying embers of a campfire. There are limitless ways to enjoy the sense of sight. So, instead of just using your eyes to watch the road when you're driving or to scan the computer at work, use your eyes to drink in all the visual pleasures God has so richly given us.

THE SENSUALITY OF TOUCH

Here in Colorado, the climate is extremely dry. On the positive side, it's so dry that you can leave a box of crackers open for a week and they won't get stale. You can walk through the grass in the morning and your shoes won't get covered with dew. For most of the year, there's not even the possibility that a rainstorm will ruin your picnic.

On the negative side, though, the dryness is horrible for your body. It makes our skin crack and hair split. Oh, the frustration! When my fingers begin to snag my hose, that's when I know I'm in trouble. My sense of touch is being lost, or at least dulled. What to do?

Baby oil, and lots of it, can be the cure for dry skin. A bottle of it does wonders for me. Once my fingers and hands feel soft again, I'm ready to start enjoying my sense of touch.

These days you can find body scrubs at almost any store. They're a popular gift item too. In fact, I have two different bottles in my bathroom from friends: vanilla and plumeria scents. Sounds yummy, huh? If you don't already have any body scrubs, treat yourself and get a loofah brush or sponge. Indulge your hands and feet, arms and legs, in a scrub down. Dry, rough skin will be gently polished, and your overall skin texture will be improved. What a delight!

How about giving your feet a treat? Some evening while you're reading a book, studying, or watching television, get out a large pan. Fill it with the warmest water you can stand, then slip your feet inside. Talk about a great way to get off on the right foot!

Did you ever have a rabbit fur coat when you were a little girl? I did, and I sure was proud of that jacket. (If you're an animal-rights activist, forgive me. I honestly wasn't trying to be cruel when I wore it.) I really enjoyed the Sundays that I got to wear my coat. It was warm, pretty, and snugly. Best of all, though, it was soft. I loved to sit in church and run my fingers through the fur. How many sermons passed through one ear and out the other while my hands lingered on that coat!

Now, I'm not recommending that all of us grown-up girls go out and buy fur coats. However, I would suggest that we use our sense of touch to enjoy things such as that. Get out your mom's old mink coat and run your fingers through it. Touch the leather on your boyfriend's jacket. Feel the softness of a silk blouse.

If you have a pet, or if one of your friends has one, give it a good rub. Your fingers will enjoy the sensation—and your pet will love the attention.

Besides giving a pet a massage, how about getting a massage for yourself? It's an incredible stress reliever. Sound too

> CREATE YOUR OWN BATH SALTS
> *Simply mix 1/2 cup table salt, 1 tablespoon baking soda, 1 tablespoon borax, and add 1/4 teaspoon of any essential oil— which you can buy at a natural foods store. Add this mixture to your bath water. Or you may find that you enjoy soaking in plain Epsom salts just as well.*

expensive to indulge in? A cost-effective way to get a great massage is at a massage school. Usually the students have a clinic where they practice on people for a reduced price. See if there's a listing in your yellow pages.

Volunteer to work in your church nursery one week. As you take care of the babies, touch their soft hands and feel their chubby little cheeks. I'm not sure that there are many things more delightful to the touch than a brand-new baby's skin.

The sense of touch truly is a wonderful way to enjoy our sensuality.

God gave us our senses, of course, for utilitarian purposes. If we could not hear the warning whistle or see the red light we would definitely be in trouble. Certainly, though, God also meant for us to use our senses to a far greater degree. By taking the time to enjoy our sensuality, we can add pleasure to our lives. Our stressful and sometimes monotonous routines will be enriched by deliberately delighting in what we taste, touch, smell, hear, and see.

Sherri got it right when she decided to be a sensual woman. That's the type woman I want to be too: enjoying all the senses

God has given me. In fact, I'm going to go make a cup of flavored coffee and watch the sunset. Will you join me?

 *COFFEE TALK*

1. How have you traditionally dealt with stress in your life?
2. When was the last time you pampered yourself? How do you think God viewed this?
3. What will you do in the next ten days to specifically enjoy each of the senses God has given you?

---

[1] *Merriam-Webster's Collegiate Dictionary,* 10th ed., see "sensual."

Finances

Millions of stars brightened the black sky above the dense tree line. The river running through the thick forest put a slight chill into the air, making it a perfect evening to be wrapped in a sweater and a sleeping bag.

At a small campsite, Laurie and her friends lit a match to a pile of cardboard, paper, and wood. In an instant, the bright red and orange flames illuminated the campsite. They warmed their hands and then reached for marshmallows to roast.

"Get some more logs," someone called as the fire started to sub-side. Laurie ran to their makeshift woodshed and grabbed two pieces of wood. As she added the wood one log at a time, the blaze became more intense, until it gradually turned into a majestic bon-fire. The flames rose high into the dark, and the group stepped back to enjoy its roaring beauty.

As Laurie watched the fire, she remembered a news story. A wildfire had ripped through the northern part of their state, burn-ing every blade of grass and every pine and oak tree in its path. The footage she saw was devastating, with hundreds of firefighters bat-tling the flames and wildlife attempting to escape its rampage. How *could this enchanting fire they were watching turn into a disastrous inferno?*

Like fire, the money we are entrusted with can either bring us peace or terror. If we wisely add money to our savings and investments, we can watch it grow like the flames of a soothing campfire. But if we spend recklessly or are careless with our finances, they could quickly get out of control and begin engulfing everything around.

If you lost your job tomorrow, would you have enough money to live on until you found new employment? Is your credit card balance so high that you dread receiving the next statement, because there is no way to pay it off? Or do you keep buying new things on credit because you don't have any cash? If these areas are out of control in your life, the campfire has turned into a wildfire.

With proper planning and control, however, you can build a steady and secure fire that gives you comfort instead of fear. By budgeting your money and putting aside a little every paycheck, you can save enough money to buy that car or take the vacation you've been wanting, and you can gradually build your financial security one dollar at a time.

- Twelve -
THE BUDGETING WOMAN
Controlling Your Finances

Chelsea sighed as she waited in the seemingly unending line at the ATM machine. It was Friday night, and she was going to a movie and to eat out with her friends. They were waiting for her at the theater while she was waiting to get some cash.

Every moment that she waited, agitation filled her stomach. Not so much from the long line, although that was irritating enough. Her agitation came as she mentally ran through her finances. The forty dollars she was about to withdraw from the ATM machine was all she had left until the end of the month—ten days from now. At the beginning of the month, Chelsea had gone on a shopping spree, impulsively purchasing two pair of shoes and a few new outfits. That same weekend, she got a perm too. It had been a really fun weekend, and she loved her new look. But now new hairdos and clothes aside, she was financially strapped. When her turn came to use the ATM machine, Chelsea swallowed hard, knowing that after she used this last forty dollars for entertainment, she was not going to be able to buy anything else for the next ten days.

As she put the money in her wallet and made her way to the theater, Chelsea grimaced at the thought of what her father would say: "Chelsea, you need a budget!" *He'll never know.* She pushed the mental rebuke aside as she saw her friends waving to her. Like Scarlet O'Hara, Chelsea told herself, "I'll think about it tomorrow," and purchased her ticket.

WHY BUDGET?

You've heard it before: you should budget your finances. Perhaps your aunt who is an accountant gives you this admonition each family Christmas. Maybe your father asks you about it every time you talk with him on the phone. Or maybe your organized roommate reminds you by her example, when, each month, she sits down at the kitchen table to work on her budget. Maybe your own conscience is nagging you. But you still haven't organized your finances and made a budget. Why not?

Is it because you enjoy that all-of-the-sudden horrible feeling in the pit of your stomach when the check you wrote yesterday is bouncing today? Does your idea of a rosy future contain candlelight—because your electricity has been shut off? Do you enjoy feeling guilty for spending thirty dollars to go to a concert when you should have used that money for your phone bill? Or do you not have a budget plan because you enjoy being bogged down in debt? We seriously doubt that any of these are true of you.

As a Christlike single woman who is seeking balance and fulfillment, orderly finances should be a priority in your lifestyle. You want to be prudent about your money, controlling it rather than letting it control you. You want to create financial security for yourself so that you can take care of yourself now and in the future. You like the financial freedom of both paying your bills and having money left over to enjoy the perks of life. And it's not an exaggeration to say you abhor debt.

Financial freedom, security, and confidence are only three

of many reasons why we should all budget. As a single woman, it depends on your own initiative to make these happen in your life.

HOW WILL A BUDGET HELP ME?

"Well, financial security sure sounds appealing, but how will a budget help me accomplish that?" Chelsea asked when we later discussed her dilemma. Budgeting will help you in two ways.

First, a budget enables you to establish financial priorities in your life. As you think through what you will spend your money on, you will be more likely to use it for what's important to you rather than what is urgent or impulsive. Have you ever tallied up the small things that you spend money on each week? Coffee, sodas, lunches, movies? It adds up fast, and that amount can significantly affect what you have left in your bank account. When you *plan* how to use your paycheck, you will be more likely to use the money for things that are significant to you rather than for impulse purchases.

A budget also enables you to organize your finances so that you can keep accurate records and systematically pay your bills. No more "Oops! I forgot to send in my utility bill!" "Did I pay my rent this month?" "Can I afford to support this charity?" "I can't give my tithe this month!" With a budget, you will know exactly how much you have to spend in the different areas of your life. You will pay your bills on time, and you will still have money left over to enjoy life and to plan for emergencies.

As you establish your financial priorities and organize your finances, a budget will enable you to be a good steward of what God has entrusted to you. No matter whether you make a lot or a little, you will be able to use your money—God's money—wisely.

IS IT SIMPLE?

"I just bounced three checks! I thought I had enough money to cover them, but I didn't," Stacey lamented to me (Tosha). "Now the bank wants money for overdrawn charges, and I owe fees to the stores where I wrote the bad checks. This is going to cost me a bundle!" she moaned.

I nodded in sympathy, hating to think of how much money Stacey was going to be out for her mathematical mistake. With her bachelor's degree in math, she was quite adept at numbers. Confident in her ability, she had always kept her finances in her head. In spite of her math degree, though, Stacey looked at budgeting as a complicated process. So, she just put her entire paycheck in the bank and kept a running mental tally of how much she spent until her next paycheck. This plan usually worked well. However, a week-long vacation followed by a minor car accident had caused a blip in Stacey's normally efficient mental calculator. Now she owed a lot of money—and would have nothing to show for it.

If creating a budget seems too complicated, how much more complicated (both in terms of money and time) is it to work yourself out of a situation like Stacey's?

Despite the fact that it is much more complicated to fix a financial mess than to create a financial plan, the main reason people don't have a budget is that it seems too complicated or time-consuming. I've heard some singles say that they will not start keeping a budget until they get married, have a family, or buy a house. Others say they don't keep a budget because it seems too rigid and inflexible.

However, a budget need not be complicated, inflexible, or time-consuming. You should simply choose and implement the plan that works best for your lifestyle. Then, with just the investment of taking the time to create a budget and then the discipline to maintain it, all the benefits of budgeting are yours to enjoy. Today is a great time to begin that process.

OKAY . . . SO HOW DO I MAKE A BUDGET?

While attending seminary in Dallas, I had the privilege of working for a gentleman who had worked in the finance industry for many years. Fresh out of college, I was as green in the finance field as I was enthusiastic, but he took a chance and hired me anyway. For the next few years, I worked as the assistant in the financial aid office, doing everything from creating scholarship letters to writing loans.

One of my favorite parts of the job, though, was on the rare occasion that the office was empty and the phones were silent. I then would ask my boss all sorts of questions about finances, and he would patiently answer them for me. Among other things, he taught me that the process of establishing a budget has three basic steps: determine your financial priorities, organize your finances, and choose a budget style.

Step One: Determine Your Financial Priorities
What is truly important to you? God's Word reminds us, "Where your treasure is, there your heart will be also" (Matt. 6:21 NRSV). Usually what is in your bank account will go to what is already important in your heart. This is key to remember as you plan your financial priorities. Regardless of whether they are important to your family or friends, these priorities are

important to *you*. And that's what counts.

Primary items for all of us are: housing, groceries, and transportation. Other items of importance include clothing, insurance, and personal care. Beyond those basics, though, what is important to you?

A financial priority that every believer should have is tithing. As a balanced, Christlike woman, you should give back to God some of what He has given to you. This priority is a matter of obedience, because the Bible commands us to give. Don't forget to include this vital area in your list of priorities.

In addition to your tithe, you also may want to support your local crisis pregnancy center or give gifts to needy children at Christmas because you enjoy giving money to good causes. If this is true, then benevolence is one of your financial priorities.

You may like spending time with your friends, going to movies, concerts, or special events—most of which cost money. If this is true, then entertainment is a financial priority.

You may have dreams of building your own home, taking a special vacation to Europe, or buying your next car with cash. If any of these are true of you, then saving is probably a financial priority.

Photography, arts, horseback riding, or other hobbies may be a priority for you. You may need to get a new pair of eyeglasses next year. Before you start creating your budget, determine what your financial priorities are for the year.

When you weigh your priorities, you will be able to determine where things go on their relative value scale. Entertainment may be important to you, but sponsoring an impoverished child may be even more important. You may like to have new clothes; however, you would rather keep wearing what you have and put more money into savings for a down payment on a new home. You may enjoy going on vacation, but instead of spending your money on one week of holiday, you would rather do fun things throughout the year.

Take a few minutes to think about your financial priorities and jot them down, perhaps at the end of this chapter. As you write them down, assign a dollar value to each. You've just accomplished the first step of creating a budget. That wasn't too hard, now was it?

Step Two: Organize Your Finances

After prioritizing your finances, the next step is to organize them. If organizing is not your favorite thing to do, hang in there. This step will take a few hours, but once it's done, you won't have to worry about it for another year.

You can organize your finances, first of all, by determining what your regular, monthly income is. For the sake of ease, use your take-home income for this figure. Most of us have income solely from our paychecks. However, you may have income from other sources, such as savings, an inheritance, or a second job. If you depend on this money to make ends meet, figure it into your monthly take-home income. If not, create your budget solely using the figure from your main paycheck, and allot the irregular money for savings or unexpected expenses.

Second, after you determine your regular monthly income, determine what your regular, monthly expenditures are. These will fall into two categories: fixed expenses and variable expenses. Understanding which categories your expenses fit into will help you choose a budget system that works best for you.

You may need to keep a running record of your expenses for

DEFINITION OF TERMS

Fixed expenses: A fixed expense is one that is fairly consistent in cost. Most of the time, you will not get a receipt for fixed expenses; rather, your canceled check becomes your receipt. Examples of fixed expenses include: tithe, housing, loan payments, car payments, utilities, insurance, or savings.

Variable expenses: A variable expense is one that can change a lot from month to month. One month you may have a lot of expenses in one category, then the next month you have very few or no expenses in that category, neither of which harm your overall budget. Examples of variable expenses include: groceries, entertainment, gas, medical copayments, or haircuts.

several months so that you know about how much you spend in each category. Accurately record how much you spend and what you spend it on. These records will be worth the effort when it comes time to start budgeting. If you do this, you will soon have some realistic figures with which to create your new budget.

We suggest that once you know these figures you make a budget plan that operates on a yearly basis. You may choose to run your budget from January to December (because you like to start things fresh each year), or from July to June (when you usually get a pay raise). If it is midyear, however, and you want to have an annual budget, don't wait six months to start budgeting. Get started with a half-year budget and switch over to a full-year budget at the beginning of next year.

Whew! You've now completed the second step of creating a budget. You've determined your financial priorities and organized your finances. Just one more step to go.

Step Three: Choose a Budget Style

We women are sometimes notorious for not being able to make up our minds. If you are a decisive woman, then this step will be easy. However, if you are like many of us, you are going to need to choose a budget style and stick with it. Just be reassured that this is not a terminal decision—you can change budget style next year, if need be!

The cash envelope method. If you have never operated with a budget before, a great way to start is with the cash envelope method. Using this system, you will pay all your fixed monthly expenses with a check and all your variable expenses with cash. The beauty of this system is that it will help you pay your important bills on time as well as teach you to stop spending when you run out of money. You'll clearly know when you have no more to spend for the month: when you peer into your envelopes, they will stare back at you empty!

Samantha had never used a budget before, so when she started, she wanted the easiest system possible. The fewer records and the more control, the better, in her opinion. So she chose to use the cash envelope method. Here is how she does it.

Her paycheck is automatically deposited at the beginning of each month. At that time, Sam writes the checks for her fixed expense bills, and she subtracts that money out of her checkbook register. While she's doing this, she goes ahead and puts those checks into envelopes, ready to mail before their due dates.

Then Sam makes a trip to the bank for cash. (Yes, one trip to the bank, which keeps her from making repeated trips to the ATM machine!) She gets $290 in cash for all of eight of her variable expense envelopes (groceries, gas, haircut, dry cleaning, clothing, entertainment, gifts, and miscellaneous). Once she gets home, Sam pulls out her envelopes and puts the right amount of cash into each. She keeps her gas envelope in the glove compartment in her car, and she always sticks the miscellaneous envelope in her purse. The other envelopes stay locked at home in a safe place until she pulls money out during the month for expenses.

When Sam was putting the allotted money into each envelope this past month, she was pleased to see that she had $60 already in her clothing envelope. For the prior two months, she had not spent any money on clothes, choosing rather to save it for a big purchase. With the additional $30 added to the $60 already in the envelope, Sam had the great feeling that it was about time to go shopping. She uses this method all the time to save for hair highlights or for special gifts that cost more than one month's allotment.

On the other hand, there have been months when Sam overspent well before the month ended. One time she spent most of her allotted grocery budget on a special meal she prepared for a large group of friends. After that evening, eleven days were left until she got her next paycheck, and she had a whopping $10 left in her grocery envelope. Rather than using her credit card or taking money out of savings, Sam chose to use that ten dollars to buy some cheap foods, like rice, bananas, macaroni and cheese, carrots, and peanut butter, to tide her over until the next paycheck came along. Two days before the month ended, she started PMSing and absolutely craved salty pretzels. Since she did not use all her gas money that month, Sam just took a few dollars from that envelope, went to the store, and bought the best pretzels she could find.

The cash envelope system requires discipline and flexibility. When money in an assigned envelope runs out, you will have to discipline yourself to not spend any more money. Charge cards and checks are out of the question. On the other hand, you should allow yourself some flexibility. Borrowing from other envelopes is absolutely fine—as long as you don't spend more than the sum total of all your envelopes. As you watch the money in your envelopes dwindle each month, you'll be surprised at how closely you guard the little purchases you make along the way.

Converting to the cash envelope method may seem a little intimidating, because you will need all the cash for the month at the beginning of the month. Slide into this system a little bit at a time, if you need. Only get enough cash for two weeks, if you get paid twice a month. Or, just get cash for a few categories at first, adding a new category each month until you have all of the envelopes working.

The journal entry method. You may be a person who does not like operating with cash. You would just as soon use your credit card or checkbook when it comes to paying for things. If that is the case, you may find it a lot easier to use the journal entry method to keep track of your expenses.

When Stacey decided to go to a more reliable budgeting system than the one in her head, she chose to use the journal entry method. With her mathematical background, she enjoys working with figures and numbers, so this method is a natural choice for her. Here's how she does it.

One evening, she took a few minutes at her computer to create a grid with about ten columns and fifteen rows. In the first column on the left-hand side, she typed in each of her budget categories. Then, in the second column, she typed in her budgeted amount for each category. Stacey printed twelve copies of this grid (one for each month) and put them in a budget notebook.

Each month, Stacey writes out the checks for her fixed expenses when she gets her paycheck. After writing out the check, she hand records it on her budget journal page. Like Sam, she puts the checks in envelopes, ready to mail before they are due. Unlike Sam, Stacey does not get cash for the entire month. She only gets about $25, which is her miscellaneous money for various small expenses.

Throughout the month, Stacey writes checks for all her purchases and saves her receipts. About once a week, she grabs all her receipts and records each expense in the appropriate row of its category. As she writes in what she has spent, she takes a mental note of which categories she has reached or has almost reached the limit in.

Stacey's budget journal page for June looked something like this:

JUNE BUDGET	Budget Amt.	Date/Amt.
Fixed Expenses		
Tithe	$140.00	6/1, $70; 6/15, $70
Rent	450.00	6/1, $450
Utilities	60.00	6/1, $60
Health Insurance	35.00	withdrawn from payck.
Savings	75.00	auto. dep. 6/1, $75
Car Payment	285.00	6/1, $285
Car Insurance	45.00	6/1, $80
Variable Expenses		
Groceries	$90.00	6/1, $26; 6/10, $32
Gas	60.00	
Hair Care	15.00	6/10, $15
Clothes/Dry Cleaning	35.00	6/5, $12
Entertainment	50.00	6/7, $15
		6/15, $21
Miscellaneous	35.00	
Gifts	20.00	6/10, $15
TOTAL	**$1395.00**	

On a rare occasion, Stacey will need to purchase something when she does not have her checkbook with her. If she knows she has the money in the bank to cover it, she might choose to pull out her credit card. Then she goes home with that receipt just as she would any other, recording it in her journal. When the credit card bill comes, she has the money sitting in the bank waiting to make the payment.

If you use the journal entry method of budgeting, you will have to know how much you can spend each month, keep up with your receipts, and update your budget journal periodically. All together, it's not that time-consuming; it's just a matter of being organized.

Stacey and Sam both discovered how simple it is to keep a budget, and they are now confident in managing their finances. You, too, can experience this confidence with a budget.

Other methods. If the cash envelope or journal entry methods of budgeting do not appeal to you, keep looking until you find a method that works for you. Perhaps you can create your own personalized variation of the cash and journal methods. Or you may choose a totally different route. If you are a computer guru, you might create your own computer spreadsheet. You may do well to look through an office supply store and select a computer budgeting program such as Quicken. Before you decide to go this route, though, make sure you are committed to getting on your computer and entering all your payments. If you have a friend who handles her money well, talk to her about what budgeting method she uses.

No matter which method you choose, having a budget will help you establish your financial priorities and organize your finances. No worries that yesterday's checks are bouncing or that debt is going to consume you, because you will have control of your finances. No living from check-to-check, because you will have a financial plan to carry you through the year. No guilt about going to occasional special events with friends, because you will have the financial freedom to do so.

Chelsea's financial motto of "I'll think about it tomorrow" finally changed when she got into such deep financial waters that she had to be rescued with a life preserver. That life preserver was a budget—something that would have protected her from getting into financial trouble in the first place.

A prudent woman will give thought to her finances long before she encounters financial trouble. Today is a great time to start.

 ## COFFEE TALK

1. Has budgeting been a successful endeavor for you? Why or why not?
2. What are your financial priorities, and what dollar amount do you assign to each of them?
3. One of the Spirit's fruits is self-control (Gal. 5:22-23). How does that attribute apply to budgeting?

- Thirteen -

THE SAVING WOMAN
Putting Money Aside

IN THE HOUSE OF THE WISE ARE STORES OF CHOICE FOOD AND OIL,
BUT A FOOLISH WOMAN DEVOURS ALL SHE HAS.
PROVERBS 21:20, PARAPHRASE

"I can barely make ends meet, much less set aside money to save!" Jeanette groaned in exasperation.

A few friends were sipping tea with me (Tosha) when the conversation turned to finances. Budgets and bills, pay raises and salary cuts were our topics when we began talking about creating budgets that would enable each of us to pay our bills as well as save. Before we got too far into that discussion, though, Jeanette was frustrated.

"I've tried to save before, but it just doesn't work out for me! If I could just make more money, this wouldn't be a problem," she continued.

After a couple of sympathetic nods and a few suggestions, the usually unopinionated Hailey spoke up. "I think that even if your salary never increases, you can find ways to save money!" Startled by her bold statement, we hushed and waited for her to continue. Carefully emphasizing her first word, she said, "*Anybody* who is willing to give it a try can save money. I know, because that's what happened to me." We knew that although Hailey had come from a poor family she completed graduate school without debt and was just about to purchase her own townhome. I had never stopped to consider how she had done so, though.

We continued to listen with vested interest as Hailey told us her story: how she got out of debt, paid her way through school, and had a down payment.

WHY SAVE?

"Before I began trying to save money, I came up with some financial goals. That's where you've got to start," Hailey told us. Retirement, emergencies, a down payment for a home, luxury items, special occasions, or long-term goals are a few of the reasons women should save money.

"I thought retirement was so far off that it was not a necessity in my budget now," Hailey began. "But once I got out of school, I realized I shouldn't wait any longer." By starting to save for retirement while you're young, your money will compound until you have a healthy retirement fund when you need it.

"Did you know that some financial experts advise that you have at least three months worth of salary in savings to prepare for the unexpected?" she continued. As we all shook our heads, she reminded us that if a financial emergency should arise, be it a car repair or a hospital bill, savings are what could tide us over.

"I don't know about you guys," Ann spoke up, "But I've always wanted to own my own home." We talked about how we could start saving for our down payments, possibly by setting aside some money from each paycheck. The money contributed to a dream home account will eventually build up into a nice nest egg.

"What about those luxury items you want, like that hope chest you mentioned earlier, Carolyn?" Hailey went on. A luxury item is anything you would really like to have but can live without. While you should not go into debt for luxuries, saving for them is a great idea. Luxury items may include a nice living room set, patio furniture, a VCR, a camera, a laptop computer, or a guitar. "When you finally get to splurge on your luxury item, you'll enjoy it even more because of the anticipation you've built while saving for it," she said with a smile.

"I think saving is especially fun when you have a special event as your goal," Laura chimed in. She told us about a vacation she took with three girlfriends to gorgeous Vancouver Island in Canada. Nine months before their trip, they made the plans and began saving for it. When their getaway week finally arrived, the trip was completely paid for out of their special occasion savings accounts. Maybe your special occasion is a vacation like that, a reunion, a weekend getaway by yourself, or a plane ticket home for Christmas. "Because we paid for our trip with money we'd saved," Laura said, "we had so much more fun than if we had to work to pay for it after we got back."

"Personally, my biggest motivation for saving was graduating from school without thousands of dollars in loans," Hailey concluded. Then we started talking about each of our long-term goals. More education was Ann's priority. Laura's old car was on its last wheel, making a new vehicle a necessity. Another girl's goal was to backpack through Australia while she was still in her twenties. Jeanette added that she wanted to take a month-long trip to Europe. I told my friends that I'm setting money aside for a grand piano. We laughed that while a piano is a dream purchase for me, it is of absolutely no interest to my friends. All our goals and reasons were different, but without a doubt each was worth saving for.

Why should *you* save? Whatever your personal long-term and short-term financial goals are, it is important that you identify them and start saving for them.

"Okay, okay! I get the point!" Jeanette joked. "But how am I supposed to find ways to save?"

ENTERTAIN ECONOMICALLY

As a single woman, your friends usually become your family, and it's important to spend time with them. Your weekend schedule may look something like this: a movie and pizza with friends on Friday night; lunch and shopping with a girlfriend on Saturday afternoon; lunch with friends after church on Sunday; then ice cream with another friend on Sunday night. All weekend long, you're spending money to spend time with your friends, not to mention the dollars that you spend during the week with them.

As you try to save money, learn how to entertain yourself and your friends economically. How about having a game night? Or renting a few videos and having your friends bring some of the snacks for a movie marathon?

Instead of going out for dinner on Friday night, organize a progressive dinner with your friends. At each home along the way, eat a different course: appetizer, salad, main dish, or dessert. This can be great fun without the restaurant expense.

During the summer, go to the park for a game of volleyball and a picnic. Camping at a national park is fairly cheap, especially when you go as a group. Organize a Friday night getaway with your friends.

During the winter, have a picnic in your living room. Or, since you can't go camping, organize a girls' slumber party. Make it really fun by giving each other manicures, pedicures, makeovers, or, if you dare, haircuts and perms.

Many ideas for entertaining are not only great fun but also

economical. As your friends see how much fun you can have without spending a lot of money, they will follow your lead in planning inexpensive entertainment. By starting this trend, you and your friends will be able to save money for long-term goals.

GIVE CREATIVELY

Sometimes it seems like every week there's another event that needs to be commemorated with a gift. Birthdays, weddings, baby showers, and Christmas. All very special and significant times in peoples' lives, but expensive when you need to give gifts. Thirty dollars for this person, twenty-five for that event, fifteen for this gift, nineteen for that present. It adds up fast.

None of us want to be a Scrooge, though, because giving is fun. So, here are some ideas to keep the costs down.

If you're a photographer, take a picture that would be meaningful to the recipient and frame it to match her home. If you're an artist, draw one. If you're good at needlepoint, make a special cross-stitch for the event. If you're a seamstress, sew something useful for the person's house, such as a ruffle for the kitchen window or a cover for a table.

In the past, I have made pillows, wall hangings, and Christmas decorations. Melanie has made dried flower arrangements, potpourri baskets, and jars of tea mixes.

You may not enjoy making things, and that's perfectly okay. However, you can still give creatively and inexpensively. Next time you go to the store and find some bargains, think through coming events. If pretty lingerie is on sale, think of friends who have bridal showers in the next few months. If you find some adorable, sale-priced baby clothes, think through which of your friends are pregnant. If you like giving Christmas decorations, then shop at the after-Christmas sales. If you know that your mother loves eclectic picture frames, buy several when you find them on the clearance rack to use for Mother's Day, her birthday, and maybe even Christmas. If you like to give dolls to needy little girls at Christmas, then don't pass up a bargain dolly! Sweaters, stationery, home decorations, and other nice gift ideas can all be found on clearance racks occasionally. Take advantage of the deals.

It may seem like storing gifts purchased or made in advance will take up too much space. However, I set aside a shelf in my closet just for storing gifts. If you don't have a spare shelf in your closet, I'll bet you have space under your bed. Boxes that slide under bed frames can be purchased inexpensively. Get a couple of those to use as gift storage boxes.

DRESS FOR LESS

Most women like to spend money on clothes. Whether we feel best in a pair of jeans, in a professional suit, in casual shorts, or in a dress, we all like to look good. Your biggest temptation may be a trip to the mall where thousands of great outfits are displayed on store mannequins. Or you may be most enticed by a home shopping magazine, such as L. L. Bean or J Crew. Or is a trip to the outlet mall your biggest draw?

You may already have a certain amount budgeted for clothing. However, if you're looking for ways to save money, this can be a great place to cut back. And that doesn't necessarily mean that you won't purchase any new clothes. It may just mean that you begin shopping in new places.

Whether your closets and drawers are bulging or sparse, events in your life may necessitate some new clothes. Last year,

> *Before some of us purchase more clothing, we need to either wear out or give away some of the things already in our closets. After several years of purchasing the latest trends, closets begin to bulge. You may want to donate some items to an organization such as the Salvation Army. Call a women's shelter to see if they could use any donated clothing. Or clean out your closet when your friends clean theirs, then have a big group yard sale.*

our friend Renné got promoted to office manager, and she needed to start wearing business suits to work. She went to the mall looking for nice suits, only to find them priced out of her league at up to $250 apiece. Instead of charging several on her Visa card (and justifying the purchase with thoughts of her upcoming raise), Renné started searching for sales and alternatives. A financially savvy friend recommended that she find a clothing consignment shop. Because she had never purchased second-hand clothing before, Renné was hesitant to follow her friend's advice. But she looked up several consignment stores in the phone book anyway.

The next Saturday, she set out early in the morning to visit three stores. The first was a dive, with worn-out clothes and not-so-great prices. Disappointed, she almost gave up the search and headed to the mall. But on her way there, she passed the second consignment store and decided to try once more. To her surprise, she found the store as clean as a department store and the clothes were almost as nice as new. As she looked around, she saw designer dresses, name-brand outfits, and fashionable shirts and pants. Then, Renné found four well-kept, name-brand suits that perfectly fit her, each for just $25. It didn't take her long to decide to purchase them. Although they all looked clean, she still did not feel comfortable wearing other people's clothing. So, on her way home, she dropped them off at her bargain dry cleaners, where each item costs just $1.50. Three days later, her suits were ready. She picked up her newly laundered items, paid less than $20 for the service, and went home with a new wardrobe. Including the price of dry-cleaning, she got four new suits at a consignment shop for much, much less than the price of one at the mall.

Whether you need suits like Renné, just want some new shirts and pants, or need some sweaters for the fall, shop at consignment stores or discount stores before you ever pay full price at a clothing store. Sidewalk sales and clearance racks can also be great ways to dress for less. The money you save can put you one step closer to your financial goals.

AVOID WASTE

The $1.29 head of lettuce sitting in her vegetable bin had been fresh and crisp when Carolyn first bought it. But when she got it home, along with the tomato, cucumber, and pepper, a salad just didn't sound appetizing. So she ignored the veggies and ordered a pizza. Two weeks later, the pizza was long gone, and the vegetables were sitting in her refrigerator turning into green scum. Almost four dollars worth of groceries needed to be dumped in the garbage.

As we try to save money, we should start with avoiding waste. Sometimes, though, that's difficult to do. As a single woman, it's hard to use up a whole loaf of bread before it starts to mold or a gallon of milk before it starts to sour. What can you do to avoid waste? Put half the loaf in a freezer bag until you need it, and put a pinch of salt in your newly opened container of milk. It will last longer!

Throwing away leftovers is also a big waste. If you absolutely hate the thought of eating leftovers, then cook smaller portions or be creative in "remaking" a meal. For instance, if a pot roast tastes wonderful to you the first day but you hate pot roast leftovers, then try making beef stew out of the leftovers for the next day's meal. You might be surprised at how good it tastes, and you'll avoid waste.

A rubber spatula can be a great asset in avoiding waste. It will get the extra soup out of a can, peanut butter out of a jar, or cookie dough out of the mixer.

Avoiding waste can be as simple as resoling your shoes and not letting your scissors rust. Turn off lights when you leave a room, and don't let water run for long. Get that last dab of hair gel out of the container before tossing it. Mend your clothes by sewing the holes in your socks, reattaching buttons, and repairing torn hems on pants or skirts. If you don't know how to do this, ask a friend who sews to show you how.

Instead of throwing away shoes that have scuff marks on them, dip a Q-tip in nail polish remover, then lightly and gently rub it over the scuff marks. Or use shoe polish. Your shoes will look as good as new!

One pair of wet jeans in the dryer is a wasteful dryer load. How about hanging your jeans on the shower curtain rod to dry overnight?

Another way to avoid waste is to hold onto your receipts. If you realize you don't need an item, you can easily take it back to the store for a full refund if you have your receipt. Rather than something sitting unused on your shelf, get your money back.

Observe your lifestyle for a week and figure out a few ways that you can avoid waste. What you can save will be worth the effort.

REUSE

It was 11:25 at night and I was washing out the crumbs in my sandwich bag. My roommate casually remarked that she threw her used sandwich bags away, but I just couldn't do that. "It just takes me a few seconds, then I can reuse it for tomorrow's lunch," I responded.

Call me crazy, call me weird. But whatever you do, don't call me wasteful. In the throwaway society that we live in, I still think a few things are worth reusing. Sandwich bags, paper lunch bags, empty plastic sour cream containers, and foil are just the beginning of reusable magic.

Recently, my family had professional pictures taken. When my photographs arrived, I hurried to the store to find some new picture frames. To my disappointment, none of the gold frames I liked fit my small budget. So, I bought a can of gold spray paint and went home to dig out some old wooden picture frames. I cleaned the frames, sprayed them with gold, washed the glass, and—voila!—I had new picture frames! Not only did I save money, but I reused items that had been taking up space.

When it comes to reusing items, be creative. While we don't want our homes loaded down with junk that we'll use "someday," some items are worth using again before we trash them. So, before you throw away that jar of leftover pickle juice, reuse it! (Marinate chicken in it before cooking.)

GROCERY SHOP SMART

There are two kinds of grocery shoppers: unwise and wise. The first kind of shopper goes to the grocery store and buys whatever looks tasty. This person will, many times, have a large grocery bill to show for a small amount of food, because she put little forethought into her shopping.

The other kind of grocery shopper is the one who goes to the store with a plan. She wisely plans to get the most out of her grocery dollar. This shopper:

• Makes a list and sticks with it.

• Buys store brands or generic brands, when possible.

• Cuts coupons for items that she regularly uses (and remembers to take her coupons to the grocery store).

• Shops grocery stores that offer double coupon savings.

• Watches the newspaper for store specials, called "loss leaders." For even greater savings, she uses her coupons on these.

ORGANIZING A COUPON FILE

If coupons have always been a fearsome task for you, try this strategy. Buy a four-by-six index card file, and gather fourteen index cards. At the top of twelve cards, write the name of the month and its number (for example, December—12). On the top of another card write "No Expiration Date"; then on another write "Coupons to Use This Month." As you cut your coupons, make stacks by their expiration dates. Then, when you're finished cutting, stuff the coupon stacks into the card file behind the appropriate month's card. Before you go shopping, pull coupons that you intend to use and place them behind the "Coupons to Use This Month" card for easy reference.

Despite the best intentions, there are seasons in every woman's life when she literally does not have time for one more thing. If coupons and store ads are too time consuming right now, buy generic brands and be done with it.

However, in other seasons of life, the investment of a few minutes of cutting coupons, surveying ads, and making a trip to the double-coupon store can be worth quite a bit. The money you don't spend on your groceries can be put into your savings.

BUY IN ADVANCE

Buying in advance is a great money-saving strategy, whether you're shopping for groceries or clothing. The key is to buy items when they're on sale—really good sales.

Hailey told us she had just found cans of tuna on sale for 33 cents apiece; usually tuna costs 99 cents a can. She admitted that tuna fish is not her favorite food in the world, but, when she's hungry and the cupboards are empty, it sure tastes good! So she stocked up and bought six cans. That's enough to last her for awhile. Savings? She spent $1.98 on what normally would have cost $5.94.

After Hailey's suggestion, Kate drew our attention to the pair of leather, lace-up shoes she was wearing. "These are the best shoes I've ever had," she said. A few weeks prior she found a pair of identical shoes at the outlet on sale for $7.50. Kate bought the sale shoes and put them in the back of her closet for when her current pair wears out. That may be a year from now, but rather than paying $40.00 to replace them then, she paid $7.50 now. Savings? $32.50.

To save money, buy two tubes of toothpaste (with your double coupons) when your favorite brand is on sale; buy sale-priced tampons now rather than waiting until the day you need them; and stock up on pantyhose when they are discounted.

At first this system of purchasing may stretch your budget because you're buying extra things for future use when you still need to buy things for now. However, after a few months of buying sale items in advance, you'll find that your supplies carry over from month to month, and even from year to year.

> *A savings rule of thumb: No matter how good the bargain is, don't buy anything on sale that you would not have paid full price for. If you don't use an item, it's not a bargain!*

AVOID TEMPTATION

"It almost never fails," Laura admitted. "If I'm at the store, I'm going to buy something." Window shopping doesn't get her into as much trouble, she told us, as browsing the sale racks in the back of stores. As a self-described sucker for a bargain, Laura finds lots of good bargains. That's a good thing—most of the time. It's a bad thing, though, when she does not have any money remaining in her month's budget. Then looking for bargains can get her into trouble.

As an example, Laura told us about one time she found a $300 jacket on sale for $85. Such a good deal could not be left behind. Not having $85 in her pocket, she grabbed the credit card shouting her name from her wallet. *I'll just buy it now and pay for it next month,* Laura rationalized. Never mind that no matter how lovely this jacket was, she had three other perfectly good ones in her closet. Never mind that her monthly clothing budget was only $35, and she'd end up paying interest on the jacket. Never mind that she really needed a white sweater more than she needed another jacket. The temptation was too much, overriding better judgment. Laura left the mall owning a great jacket, but owing a lot more than she needed to at the time.

Ever had that happen? It's often a good idea to buy things when they're on sale and save them for later. However, during a financial crisis, which we all have now and then, avoiding temptation is an even better idea.

Avoiding temptation can come in different forms. Some women discipline themselves to use their credit cards only for emergencies. Other women, who have the cash envelope budget system, buy everything under $100 with cash. Almost all of us can avoid temptation by avoiding all malls, clothing stores, and outlets when we don't have any expendable cash.

After instituting all of these temptation-prevention policies in her life, Laura was in the store one day and found a nice skirt on sale for fourteen dollars. Unfortunately, it cost exactly ten dollars more than she had in her purse. The nearest ATM machine was two miles away. After debating about whether she should go get the cash, cheat by using her credit card, or just pass up the sale, she finally decided to do the last. Laura handed the skirt back to the clerk and left the store.

Proudly, Laura told us that three months later, she was back in that same store and found the exact skirt back on the sales rack for four dollars! She had avoided temptation earlier and was rewarded with not just a good buy but a *really* good buy!

DON'T BELITTLE A NICKEL

Do you remember picking up change you found on the sidewalk as a kid? I do. Pennies were great, nickels and dimes were a find, and quarters were absolutely incredible. The day I found a dollar bill was a hallmark in my childhood.

Now we're big girls, though, and we bypass the pennies lying on the floor beside our chairs. No big deal if we drop a nickel or lose a dime. A quarter that falls into the trash is not that much. It's just small change, we reason. It won't make a difference in our savings.

So we waste a quarter on Monday, bypass two dimes on the sidewalk on Tuesday, misplace a nickel on Wednesday, joke about the head-side-up penny on Thursday (and leave it lying there), and spend fifty cents on a candy bar on Friday. It's not that much, after all—just $1.01 for the week.

Some calculations are worth noting, though. Wasting $1.01 a week for a year means wasting $52.52. That's enough to buy that nice purse I've been wanting. Hmm . . . I could have done without those candy bars on Fridays!

So, instead of bypassing or wasting insignificant amounts of change, save your change. Melanie keeps hers in a small box under her bed. I keep mine in a bear-shaped jelly jar. It doesn't matter what you use to hold your change. The important thing is that you don't belittle even a nickel. Save it!

KEEP THE WALLET (ALMOST) EMPTY

I had anticipated this Mother's Day for months. When my mother came to visit, I planned to take her to a cute tearoom that had the most quaint atmosphere and delicate food you can imagine. It was going to be an extra special way to honor her.

We arrived promptly for our reservation and were seated. After ordering, we sat back and enjoyed our time together. Everything went just the way I had imagined, until the check arrived. It was tabulated correctly, and I reached into my wallet for my credit card. To my dismay, it was not there. Frantically, but trying to appear calm lest my mother notice, I dug in my wallet and then in my purse looking for my card. It was nowhere to be found.

This was back in the days when I used my credit card to pay all my bills. The convenience was great, the balance could be paid off each month without interest, and I didn't have to worry about cash. Didn't have to worry, that is, until I lost my credit card and had a bill to pay.

At this point I swallowed my pride and asked my mother if she would loan me the money to pay for our meal—*her* Mother's Day gift. She graciously did, and I didn't have to spend the afternoon scrubbing dishes in the kitchen. But on the way home, she gave me the "every woman ought to keep twenty dollars in her wallet just in case" lecture. Embarrassed by the fiasco, I could only nod silently in agreement.

With my mother's admonition in mind, I still believe it is important to keep our wallets (almost) empty. If I have money in my wallet, I'm usually going to spend it. If Laura would have had fourteen dollars in her wallet when she found that nice skirt, she would have purchased it without hesitation. However, by not having the money with her, she was able to restrain herself. I'm sure you can add plenty of examples of your own.

It's a good idea to keep a twenty-dollar bill tucked in the back of your wallet for "emergencies only." It's a great idea to keep two quarters for emergency phone calls. And take money with you when you have a special event like my luncheon. But other than that, be careful how much cash you carry. Avoid the ATM machine as much as possible. Keep your wallet (almost) empty.

LIVE BENEATH YOUR MEANS

When it comes to saving money, it's not too difficult to avoid waste, to reuse items, and to grocery shop with a plan. And saving your change and avoiding temptation just make sense. However, when enacting your money-saving strategies, living beneath your means is something that takes discipline. A lot of it.

At her first job, Hailey was promised a thirty-five cents an hour raise after working there for three months. That does not sound like a lot of money now, she admitted, but when she was in high school, it was exciting. She looked forward to that raise for twelve weeks, thinking about how much more valuable her time would be when she got paid thirty-five cents more an hour. She told us about her visions of what she was going to do with all that extra money.

Then the day finally came when she got the raise. The new amount of her paycheck seemed huge. But, inevitably, it slipped down the spending hole just as fast as her smaller paychecks had.

The same thing happened with her first job out of college. By this time, pay raises didn't come in the form of cents. If they came, they were in dollars. But the increased money in Hailey's paycheck went for bills, entertainment, this or that just as fast as all the rest of her money did.

Then, Hailey told us, she finally learned one of the most important principles of saving: living beneath her means. It goes something like this: If I earn enough to live in a two-bedroom apartment, I could live in a one-bedroom and save the difference. If I can afford to spend $100 a month on entertainment, I could spend just $75 and save the difference. If I can afford the $1,000 stereo system with awesome speakers, I could purchase the $600 system with great speakers and save the $400 difference.

Living beneath your means is contrary to the standard in our society. Most would agree that the majority of Americans live above their means. Credit card companies give you the opportunity to buy, buy, buy today and then pay tomorrow, tomorrow, tomorrow. The advertising line goes something like, *you deserve it today, so get it now.* Merchants tell you not to wait to purchase that luxury item. Whether it's qualifying for the larger apartment, affording more entertainment, buying the top-of-the-line stereo system, or something else, we are encouraged to spend all we can afford—and then some.

However, living beneath your means has multiple benefits. More than any other method of saving, living beneath your means will enable you to build a financial reserve, possibly to use as an emergency fund. In an economy where losing your job or taking a pay cut is a real possibility, living beneath your means will help prepare you for living on less, if need be. Should an emergency arise, you won't need to run to your parents for help; you won't have to despair because you are your sole provider. Rather, you will be able to confidently drive to the bank and withdraw money that you have disciplined yourself to set aside. And, if an emergency never arises, you can use that money for a significant large purchase, like the down payment on a house.

As you review your budget, ask God to give you insight about where you can reduce your cost of living. Then make the changes necessary to live beneath your means.

YOU CAN DO IT!

As we talked through ways to save, I watched Jeanette's eyes start to brighten. I could almost see the wheels turning in her mind.

Finally she said. "Cutting coupons just isn't my style—I don't spend much money on groceries anyway. But I *could* use some of those ideas . . ." She paused, with the look of deep thought on her face. Then she continued, "I really need to organize my budget too, so I can figure out how to live on less. I guess saving money might not be so hard after all!"

My friends and I laughed, and I prodded her, "So, what's this about a trip to Europe . . ."

 ## COFFEE TALK

1. What financial goals do you have that make saving a worthwhile endeavor for you?
2. How does living beneath your means impact your contentment level, especially as related to Paul's words in Philippians 4:11-13?
3. What two money-saving ideas can you start using this month?

RESOURCES

Dacyczyn, Amy. *The Tightwad Gazette*. New York: Villard Books, 1992. Authors' note: *The Tightwad Gazette* series (look for the 1995 and 1996 editions also) contains lots of ideas for saving money. Some might be labeled extreme, but others are really great ideas. Look through these books before you purchase them to make sure they contain information that is helpful to you.

Hunt, Mary. *Complete Cheapskate*. Nashville: Broadman & Holman Publishers, 1997.

Hunt, Mary. *The Financially Confident Woman*. Nashville: Broadman & Holman Publishers, 1996.

- *Fourteen* -
THE SENSIBLE WOMAN
Buying and Caring for Your Car

DISCRETION WILL PROTECT YOU,
AND UNDERSTANDING WILL GUARD YOU.
PROVERBS 2:11

It was almost noon, and I (Melanie) was dreading my lunch hour. I checked my watch again, ten more minutes, and the excuses started rolling through my mind: "I'm not feeling so great," "It's a crazy day. I can't break away from work," or simply, "I've changed my mind." But I couldn't make an excuse. I had to follow through on my plan.

Where was I headed? The dentist office? I wish. The gynecologist? No problem. I can deal with those as much as I dislike them. But it's anguish for me to attempt negotiating a deal when I'm lacking knowledge. And car buying is on the top of the list.

My lunch appointment was to be spent looking at a used car that I had circled in the classifieds. It was no use trying to break my engagement. The Honda that my dad helped me buy was slowly dying, and it couldn't even scale a small hill (not to mention a mountain) over thirty miles an hour. I had procrastinated about purchasing a new vehicle, but I knew that if I put it off any longer, I would be completely vehicle-less.

So off I went to look at the red Nissan Sentra. Aside from the slight hail damage that brought the price of the car down, it looked to me like it was in good condition. I drove it around the neighborhood, and then I asked if I could take it to a local mechanic (another task I loathe) to check out the insides. After a thorough inspection and a bill of seventy dollars, the mechanic found about $500 worth of repairs, including brakes and alignment. The car seller agreed to bring the price of the car down, and I agreed to pay for the repairs. And then it was done. I had a new-to-me car that drove up mountains at fifty-five miles per hour, and after getting the initial repairs, my constant fear of breakdowns was eliminated. However, I was determined not only to take care of this vehicle but to educate myself in the area of automobiles so I wouldn't dread my next car purchase.

Taking care of a car isn't just a male responsibility. As single women, we need to educate and prepare ourselves for life's necessities, and transportation is key. Unless you live in a major city with an intricate and safe public transportation system, you will probably need to purchase and maintain a vehicle for both work and play. How do you start this process? First you need to select a car.

CHOOSING YOUR CAR

The thought of buying a car makes many of our hearts race with anxiety. We're not exactly sure where to begin, and we don't want to appear ignorant about this process. Several years ago, my roommate Connie decided that she needed a new car. Instead of mulling over her fear, she decided to be proactive. She made a list of what she was looking for, researched the kind of vehicle that would meet her needs, and then visited several dealerships searching for a bargain. By preparing for her venture, she was secure and confident in what she wanted and no dealer was able to sway her decision.

Make a List

Where should you start in your quest to buy a car or truck? The first thing to do is create a list of exactly what you want. You should have two tiers on this list: the first tier should be a list of nonnegotiable items, and the second tier should be a list of extras you would like to have on your vehicle. "The beginning point is to know exactly what you want to buy," say Ron and Judy Blue in *A Woman's Guide to Financial Peace of Mind.* "That way, your bargaining is over price and not features. Anyone who's selling a car will want to convince you of the value of the features. But if you've already decided on the features you want, all you're talking about is the cost to buy those features, and you can compare apples to apples."[1]

On the nonnegotiable list, you may include items like high safety and maintenance rating, good gas mileage, antilock brakes, airbag, two or four doors, automatic transmission, air-conditioning, or front wheel drive. Everything you include on this list is absolutely critical in making your purchasing decision.

On the second list include items like a CD player, power windows, sun or moon roof, four-wheel drive, convertible top, heated seats, or power locks. This is a wish list that can be changed pending price and availability. However, if power windows are your favorite feature in the truck you want to purchase, make sure to put it on the first tier.

Research the Vehicle

Once you have determined what you want in a car, it's time to learn what is available to match the needs on your list. Start by going to the library and matching your needs with several cars in *Consumer Reports.* This reliable resource rates vehicles in a variety of areas, including safety, and will tell you what features are on different vehicles.

Once you have determined which specific vehicles interest you, look up N.A.D.A.'s appraisal guides (otherwise known as a "blue book") in the library reference section, at a local bank, or at your credit union. The blue book will tell you approximately what each vehicle is worth (its resale value), so you know if it is in your price range. Edmund's Used Cars internet site can also assist you with pricing by listing exactly what each feature on your potential vehicle is worth.

The average cost of a new car is $18,500, while the average used car costs about $11,000.[2] Because a car quickly depreciates in its first year, we recommend you invest in a well-maintained used vehicle instead of buying something straight from the factory.

> *Internet sites like www.autobytel.com,* Consumer Reports, *or your credit union can give you information on car values, warranties, a loan versus a lease, and where you can find the vehicle you want.*

Start Looking

You've narrowed down your options and are prepared to start searching for your car. Look in your newspaper's classifieds or on the bulletin boards at your church, work, or apartment house to begin the hunt. The classifieds will have a smaller selection than a dealership, but you may get a great price. You can also place a "car wanted" ad in the newspaper. If you decide to purchase a car through the classifieds, follow the same process as if you were purchasing it through a dealer.

If you don't find what you are looking for in the classifieds, it's time to head to your local car dealership row. This is the part many of us dread the most, but with the research you have done, you should be prepared to get exactly what you want.

LEASING

Some people recommend leasing a vehicle instead of buying, because you can trade the car in every couple of years for a newer model, and the dealer is responsible for any maintenance problems. Leasing is a good option for someone who only needs a vehicle for a short time or can write the car off as a business expense. However, we don't recommend leasing for the long term, because you don't have an investment when your payments end. While it is easy to obtain a lease, you can also purchase a car for a small or even no down payment. If you are planning on leasing, make sure to find out all of the costs involved as well as the mileage and other limitations placed on you from the dealer. Also, make sure you have the option to purchase the vehicle at the end of the lease if you decide you want to keep the car.

Prepare to Hunt

As you head to your local lineup of car dealerships, ask God for His wisdom and strength. If you aren't an assertive negotiator, ask a friend or parent who enjoys negotiating to help you search for a car.

You won't be at a dealership for more than a minute before a salesperson will approach you to offer you assistance. Unfortunately, it is hard to trust car salespeople, even if they appear to be nice (and sometimes they genuinely are!). Because they make their living off of commission, they want to sell you a car at as high a price as they can, and a shady salesperson may even lie to make a sale.

Isn't it sad that we have to approach buying a car with such a skeptical attitude? Second Timothy 1:7 (NKJV) says, "For God has not given us a spirit of fear, but of power and of love and of a sound mind." With the sound mind He has given us, we can discern which purchasing decisions are wise and which are unwise. Following are some practical suggestions that will help prepare you for the world of car buying.

• Even though you have researched the car, it is wise to ask the salesperson questions about the car you want. If this new information contradicts what you have previously learned, you may have reason to suspect this person's honesty. Move on to another dealership.

• Never purchase a car after only visiting one place. See what several dealers have to offer.

• Don't let a salesperson sway you from what you had originally researched and wanted. They will want you to buy a more expensive vehicle or at least one with more features. If you think another car will be better than the one you researched, go home and do your homework before you make the buy.

• Don't feel bad about spending time at a dealership and then not buying a car. It is their job to give you service, and it is your job to get a good deal on a car. If they don't give you a good deal, you need to look elsewhere.

• Recheck the blue book price of the car you want to purchase. Look for any price differences with mileage or added features. Purchase the car for this price or less.

• Test drive the car by yourself or with a knowledgeable

AN EXPERT'S TIP

Ask the dealer if this is a one-owner car and if you can have the name and number of the original owner. If it's available call and ask why he or she decided to sell the vehicle. Also, ask the dealer for the owner's manual with a maintenance record as well as receipts from oil changes and repairs. A bit of detective work could save you some major expenses or give you the security of purchasing a well-maintained car.

friend. If salespeople ride along, they may distract you from listening and feeling how the car runs. Things to check out include: the brakes, to see if they squeal, are spongy, or go all the way to the floor; the clutch, to see if it's tight; the heat and air-conditioning to make sure they work; the stereo; the steering, to see if it's straight or has excessive movement before the wheels turn; the oil, to see how dark it is; under the car for oil, transmission fluid, or coolant leaks; unusual vibrations or hesitation when you accelerate; and the tires for wear on either side (indicates alignment or balancing problems). Also, get out and press on all four corners of the car to see if it bounces up and down. If not, the shocks are probably bad.

• If you are serious about buying a certain car, take it to a reputable mechanic for a thorough and reliable check (investment is about seventy-five dollars) instead of relying on the dealer's inspection. The mechanic will check the car's "insides," including oil consumption, shifting, the CV joints, and any knocks in the engine. The dealer should then fix everything on the car before you purchase it.

• Ask for anything you want the dealer to do prior to buying the car. If you don't ask, you won't get, and they may even be willing to do things like install your current CD player into your new car.

• Don't stay too long at one dealership. They will do everything they can to keep you there so you won't have time to look other places. Tell them that if you're interested you will be back; then leave them your name and phone number in case they have a good deal they want to call you about.

• Never buy a car the same day you find it. If you're in a hurry, you may get a bad deal.

• Don't mention trading your current car in until after you get a good price on the newer car. Find out what your current car is worth from the blue book; then expect them to give you what it is worth for a trade.

• Be prepared for tricky negotiations. If you ask for something unusual, the salesperson will say he or she has to talk to the manager about it. I have a friend who tells the salesperson she will walk out if he or she is not back in ten minutes so her time is not wasted with intentional stalling.

• Read and understand everything you sign, including every word of fine print.

• Don't take any "promises" to be actual truth. Unless a promise is in writing, it won't happen.

• Be prepared to leave if you don't get a good deal. If you aren't willing to walk out, you probably won't get the best deal.

If you are assured and wise in your car search, you will make a good purchase. At the end of your search, you will also have the confidence that only comes from accepting and conquering new challenges.

Finance Your Car

You've done your homework, maintained your cool, and negotiated the exact car you wanted for a great price. But if you don't pay cash for your car, how do you finance it for the long run?

First, put as much of a down payment on it as you can afford. While you don't necessarily need to put money down on a car, you will save hefty interest payments if you have money to invest up front. Better to save for a small down payment than to pay interest on the entire cost.

> Every vehicle is assigned its own unique number called a VIN (vehicle identification number). You will need this number to finance, insure, and register your new car.

Second, be prepared for the additional fees that will be added to the purchase price. In the U.S., each state has a unique set of tax laws for car buying, including potential property tax. Check with your Department of Motor Vehicles to find out what additional costs you should expect, including taxes, title, registration, and license plate fees.

You will also have the option to purchase a warranty at this time. When Dana bought her car, she purchased an extended warranty on it, and over the course of the next two years, she took the car back repeatedly for repairs. However, Virginia bought an expensive warranty and never had to use it. She wished she had spent her money on something else.

Warranties come in all different sizes and shapes. A reputable dealer will usually offer you a good limited warranty like a ninety-day warranty, where you would only pay 50 percent of the labor costs and 15 percent of the parts if something goes wrong. If you're not offered a good limited warranty, this could be an indication that the car is not in good mechanical condition.

Your dealer will offer you additional warranty options for an extra price. These options cover either certain parts of your car or the entire vehicle. Private companies also handle warranties that may be less expensive than what the dealer offers. If the car you are buying has low mileage, an extended warranty is generally not necessary because the two major components, the engine and transmission, should have a lot of life left. Conversely, even if the car has high mileage, an expensive warranty may cost more over the period of time you own the car than the cost of the repairs.

Because you just had the car inspected and fixed, it should be in good condition. However, cars do break down unexpectedly, as we all know. You need to weigh the pros and cons of buying the warranty—think through the risk of purchasing one and not using it versus not buying one and then having to spend a large amount of money fixing your car. Research your options and then decide. If you haven't decided when you buy your car, ask if you can have an extended time to make a decision. They may try to pressure you to buy it immediately, but ultimately they'd rather wait for you to make up your mind than lose your purchase altogether.

The third step in financing a car is to research what interest rates you can get on a loan through local banks and loan companies. Once you have decided on a price for your car, your salesperson may pass you off to a manager to discuss financing and sign mounds of paperwork. The dealer may be able to give you a good interest rate on the vehicle through a company they work with.

You should be able to drive off the lot with your new car,

but it will take several days for them to approve your loan. During this time, see if you can get a better interest rate, and if not, the dealer will have the final paperwork for you to sign in about a week.

> *If you purchase a high-priced car and have to sell the vehicle a year or two later, you may get stuck owing money. What an awful feeling to sell your car and still have to pay $2,000 or more on it! While you should purchase a car that will be reliable and safe, also purchase something you can afford.*

Don't be swayed by having low payments for five or seven years. Ask the dealer or loan officer to quote you the entire interest for a two-, three-, and four-year loan so you know exactly how much interest you will be paying. If you are able to afford a higher monthly payment, go with that option and pay off your loan quickly. The faster you pay for your car, the less interest you will owe.

Celebrate Your Purchase

When Amy Jo purchased her new Honda, she celebrated by sending all of her friends and families a "birth announcement" with the information on her new car. She included the name she had chosen for it, the weight, the length, and a large picture of her sitting on her red Accord. The recipients of her announcement enjoyed the unique mailing, and she was able to enjoy her new purchase by sharing her excitement with others.

Be creative in celebrating the intelligence, confidence, and responsibility you displayed in purchasing a new vehicle. When I bought my Toyota, I immediately went on a long weekend road trip with a girlfriend to "break the car in." The Tercel climbed steep mountains, drove a tremendous number of miles before running low on gas, and survived many back roads filled with gravel and rocks. We enjoyed the mountain views as much as we enjoyed riding in my new car. Purchasing a vehicle on your own is worthy of a fun celebration.

MAINTAINING YOUR CAR

The key to maintaining your vehicle is to read and follow the owner's manual that should have come in your car. We know— "Yawn!"—but this little book will answer questions on how and when to maintain your car. It will tell you everything from how to change your headlight to when you need a tune-up. It will also explain how you safely jump-start your car if the battery dies, change a flat tire, and operate your stereo.

If you don't have a manual with a used car, ask your dealer or call the manufacturer to obtain one. Just like taking the time to research the type of car to purchase, it is important to learn all about the type of car you actually bought. A poorly maintained car can result in unexpected expenditures and safety hazards.

Putting gas in the car isn't the only thing you should do on a regular basis. You should also be checking the oil every month (or more if you travel a lot or it tends to run low) to make sure your engine has the lubrication it needs. When you check the oil, also check the water level, windshield fluid, transmission fluid, power steering fluid, brake fluid, air filter, and the air in your tires. These are all things you can easily add yourself. The oil, transmission, and power steering fluids have dipsticks you can pull out to check, and the brake fluid usually has markings on the side of the master cylinder to determine if the fluid is too low. Pull out your manual to determine what kind of fluid to put in as well as to find out where each of these fluids is located (also read your manual to find out what grade and viscosity of oil to put in). At the same time you check all of your fluids, test all your water hoses for leaks. Do this by waiting until your engine is cool and then squeeze each radiator hose. If any of them feel extremely soft or squishy, it's time to have a mechanic change the hose.

If you don't know how to check or add these items, ask a friend or your mechanic. Some vocational schools or churches offer short seminars on basic car maintenance. The more you learn, the more confident you will feel.

Your manual will give you an in-depth schedule on when you should change the oil in your car and have a mechanic give it a tune-up. You should also have a mechanic rotate the tires on your car once a year to allow them to wear evenly.

As you follow the manual's maintenance schedule, keep a notebook in your car and record the date each time you have work done on your car. Also keep the receipts of the work done so when it comes time to sell the vehicle, you can show that it was regularly maintained.

Be continually alert to how your car is running. Several years ago the engine on my Nissan started making a horrible noise. Instead of stopping to have someone check it, I continued to drive for several days before getting it inspected. By the time I took it to a mechanic, there was no hope left for my engine. The radiator had gotten clogged, the cap had blown off, and the cooling water in my engine was gone. What could have been relatively simple maintenance turned into a nightmare. The parts inside seized up from the intense heat, and I was off on a search for my next vehicle.

Please don't follow my example! Here are some warning signs to alert you to a potential problem:

• Difficult time starting the engine or the engine runs rough.

• Leak under the vehicle (other than water dripping from the air conditioner).

• Unusual engine or other noises.

• Engine getting excessively hot (the little arrow on your dashboard temperature gauge will be on the H instead of midway between the C and H).

• Low or overinflated tires.

• Loss of brake and clutch effectiveness (you have to push down really hard to make them work).

• Vehicle pulls to one side of the road when you are steering straight.

• Loss of power when you accelerate.

AAA (American Automobile Association) offers many benefits to its members, including their Approved Auto Repair program. When you take your vehicle to an AAA-approved mechanic, they will give a written estimate and price guarantee for your repair, a limited warranty on the repair, and a free maintenance inspection on those items that frequently contribute to breakdowns.

The fear of taking our car to a mechanic often makes us tremble. It is unfortunate that mechanics have the reputation (and sometimes rightly earned) for taking advantage of naive women. However, you can make a few preparations to ward off any schemers.

The first is to research your mechanic before a problem occurs. If you have a sudden breakdown, it is best to know up front whom you should go to for help. Ask a trusted friend where she takes her car, and then call the Better Business Bureau to see if anyone has ever reported that mechanic for misconduct. Another sign of a potentially good mechanic is if that person is ASE certified. An ASE certification means the mechanic has passed a series of twelve automotive tests by the national organization. ASE also keeps a file of complaints about certified mechanics, similar to the Better Business Bureau.

The second preparation is to know your car. Study your manual so you know what makes your car work. Every vehicle has seven major systems: the electrical, fuel, cooling, brakes, steering and suspension, lubrication, and transmission system. If you take a look at a book like *Auto Repair for Dummies,* by Deanna Sclar, you should be able to determine which system has a problem and what may be needed to fix it. If your mechanic says you need a new head gasket when your brakes are squeaking, you would know that you probably should be looking for a new mechanic.

Third, ask up front for a written estimate of what it will cost to repair your vehicle and say you don't want anything fixed without your approval. If the mechanic is putting in new parts, ask for your old ones to guarantee they were replaced.

When you get your written estimate, if the cost is extremely high or if the diagnosis doesn't sound correct, say "thank you" and leave. Take your vehicle to another mechanic and ask him to take a look. Don't tell him what the initial diagnosis was, and see if he has the same concerns. A second opinion can be a valuable one.

If you still don't feel comfortable, ask a guy friend to come with you. Even if you do the talking, having a man there often makes the mechanic more accountable. Sad, isn't it?

By properly maintaining your car, it should run smoothly and be safe to drive. And next time you have to visit a mechanic, you can be confident that you know exactly what to ask for to get the results that you need.

> ### SAFETY TIPS
> *1. Always wear your seat belt.*
> *2. Lock both doors immediately when you get in.*
> *3. Carry a cell phone.*
> *4. Maintain your car to prevent breakdowns.*
> *5. Don't drive on lonely, back roads at night.*
> *6. Be alert when walking in parking lots. If you feel that someone is stalking you, go back into the building instead of opening your car door.*
> *7. If someone gets in the car with you, draw attention to yourself by running the car into a building or barrier.*

WINTERIZING YOUR CAR

Fall in Colorado can be tricky. You never know if you are going to wake up to a breezy cool day or a flurry of snow. One October, though, we got a surprise from the skies. It started out like any other fall Friday. It was sweater weather, a little breezy, and slightly overcast. By the afternoon, it started to snow just a little, and the newscasters told us we might actually get a couple of inches of the white stuff over the weekend.

By Friday night the several inches of snow turned into several feet, and we got pounded on Saturday with harsh winds and piles of dense snow. The city officially closed all the streets, but hundreds of unfortunate people were stranded in their cars along our highways. They had slid off the road, run out of gas, or just could no longer drive in the extreme conditions. The army sent Humvees out to rescue the stranded, but many of these locals and tourists had to live in their cars for more than twenty-four hours. Several people lost their lives that night, but the majority had been prepared and made it home the next day.

How do you prepare for a winter emergency? Those of us who live in a snow-prone state need to winterize our cars each year to prepare for the onslaught of cold weather and icy roads.

You can winterize your car inexpensively by using a wire brush to remove the dirt and corrosion from the battery terminals and by coating them with a special grease or lubricant from your local automotive shop. Also, add windshield washer and antifreeze fluid, and replace your windshield wipers with blades that are rubber-clad to discourage ice buildup. You can do each of these yourself with the help of your car manual or a friend.

A mechanic should help you winterize the more technical elements of your car. Check the battery if it is more than three years old to see if it's going to survive the cold months and check the antifreeze in your radiator. Check your exhaust system so you don't have a problem with a carbon monoxide leak, and inspect your brakes to avoid skidding on slippery surfaces. If you don't have either winter or all-weather tires, have the correct tires put on your car.

If you live in an extremely cold area, you may want to invest in an engine heater that will warm your car's antifreeze and circulate it constantly through the engine. This will mean your car is almost instantly warm when you start it in the morning. Also, you can purchase a block heater that will directly heat up your engine's oil.

No matter how much you prepare for the cold, snow and ice storms still may pose challenges for you during the winter. If you do get stuck, put sand, salt, or kitty litter under either your front or rear wheels for traction (depending if your car is front- or rear-wheel drive). Then slowly try to rock your way out by going forward and then in reverse. If you accelerate too quickly, you may just spin out and not make any progress. Let your wheels make contact with the sand, and then gradually move the car.

WINTER DRIVING KIT

Small snow shovel, blankets, gloves, ice scraper, cell phone, candy bars, first-aid kit, dried fruit and nuts, full water bottle, sand, salt, or kitty litter for traction, flashlight, jumper cables, white handkerchief, "help needed" sign, flares, coffee can with large candles and matches to create a small furnace.

If you do get stranded, use your cell phone to dial for help. The Federal Communication Commission requires that all cell phone carriers provide the 911 service for free. So even if you don't have a phone carrier, you should always be able to use your cell phone in an emergency. When you are driving, be aware of your location so that when you dial for help, you can quickly tell your rescuers where to find you and your car.

If you don't have a cell phone and are stranded in a nonresidential or noncommercial area, turn on your flashing lights and wait for help to arrive. Just as your parents taught you as a kid, it is unwise and unsafe to get in a car with strangers. Simply request that they call an emergency vehicle for you when they get to the next town.

By preparing your car for winter, you should be safe to drive in icy weather, but it is smart to always be prepared for winter emergencies. Not only will you be prepared for a crisis, but you will have peace of mind for the entire blustery season.

SELLING YOUR CAR

The odometer went past the 100,000-mile mark two years ago and the 150,000-mile mark last month. The mechanic knows you on a first-name basis as you make your once-a-month repair visit to inquire about a new noise or leak. Even though you're attached to your car after driving it for eight years, the time has come to say good-bye.

Like buying a car, you have two options to sell your vehicle. You can advertise in the newspaper, or you can trade it in at the dealer to help with the cost of a new car. If it's in really bad shape, you can sell it to a junkyard so they can use it for parts, but don't count on getting much money for it.

When it comes time to sell, look up the make and model again in N.A.D.A.'s blue book and on Edmund's Used Cars internet site to find out what the current resale value is. This will let you know what the car is worth. If the car is damaged or has high mileage, expect to receive less than the resale value.

To sell it to an individual, take out an ad in your newspaper's classifieds and put a sign in the window. Some areas have a specific lot where people go to view used cars. Find out where that is and display your vehicle.

You can make repairs prior to selling it or let the potential buyers know you are selling it "as is." They may want to have an inspection done on the car, so be prepared to negotiate a deal if the car isn't in good condition. Once you have agreed on a fair price, you will exchange the title for their payment.

If you use your car as a trade-in at a dealership, you don't have to take it in for repairs. The dealership has mechanics on-site who will check out your car after you have traded it in and make any repairs before they resell it. Expect the dealer to give you the blue book price on the vehicle that you are trading in and deduct that from your new car's price. Remember, don't agree to trade the old car in until after you secure the new vehicle at a good price.

After my Nissan died, I launched back into the car-buying process. This time I decided to purchase a newer used car from a dealer. Armed with my research, a little more knowledge, and a patient guy friend, we headed off to wheel and deal. After hours of tough negotiation, I finally got the car I wanted at a price I could actually afford. I felt like I had conquered the world!

With my new purchase came the willpower to actually take care of this machine. By reading the manual, I have learned how to maintain my car; and by doing a bit of research, I've learned what makes this car run well. I hope you, too, feel the excitement of conquering the vehicle-buying process and the security of owning a well-maintained car.

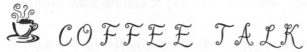

COFFEE TALK

1. What do you need to learn about maintaining your vehicle? Can you challenge yourself to learn something new about it every month?

2. What have you done to prepare for a winter emergency or vehicle breakdown?
3. Processes like buying and maintaining a car often strip us of our self-confidence and create terror. What does the Bible say about promoting confidence and eliminating fear? (See Luke 12:22–34, Eph. 6:10–12, Phil. 1:6, 2 Tim. 1:7.)
4. What other challenges do you want to overcome in your life? What first step can you take to overcome one of these challenges?

RESOURCES

Cerullo, Bob. *What's Wrong with My Car? A Quick and Easy Guide to the Most Common Symptoms of Car Trouble*. New York: Penguin Group, 1993.

Gillis, Jack. *The Car Book 1999: Jack Gillis' Guide to This Year's Best and Worst*. New York: HarperCollins, 1998.

Hazelton, Lesley. *Everything Women Always Wanted to Know about Cars but Didn't Know Who to Ask*. New York: Doubleday, 1995.

Howell, Donna. *The Unofficial Guide to Buying or Leasing a Car*. New York: Macmillan, 1998.

Nunn, Richard V. *Glove Compartment Guide to Emergency Car Repair*. New York: Rand McNally & Company and Roundtable Press, 1986.

Ramsey, Dan. *The Complete Idiot's Guide to Trouble-Free Car Care*. New York: Alpha Books, 1996.

Sclar, Deanna. *Auto Repair for Dummies*. Berkeley, Calif.: Ten Speed Press, 1988.

---

[1] Ron and Judy Blue, *A Woman's Guide to Financial Peace of Mind* (Colorado Springs: Focus on the Family Publishing, 1991), p. 63.

[2] Jerry Edgerton, *Car Shopping Made Easy* (New York: Warner Books, 1997), p. 138.

Pursuits

Raindrops from the dark clouds briskly pelted the 747's silver wings. People from all over the world rushed through the packed airport and slowly filled the belly of the plane. At 3:06 P.M., the flight attendants pulled the doors shut, and Marcy buckled her seat belt.

Out of her window, she watched the mechanics meticulously examining the plane's exterior. She looked forward to getting into the air, away from the rain and the wind at this interim stop. Her excitement was suddenly shattered, though, when the captain came over the intercom and said there was a delay. The professional woman beside her grunted with anger, grabbed her purse, and demanded to get off. Marcy watched her stomp down the aisle, and after an unpleasant confrontation, the flight attendants reluctantly let the irate woman go.

For the next hour, the mechanics worked diligently to fix an oil leak, and when the repairs were finally complete, the captain told the passengers it was safe to fly. The plane slowly backed away from the gate as its passengers gazed at the dismal sky. Suddenly, the plane came to an abrupt stop. The captain's voice came over the intercom and apologized, "The control tower has delayed our departure due to the weather. We'll let you know when we can fly." Marcy heard the grumbling around her. "Can't they at least try it?" someone behind her mumbled. But the captain didn't listen to the passengers. He only took orders from the control tower, and the tower told him it wasn't time.

Minutes turned to hours as Marcy read her book and finally drifted off to sleep. They waited, and they waited, and then the captain finally explained that the tower gave them the go-ahead to take off. The engines roared, and the plane started moving. Faster and faster it went until Marcy felt it lift off the ground and watched its gradual rise through the dreary sky. Suddenly the clouds broke, and the sun's magnificent shades of pink, orange, blue, and yellow radiated across the horizon. "What an amazing flight," Marcy thought as she soaked in the incredible sunset view from her front row seat in the sky.

Do you ever feel like your life is stuck on the runway or maybe even hasn't left the gate? You want so badly to experience the world above, but things keep getting in your way. Maybe you need some more education or you've just lost the enthusiasm to pursue something new. Or maybe the control tower keeps telling you the timing isn't right—God's saying it's not yet time for you to take off.

It's easy to get stuck in a rut. Things don't seem to work out so instead of fixing the problems, we give up on our dreams, stomp off the plane, and never get to soar. Or sometimes we stay on the plane, but we sit on the runway growing more bitter and dissatisfied with the circumstances around us.

We encourage you to actively pursue the goals and talents God has given you. He has created you as a designer original with the ability to climb straight up through those clouds and soar. If you work hard to achieve your dreams and listen to God's voice, He will tell you precisely when the timing is right. Then it's the right time for you to fly.

- *Fifteen* -
THE SEEKING WOMAN
Finding God's Will

MANY ARE THE PLANS IN A WOMAN'S HEART,
BUT IT IS THE LORD'S PURPOSE THAT PREVAILS.
PROVERBS 19:21, PARAPHRASE

Chandra furrowed her brow as she described her dilemma. A group of caring girlfriends sympathetically listened and offered advice. "I just don't know what I should do! I've got this great job opportunity in Chicago, which I've wanted so badly. But Jeff and I have been going out for a month now, and it looks like this relationship has potential! Should I move when things are starting to look hopeful? I just don't know what to choose!"

Two great opportunities and one extremely hard choice to make. The job in Chicago was five states and 850 miles away. Going there would probably close the door to the developing relationship with Jeff. Yet, at the same time, it would open the door to a terrific career.

"I think you should stick with Jeff. He's the type of guy you've been hoping for!" one friend offered.

"No way—you shouldn't stick around here just for a guy! I wouldn't!" another friend rebutted.

"After all," another caring friend suggested, "you've only been dating for a few weeks. You don't know if this is going to work out. I think you should take the job."

"If you don't take this offer, do you suppose you could find something locally that would be just as challenging?"

still another friend asked Chandra.

Several hours later, Chandra was alone. Her caring friends had gone home, and she was left to puzzle over the choices. She recalled their advice and answers to her questions. Some had suggested Jeff; others had voted for the job opportunity. None had given her the final piece of the puzzle. She alone had to make the decision. She lay down in her bed, knowing that she would be awake all night thinking through the options.

SO MANY CHOICES

Have you ever been in a situation like Chandra's? Maybe it wasn't over accepting a job transfer versus dating a nice guy. Maybe you had to choose whether to start graduate school or to continue working full-time for another year. Perhaps you had the dilemma of choosing where to live, when to move, or what to do in a situation. Maybe you found yourself in a relationship that you weren't sure was right for you. Or maybe you were deciding whether to commit to a career in the ministry. Perhaps you were trying to decide which church to attend or how to become involved.

When the choices abounded, did you know what to do?

One of the hardest aspects of being a single woman is having too many choices. You are not tied down by children or a husband's job. You can go just about anywhere and do just about anything. Move to California? Great! Go back to school? Think I will! Move in with a fun roommate to an apartment across town? Let's do it! Climb the next rung on the corporate ladder by moving to Chicago? Sure will! Go on a two-week mission trip next summer? Sign me up!

So many opportunities, but also so many decisions to

make. Sometimes you play a grown-up game of "eenie-meenie-minie-mo" to determine which option is best. Other times you seek counsel from trusted friends. Or you may just choose what seems like the most reasonable option. Sometimes everything works out great; other times everything seems to end in a huge jumble. When things don't work out as great as you had hoped, you end up second-guessing yourself. "What if I would have just . . ." you say to yourself, as you mentally picture where you would have been had you taken the other option. Other times you look up to heaven and ask God if He had any preference about which route you should have taken. If He does have preferences about your life, how in the world are you supposed to know what those are?

GOD HAS A PLAN FOR ME

Contrary to popular opinion, you are not just a blob floating in the universe whose destiny is controlled by fate. You are a unique and special creation of God's, who planned the days of your life before you even existed. The psalmist declared in Psalm 139:16, "All the days ordained for me were written in your book before one of them came to be." So, as you try to sort through the myriad of choices, God is standing behind the scenes with some incredible plans for you.

The Bible tells us about the plan God had for His Son Jesus, to which Jesus chose to submit. Jesus said, "I have come down from heaven not to do my will but to do the will of him who sent me" (John 6:38).

Just as God had a plan for His Son, God has a plan for each of His adopted children. The author of Hebrews encouraged readers, "May the God of peace equip you with everything good for doing his will, and may he work in us what is pleasing to him" (Heb. 13:20-21).

As a believer, you can be assured that not only has God known about the days of your life, but He is also working in your life to accomplish His will. Paul wrote to the Philippian believers, "It is God who works in you to will and to act according to his good purpose" (Phil. 2:13). Not only is He at work in you, He intends to finish what He started in your life. "I am confident of this," Paul wrote, "that the one who began a good work among you will bring it to completion" (Phil. 1:6 NRSV).

Recently a friend told me about a craft project she started about fifteen years ago. She invested a great deal of money in the supplies for the project, but she didn't fully calculate the time it would require. Disillusioned and overwhelmed, she soon put the project into storage to save for a rainy day. Many rainy days have come and gone since then, but her project has never come out of storage. She laughingly told me that it probably never will.

Unlike my friend's craft project, God has plans for our lives that He is daily working to complete. We cooperate in that by doing His will.

WHAT IS GOD'S WILL FOR ME?

As a Christlike woman who tries to be balanced and seeks to be fulfilled in her life, doing God's will is important to you. You don't do whatever you want, because you desire to make sure you are doing what God wants. But His will for your life seems so ambiguous at times. A point-by-point plan to follow would be nice, but you have not found one. So what to do?

In one verse, God sums up how we can find His will for our lives. It is such a short verse that you can almost miss the profound road map that it gives. But if you follow this road map, you will most certainly find out what He would have you do:

> Do not be conformed to this world, but be transformed by the renewing of your mind, so that you may prove what the will of God is, that which is good and acceptable and perfect. (Rom. 12:2 NASB)

God's will can be found by renewing your mind, which happens when you read and live what God's Word says. It is as simple as that.

"But the Bible doesn't tell me whether I should go to Chicago or stay here!" I can almost hear Chandra say, and she's right. The Bible seldom gives us specifics about decisions such as where to live or go to school. However, the Bible always gives me guiding principles about who I should be and what I am to do. As I heed these objective principles, I can begin to determine God's subjective will for my life.

GOD'S WILL: WHO SHOULD I BE?

I was browsing in a card shop when the beautiful colors surrounding the words on the front compelled me to pick up a card and read: "It's not just what you do." I opened it to read the rest: "It's who you are that makes a difference in my life." Immediately a dear friend came to mind, who needed just such encouragement. I purchased the card and a pretty seal to give my friend next time I saw her.

Nice cards and fancy seals aside, it's encouraging to know that that saying is true in the spiritual realm as well as the physical. Who I am is the first thing that makes a difference in God's will for my life. Before I ask Him *what* I should do, I need to become who He wants me to be. This in mind, it is absolutely God's will that I do the following.

• *Be loving.* "The commandments . . . are summed up in this word, 'Love your neighbor as yourself.' Love does no wrong to a neighbor; therefore, love is the fulfilling of the law" (Rom. 13:9-10 NRSV). Sometimes love requires me to reach out of my comfort zone and help another. Other times love requires me to hold my tongue or turn the other cheek. When determining God's will, the command to love should be an overarching principle guiding every believer.

• *Be self-controlled.* "For this is the will of God, your sanctification: . . . that each one of you know how to control your own body in holiness and honor" (1 Thes. 4:3-4 NRSV). Self-control is the ability to avoid sharing yourself emotionally and physically with every man you date. It is the ability to hold your tongue when your roommate is rude. Self-control is making time with God a priority. Self-control may also mean making dessert a luxury instead of a necessity.

• *Be patient.* "Those who wait on the Lord shall renew their strength; they shall mount up with wings like eagles" (Isa. 40:31 NKJV). If you are making a major decision without spending ample time in prayerful consideration, then you may be acting impatiently. The result could be as hampering to your pursuits as trying to fly without wings. For example, have you ever had a friend who married a guy who wasn't right for her because she was afraid nobody better would ever come along? God promises that as we wait upon Him, He will reveal Himself to us and give us strength to carry out His will.

• *Be forgiving.* "For if you forgive others their trespasses, your heavenly Father will also forgive you; but if you do not forgive others, neither will your Father forgive your trespasses" (Matt. 6:14-15 NRSV). Struggling with a heavy load of unforgiveness? Without a doubt, God's will is that you let go of it with His help. If something you're about to pursue is a reaction borne out of an unforgiving heart, beware that you are going down the wrong path.

• *Be respectful of authority.* "Let every person be subject to the governing authorities; for there is no authority except from God, and those authorities that exist have been instituted by God" (Rom. 13:1 NRSV). Could this mean that God wants me to be respectful to the police officer when he stops me for speeding? Could this mean that God wants me to pay my taxes, renew my driver's license, and obey other laws established in my country? Absolutely. It is God's will for believers to respect authority, whether in the government, workplace or church.

• *Be sexually pure.* "For this is the will of God . . . that you abstain from fornication" (1 Thes. 4:3 NRSV). No matter what your desires are or sexual background has been, it is God's will for you to be pure. Purity is a heart attitude born out of a desire to please God in every area of your life, including your sexuality. This attitude will dramatically affect your decisions in your relationship and dating life.

• *Be different.* "Do not love the world or the things in the world. . . . For all that is in the world—the desire of the flesh, the desire of the eyes, the pride in riches—comes not from the Father but from the world" (1 John. 2:15-16 NRSV). All of Kirsten's life, she had lived by the principle of doing whatever she could to get ahead financially. As a new believer, though, Kirsten began to realize that there is more to life than money. Instead of working hours and hours of overtime every month, she began to use that time to serve in her church. Being different as a Christian woman often means following principles and standards that are contrary to conventional wisdom.

In addition to these principles, God's Word tells believers that we are to be humble and compassionate (Col. 3:12), as well as thankful, prayerful, and joyful (1 Thes. 5:16-18).

To determine God's will, then, first ask yourself this question: "Am I *being* the person God wants me to be?" If the decision you are making does not line up with a Christlike lifestyle, then it is the wrong decision. On the other hand, if you are being the kind of person God's Word says to be, then you are already fulfilling part of His will for your life, and you are well on your way to knowing the rest of His will.

GOD'S WILL: WHAT SHOULD I DO?

"Which outfit should I wear today?"

When I (Tosha) heard my dorm roommate mutter these words, I thought she was talking to me. As I walked over to her closet to help her make a choice, I realized that she was not talking to me, much less conscious of my presence in the room. Slightly embarrassed, I retreated silently to my side of the room without giving an opinion.

My roommate had only been a believer for a few months. Excited about her newfound faith in God, she wanted to do everything she could to please Him. Part of this enthusiasm brought her to a Christian college.

For the next few days, I silently observed her going through the clothing ritual every day. "Which outfit should I wear today?" she would quietly ask. I finally decided that she just had a habit of talking to herself. Then, one evening before we turned out the lights, she came over to my bed and sat down for a moment of conversation. "I have a question for you," she cautiously started. "I've been told that God has a plan for my life. So each morning, I start out by asking Him what I should wear." *Oh!* I thought, finally understanding her behavior. "I can never really tell whether or not He answers me," she continued. "It always seems like I just end up making a decision. But then, this morning, I felt like He told me to wear that wool sweater and pant set." She pointed to a crumbled set of clothes lying on the floor. "Why would it be His will for me to wear wool when He knew today was going to reach 85 degrees?"

She was so sincerely perplexed that I could not even break into a smile. How refreshing to see someone who honestly wanted to know God's will for her life, down to the smallest details! But trying to understand those minute details was frustrating for this new believer.

Gently, lest I embarrass my friend, I began to explain how God has revealed in His Word general principles of His will. These are things that we should do, regardless of whether He gives us any more details. Specifics like what to wear on a hot day are not on this list (that's what He gave us common sense for); principles for how to live are.

Whether you are a new believer or have been a Christian for a long time, the following aspects of God's revealed will apply to your life. Before you seek to know more specifics about what to do with your life, make sure that you are doing these.

• *Spend time in the Word.* "All scripture is inspired by God and is useful for teaching, for reproof, for correction, and for training in righteousness, so that everyone who belongs to God may be proficient, equipped for every good work" (2 Tim.

3:16-17 NSRV). Scripture tells us how we should—and should not—live. God's will never, ever contradicts His Word.

One woman once told me that God had given her the freedom to have an affair with a married man. When I asked her where in His Word He had given her permission to do that, she angrily retorted, "He told me in my heart that this is okay." Whatever she heard in her heart was in direct conflict with what God's Word says about purity. If you think He is giving you permission to do something that Scripture says is wrong, then it is not His voice you are hearing.

• *Pray.* "Do not worry about anything, but in everything by prayer and supplication with thanksgiving let your requests be made known to God" (Phil. 4:6 NRSV). Talk to God about your choices, your options, and the decisions you must make. Tell Him what you are concerned about, then listen for His response. You may hear it immediately; you may have to wait. Just keep praying as you wait for His direction.

• *Abhor sin.* "Abstain from every form of evil" (1 Thes. 5:22 NRSV). Scripture clearly identifies what is sin for a believer, leaving no doubt about what God says is right and wrong. Unfortunately, many Christians like to stand on the line between the two, getting just as close to the edge of wrong as they possibly can. If you're dancing around that edge, don't expect God to reveal His will to you.

• *Make disciples.* Jesus commanded us, "Go therefore and make disciples of all nations . . . teaching them to obey everything that I have commanded you" (Matt. 28:19-20 NRSV). A lifestyle of pointing people to Christ is God's will for every believer. We must make sure our life pursuits are more people-oriented than thing-oriented. Careers, cars, and nice vacations only last for a short time; people will last for eternity.

• *Glorify God.* "And whatever you do, in word or deed, do everything in the name of the Lord Jesus, giving thanks to God the Father through him" (Col. 3:17 NRSV). Every action, every decision, and every pursuit, no matter how big or small, can and should glorify God. Do you sincerely desire to honor God?

During my late-night conversation with my roommate, we discussed how she could know God's will for her life. Before she needed to know specifics like what she should wear, she needed to know the overarching principles of what she should do. Her challenge as a new believer was to learn those principles.

As you seek to determine God's will, ask yourself: "Am I *doing* the things that God has already revealed to me?" If you are not spending time in God's Word, praying, avoiding sin, ministering to others, and living a God-honoring lifestyle, then you cannot know His will for your life. However, as you do the things God has told you to do in His Word, then you are even closer to knowing what the rest of His will is for your life.

GOD'S WILL: WHAT IS HIS PERSPECTIVE?

"But I *am* being the person God wants me to be and doing the things He's told me to do! I'm not perfect, but I'm really trying to obey Him!" Chandra wrote in her journal. But she still did not know whether to move or to stay. So she poured her feelings into her trusty journal and kept trying to reach some sort of decision.

I've been there too. In fact, that's where I am right now. To the best of my ability, I am being the person God wants me to be and doing the things He has told me to do, but I still don't know what I'm supposed to do about a certain area in my life: my schedule. On the one hand, I'm overcommitted and overwhelmed with all my responsibilities. On the other hand, I can't decide which responsibility is unimportant enough for me to let go of. No answers are falling from the sky either.

WHAT IS WISDOM?

Wisdom is the ability to view life from God's perspective and act accordingly. Proverbs 2:6-9 tells us the profound benefits of wisdom.

"For the Lord gives wisdom, and from his mouth come knowledge and understanding" (v. 6). That's where we get it— from God Himself. Not from television talk shows, not from self-help books, not even from our caring friends. First and foremost, wisdom comes from God.

"He holds victory in store for the upright" (v. 7a). If your definition of victory means winning the lottery or the heart of a handsome millionaire, you may not have the right definition! However, if you think of victory as Christlikeness and balance, then that is exactly what God plans for you to experience as an upright, single woman.

"He is a shield to those whose walk is blameless, for he guards the course of the just and protects the way of his faithful ones" (vv. 7b-8). As you walk down the road of life in wisdom, God is going to protect you from making wrong turns along the way.

"Then you will understand what is right and just and fair—every good path" (v. 9). God will show you the right path for your life through wisdom. The best path—not a mediocre one, not an average one, not just an okay one—is the one to which He will guide you. The best. And He will reveal it as you follow Him one step at a time.

Even while you are being the person God desires and doing the things He has commanded, perplexing decisions still arise. And with those decisions comes the gut-wrenching ache of trying to figure out what to do. Choices and options, situations and opportunities come our way, each promising to lead down a different path. If you are looking for a sign, a symbol, or an exact answer about which path you should take, you may or may not get what you are hoping for. However, you are not without direction as you study the road map of God's Word. God offers you wisdom to help you understand and apply that road map to your life.

It was a dark night, with few streetlights lighting the hotel where I (Melanie) was staying. Still, after being indoors for business meetings all day, I could not resist the urge to go for a walk before bed. When I had arrived at the hotel earlier, I noticed an empty field next to the building. Grabbing the pepper spray and flashlight from my suitcase, I headed outside to stroll and count the stars.

As I walked away from the hotel lights, it wasn't long before I needed to flick on my flashlight. Silently and thoughtfully, I moved across the field with only the small beam coming from my flashlight. When I shined the light out into the darkness ahead of me, I noticed that the beam was engulfed by darkness. However, when I pointed the light at my feet, I was able to clearly see my next step. By that light, I was able to avoid potholes, logs, and snakes. It wasn't until I took a step, though, that my next step was lit by the flashlight. Then I could see whether I could continue in that direction or if I was about to encounter another barrier.

Just as the flashlight helped me see my next step, so wisdom will direct you in the next step you should take for your life. "Your word is a lamp to my feet and a light for my path," the psalmist wrote (Ps. 119:105). Everybody in Bible times would have immediately understood this analogy, for every household had at least one single-wick lamp to light the way. On dark, cloudy nights, those lamps enabled people to safely walk from one place to another. By wisely shining and applying the lamp or flashlight of God's Word, you will begin to see God's perspective about the next step you should take. And you must keep walking so that you will find out what He has for you farther down the path.

So, the final question you should ask yourself when determining God's will is: "What is God's perspective about my options?" As opposed to the objective answers to the first two questions, "Who should I be?" and "What should I do?" the answer to this question will be subjective. That's okay. The Holy Spirit is living inside of you; He is the one who will give you wisdom about God's will for your life.

Sometimes He will choose to guide you through a specific passage or story in the Bible. Our friend Jennie was struggling with some major disappointments and decisions as she drove home through the mountains one night. In her despair, she felt so angry and tired of hurting that she didn't really want to live any longer. She felt like she couldn't go on with anything—not her music career, not her social life, not her job. As she cried out to God, Jennie peered out the windows of her car, looking for a shooting star to show her that God heard her. Not one appeared, she noted with frustration.

Somewhere on the road before she reached home, though, two passages of Scripture came to her mind. The references seemed pretty random, so much so that she almost dismissed them. Desperate for encouragement, she looked them up when she got home. To her amazement, the first passage spoke specifically about glorifying God with music, and Jennie knew she should keep singing. The second passage was from the fourth chapter of Jonah, where Jonah was so angry that he felt like dying. Fully able to identify with these feelings, unchecked tears began to flow down Jennie's cheeks as she realized how personal God was being with her. She had wanted Him to send her a shooting star to show her that He was there, listening to her hurts. Instead, He chose to speak to her through His Word. That evening, Jennie felt God lead her to continue with her music and to take some positive new steps in her life.

In addition to giving you guidance through God's Word, the Holy Spirit may show you God's perspective through the advice of other believers, through a message you hear at church, or through the words in a book. He may guide you through a series of unmistakable events such as opened and closed doors. He may impress on your heart which option to follow. He may even give you signs pointing the direction.

This is what happened to our friend Julianne, who had always hoped that God would let her live in Colorado. In anticipation of fulfilling such a dream, Julianne decided to make a survey trip to the state. She booked a flight to Denver and scheduled job interviews, all in the hopes of finding the means to make the move. Early in the morning before she left for Colorado, the phone rang. A friend in Colorado was calling to tell her about a job opening that she might want to consider. It was in a different city than she had hoped to live in, so she groggily thanked her friend for the call and fell back asleep.

Julianne arrived in Denver and immediately fell in love with the city and the mountains. It was exactly where she wanted to live. Unfortunately, none of her job interviews went well; either the positions had already been filled or she did not have the right qualifications. Disappointed, and with one day left in Colorado, Julianne was reminded of that early morning phone call. She reluctantly drove south to Colorado Springs, where the job opening and potential interview awaited.

To Julianne's surprise, she loved Colorado Springs even more than Denver. Even better, the job interview was a great success, and she was offered the position before she left. Before she made a final decision to accept the offer, she spent a day praying about it. When a song about Colorado mountains began playing on the radio, God gave Julianne peace as He confirmed that His will for her included moving to Colorado and accepting the position.

God used a timely phone call from another believer, closed doors in Denver, a wide open door in Colorado Springs, and even a secular song to guide Julianne. She wisely prayed about these things to confirm that Colorado was His will for her. Your own set of circumstances and signs will probably be totally different from Julianne's, but be open to how God may choose to speak to you.

Sometimes, however, the Holy Spirit living inside of you may choose not to show you God's particular perspective. Christians whom you respect may have no suggestions to give you—or everybody may offer you a conflicting opinion! There may not be a book even in print about your decision. The door to every option you have may stay wide open—leaving you with as many choices as ever. The sign you were looking for just may not occur. You are stuck with a decision for which you can't find an answer written in the sky.

What should you do?

Make a decision. Take a step by faith in one direction that seems like a wise choice. "What do you mean? How can I make a decision if I don't know which decision to make?" If you are practicing God's objective will that He has already revealed, and if you are seeking His perspective about your future, then God may be letting you make the decision on your own. He may be trusting you enough to let you decide how you can best glorify Him. In our opinion, that's a pretty high compliment!

This is what happened to Chandra. No signs confirmed which option she should choose, at least, not until long after she had to make the decision. She decided to stay put, continue to date Jeff, and look for another job. A year later, she is no longer dating Jeff, and she did not find another job. However, Chandra got promoted to a new position in the organization she was already working for. With her promotion came a higher salary and increased vacation time. This was exactly what she needed to fulfill a lifelong dream that had been on the back burner: having the finances and vacation time to take short-term mission trips each summer. In her situation, God had chosen to remain silent when she had to make decisions, but all the while He was working to fulfill His plan for her in a way she never even dreamed of.

He may be doing the same thing in your life. So, when you get frustrated about God's will, remember that God is always at work for your good and His glory. Sometimes He will choose to make His will obvious to you; other times He may decide to work anonymously behind the scenes in your life. Either way, He certainly has not forgotten about you.

Let's review the three questions for determining God's will for your life:

1. "Who does God want me to be?" Am I being that person?

2. "What does God want me to do?" Am I doing what He has already revealed to me?

3. "What is God's perspective about my options?" What is wisdom in this situation?

GOD'S WILL: I CAN'T GO WRONG!

Even after asking yourself these questions, you may still be hesitant. You made a decision, but you are still second-guessing yourself. "Look at these problems! Maybe I made the wrong choice!" "Perhaps I should have stayed there instead of coming here!" "I wonder what would have happened if . . ." You can drive yourself crazy with questions and thoughts such as these.

When your thought patterns begin to go down these paths, remind yourself that God is in control of your life. I personally don't understand it and I certainly can't explain it, but God is sovereign in our lives. While giving us choices and decisions, He is still in control. Scripture repeatedly reminds us of God's commitment to fulfill His will in our lives.

"'I know the plans I have for you,' declares the Lord, 'plans to prosper you and not to harm you, plans to give you hope and a future'" (Jer. 29:11). No matter what you're facing right now—a crushing circumstance, a recent breakup, health problems, the loss of a loved one, unemployment—God has a plan for your life. He has not forgotten you; He will not abandon you. Embrace Him and His plans—even when life is tough. Then see what He has in store!

"Commit your way to the Lord, Trust also in Him, And He

shall bring it to pass" (Ps. 37:5 NKJV). Have you entrusted your life and your future to God? Then be confident that He will fulfill His promises to you.

"A man's steps are of the Lord; How then can a man understand his own way?" (Prov. 20:24 NRSV). God is absolutely sovereign in our lives. He knows what our futures hold; we don't. So trust that your loving and faithful heavenly Father will lead you into the unseen, unknown, uncertain future that He has already seen, knows about, and is certain of. He will guide you one step at a time, one beam of light at a time.

I recently got up early to watch the sunrise. The darkness was slowly broken by beams of light shooting into the sky. One beam and then another and another shot across the sky as the sun steadily rose from its bed in the east. The sky filled with beautiful colors and light, until finally full daylight broke.

It is the same way with your life and mine. "The path of the righteous is like the first gleam of dawn, shining ever brighter till the full light of day" (Prov. 4:18). God's will, like a beam from the sun, shoots into our lives when we accept Him as Savior. One beam after another fills our lives until His full will is revealed for each of us.

As a Christlike and balanced single woman, you are being the person and living the life God has shown you. So be encouraged as you step out in wisdom! Follow God's leading as He shows you His perspective. Make a decision, then live in confidence knowing that He is going to fulfill His plan for your life.

COFFEE TALK

1. What choices and decisions are you currently facing?
2. When looking for God's will, why is it essential that you be the person and do the things He has already revealed in His Word?
3. What can help you determine God's perspective about a situation?
4. What do these passages teach you about God's involvement in your life: Psalm 18:32 and 32:8; Philippians 1:6; James 1:5? How do these encourage you?

RESOURCES

Blackaby, Henry T., and Claude V. King. *Experiencing God*. Nashville: Broadman and Holman, 1994.

- Sixteen -
THE CAREER WOMAN
Climbing the Ladder

I (Melanie) looked at the newspaper editor across the desk and tried to keep my hands in my lap, because they were shaking uncontrollably. "So you've worked on a Macintosh computer before?" he asked as he scanned my résumé. "Yes, sir." I then explained how I had spent my summer after college editing and designing a camp newspaper. He made a grunting noise, and I fidgeted in my seat as he continued to read the brief description of my journalism experience. Around his office were stacks of old newspapers, notepads, and books, and I longed for the day when I could have my own office.

"When did you graduate?" He never looked up from his desk, but I explained that I had just completed college that spring. "Well, we need somebody to do typesetting," he explained halfheartedly. "When can you start?"

Trying to calm my mounting excitement and jangled nerves, I took a deep breath. "Monday," I told him. "See you then," he said as he ushered me out the door. It was just another day in his life, but it was the launch of my journalism career. For nine months, I worked diligently at the newspaper office for thirty hours a week at minimum wage. I took a second job in the evenings to pay my bills, but my hardest work was from nine to four.

The newspaper hired me to do their typesetting, but in my "free time" I edited newspaper articles and laid out the weekly paper. As the weeks progressed, I asked the editor if I could start writing my own column, and he said yes. By the time I moved on to another job, I had done work for almost every department at the newspaper office. While I didn't make much money, the experience I gained was invaluable. It opened the door for me to get a job writing press releases for another company, which launched me into a public relations career.

If you seek to launch a new career, you need to follow several steps to land the job you desire. Determine what your goals are, get a good education, and then gain experience in your chosen profession.

Pursuing a career is hard work, but it is worth it when you are able to use the talents God has given you to make a living. Many people are stuck in jobs where there is no future. They don't enjoy going to work; some actually dread spending another day in the office. A balanced, godly woman doesn't settle in life. She works hard to obtain a position in the field of her dreams.

DETERMINE CAREER GOALS

If you haven't decided yet what you want to be when you "grow up," determining your career goals should be the first step in this process. When I started college, I knew I wanted to be a writer, but I didn't know which career track I wanted to take. I could have been a newspaper journalist, advertising copywriter, publicist, television producer, script writer, author, magazine editor, English teacher, or business writer. It was only after learning and experiencing each of these professions on a small, educational scale that I was able to hone in on free-lance writing and publicity.

When you initially determine your career goals, you don't need a specific track to follow. For example, you may want to be a teacher, but you don't know which grade you want to teach until you have experience working with several different age groups. Or you may want to be a business executive, but you want to explore a variety of industries before deciding which one to pursue. The key is to resolve a general career field and then, along the route, decide the specific path to follow.

If you haven't decided even a general field, the first step is to narrow down your options. One way to do this is by looking at how you spend your free time. Do you paint, read, hike, shop, play on your computer, sew, or plant flowers? Maybe you enjoy counseling a friend in need of help, teaching Sunday School to elementary school kids, or working out at your local gym.

Any of these hobbies can turn into a career. A painter may want to pursue graphic art. Someone who loves to read might make a great researcher or editor. The woman who hikes may want to look at a career in environmental science or work as a park ranger or wilderness guide. The shopper could get a job buying merchandise for a retail store. And the woman who enjoys computers could program software or create websites. The woman who likes to sew might design clothes, and the one who plants flowers could explore a career in horticulture. The good friend may want to be a guidance counselor, and the Sunday School teacher could also teach elementary school. The woman who enjoys working out may want to look at a career as a sports therapist or health expert. What do you like to do?

PURSUE EDUCATION

Once you have decided on a career goal to pursue, the next step is deciding the path you want to follow. Some careers will require several months of training while others will require many years of education. Start by asking a librarian which resources would assist you with your research. The librarian should guide you to a group of references like *Career Discovery Encyclopedia* and *Encyclopedia of Careers and Vocational Guidance* that will give you information on how to prepare for your career.

After you do your library research, call several people in your dream profession, and ask if you could set up an appointment to talk to them about their career. Over lunch or coffee ask them about their educational background, the path they took to launch their career, and what they would suggest to get yours started. If they have time, they will probably be candid with you—some of their answers may surprise you.

For example, when Sue decided she wanted to be a travel agent, she called several local travel agencies to find out what they were looking for in a new employee. Sue had been planning on going to a specific school that trained people to become travel agents. Her plan was to pay several thousand dollars, receive her certification, and then she would get a job. However, when she actually called the travel agencies, many of them told her they don't hire agents based on their schooling because they do their own training. They recommended she apply for a job directly instead of spending her money on school. Her research saved her money and helped her fine-tune her career plan.

While Sue opted not to pursue her certification, most career paths do require attending a technical school, college, or university. If this is the best route for you (and we highly recommend going to school), start researching which type of educational institution is best for your field. Some considerations you may have are cost, location, quality of education, and job placement after graduation. Choose your top three schools, and follow their processes to apply.

Once you have decided on a school, the next challenge is how to pay for it. Hopefully, you have been saving several years for this opportunity, and you have a nest egg to help out with the expense. If not, don't let this deter you from getting an education. Many scholarship and grant opportunities are available for students. Your local library should have a solid collection of financial aid information, and your potential school should also have lists of opportunities. Apply for both government and private grants, and find out what your school has to offer in academic, athletic, or extracurricular scholarships. You may also be eligible to apply for a work-study position or another job on campus.

When I was in college, my friends teased me because I spent so much of my free time in the library. I was constantly studying because I was relying on an academic scholarship to pay my tuition. My mother creatively assisted me by helping me fill out a stack of financial aid applications. As a result, I received government grants, school scholarships, and a work-study program. I worked hard, but the investment paid off as I searched for a job in my field after school. Because I wasn't strapped with a student loan, I was able to live on the minimum wage job that launched my career.

Student loans should be the last alternative to pay for your education. While they seem like a good source prior to college, student loans will linger for years after you finish your education.

If you must use a student loan program, talk with your school's financial aid administrator to learn a variety of ways to pay your loans off early or at reduced interest. It takes creativity and determination to explore all of the options to pay for your education. However, it will be worth it so you can concentrate on your studies and your first job instead of worrying about how to pay back student loans.

Surf the web to find sites about financing your college education. Check out sites like www.finaid.org and www.studentservices.com for extensive lists of scholarship information.

EXCEL IN YOUR EDUCATION

College is so much fun! It's a whirlwind of learning, people, events, projects, and even an occasional date. Whether you attend a university, technical college, or another type of school, you should excel in your field of choice.

While time spent in the classroom will educate you for your career, your time spent out of the classroom will also be important. You'll need a combination of book work and practical experience to be prepared when you hit the workforce. In order to do this, get involved with extracurricular activities that will help you with your career. For example, if you want to be a television reporter, get involved with the campus television station. If you want to be a powerful business presenter, join the debate team. If you want to pursue politics, work on your student government.

If your school gives you the opportunity to have an internship, do it! Paid or not, an internship gives you practical experience needed to obtain a job after graduation. While education is important, employers also look for practical experience on your résumé. Seek an internship in the field you want to pursue, and then learn everything you can while you are on the job.

Not only does school give you the opportunity to be involved, but you also may develop lifelong relationships. Don't overlook the importance of starting and maintaining friendships with people in your field. If you haven't developed close friends, you've only had half the experience.

Tosha's and my friendship started when we met during our college's television broadcasting class. We had no idea that one day we would be living in the same city, much less writing a book together. Your college friends can be the foundation for your career network as well as offer you support in your personal life for many years to come. Don't rush off the graduation platform with your diploma in hand and forget to collect your college friends' phone numbers, home and e-mail addresses. You will want to stay in touch.

PURSUE HIGHER EDUCATION

When we completed college, we waited a short time and then headed back to graduate school. Tosha earned a master's degree in biblical studies, and I got my master's in communications. While graduate school is certainly not necessary for some careers, in other fields like business, architecture, computer science, education, library science, engineering, or sociology, you will excel with an advanced degree.

In grad school your entire education is based on your chosen career. With a liberal arts education, you have to take classes in a variety of areas that don't directly relate to your career goals. In graduate school, nearly every class you take will advance your profession. If you haven't narrowed down the specific career track you want to take, graduate school should help you fine tune your options.

The application process for grad school tends to be time-consuming. Obtain applications from your top school choices and start filling them out early. Many of these applications require extensive essays and recommendations. Accept this process as a challenge that schools offer to weed out the halfhearted potentials.

Most graduate schools require that applicants take the Graduate Record Examination (GRE) before they apply. Some fields like business or law require specialized tests like the Graduate Management Admissions Test (GMAT) and Law School Admission Test (LSAT). Your library reference section should be lined with material to help you study for these tests.

To obtain information about the GRE deadline, cost, and registration information, write: Graduate Record Examinations, Educational Testing Service, P.O. Box 6000, Princeton, NJ 08541 or check out their website: www.gre.org.

FIND A JOB

Valerie had been out of college for several years and was working in temporary positions while looking for a job in the advertising field. She applied for a position at a top agency in the West, and they flew her to their headquarters for an interview. She had little career experience, but they offered her an assistant job where she would be doing administrative work in her field. However, because she wanted to start at a higher level, Valerie turned down the position and headed home to continue looking. Looking back, she regrets her decision, since the person the agency did hire moved quickly through the company's ranks until she became a manager a year later. Unfortunately, Valerie is still searching for an advertising position.

Valerie missed a good opportunity to start her career, but you don't have to follow in her footsteps. By researching and implementing a career plan, you can land a good starting position. The first step to find a job in your field is to develop a well-written résumé. Because this history of your work experience could make or break the opportunity for you to get an interview and ultimately the job, spend extra time compiling designing, and spell-checking this important document. Your one-page résumé should contain a specific objective, your contact information, your education, work background or internship, and college activities that relate to the job you seek. On the last line of your résumé write: References available upon request. If your potential employer asks for references, have a typed list of three (preferably two professional and one personal) ready. If you are want a creative position, you also need a professional-looking portfolio or demo reel.

Next, develop your job search plan. Start by researching each of the companies you'd like to work for, and then call their human resources departments to ask if they have openings. If they do, request the name of the H.R. representative who is hiring for the position you are interested in and write a cover letter addressed to this person. Send or hand deliver your cover letter and résumé, and ask if you may personally meet the H.R. representative. Leslie, who manages a team of about ten people, told us, "When I am looking to hire a new person, I am much more persuaded by an excellent cover letter than by a résumé. A cover letter should make the person stand out and answer the question: 'Why am I applying for this job?'"

Remember that the impression you leave on everyone in the interview process, including secretaries and receptionists, can make or break your opportunity to get the job. If the company does not have any openings, ask them if you may send your résumé in case a position becomes available. Most will say yes. The key here is to be willing to do what Valerie didn't want to do—start at the bottom. If one of your top company choices has a low-paying job opening that would launch you in your field, take it! By climbing the career ladder one rung at a time, you will wind up at the top.

> *Some job fields like education, accounting, and architecture require you to take regular classes or tests for accreditation. Check out if your chosen profession requires certification, and follow up on that prior to searching for a job.*

After you've pursued the companies on your top list, create a new list of companies that could be stepping stones to the company of your choice. Also scour newspaper and on-line classifieds for a job in your field. Seek positions at these stepping-stone companies with the same professionalism you do your top companies. The key at this point is to gain invaluable experience. Once you've got that, you can be more selective in future searches. For more information on pursuing a job and interview tips, check out www.womenswire.com/work.

As you aggressively search for a job, you will probably receive requests from several companies to come for an interview. This can be both exciting and intimidating. Before you go for your interview, research the company so you know things like: What is their product? Who are their clients/market? When did the company begin and how has it grown? Armed with some knowledge, you will feel a little more comfortable during your interview.

You also will feel more comfortable if you have personally prepared for the interview. Always dress your best, and bring a clean copy of your résumé in case your interviewer needs to be refreshed on your experience. Be prepared to answer questions like:

- When did you finish college?
- What jobs have you had? Why did you leave?
- What are your major strengths and weaknesses?
- Do you consider yourself a team player? A self-starter?
- Can you multitask (do several projects at once)?
- Why do you want to work for this company?
- Where do you see yourself in ten years?

Be informative and to the point with your answers. If they ask you a general question (for example, what have you done to show you are a team player?), you may want to respond with a short story . If they ask you what your weaknesses are, respond with a weakness that could be turned into a strength. For instance, "My weakness is that I take on too much work at one time, because I love a challenge. I have to be careful to focus on just several key projects at a time." Or, "I am such a detail person that it sometimes drives my coworkers crazy."

Also be prepared to ask them a few questions. For example: What are the major responsibilities in this job? Will I have the opportunity to grow? Where do you see this company in ten years?

When you go home, write a thank-you note to your interviewer expressing both your appreciation for the opportunity and your interest in the job. You may have to interview ten or twenty times before you are offered a job in your field, but don't stop pursuing your options. Keep looking at the classifieds, and if you are looking for a job in a field like teaching, counseling, or even marketing gain experience by volunteering for a local church or nonprofit organization.

While the job you are finally offered may not be your dream position, it may be the perfect stepping stone to gain experience and grow in your field. My position, for example, as a newspaper typesetter, was the step I needed to start my career in writing. If you can get a foot in the door, take it, and eventually you will open up the entire door and walk all the way in.

What are employers looking for in a job candidate? We asked a few supervisors, and this is what they told us: good communicator, flexible, organized, quick learner, pleasant personality, positive attitude, detail-oriented, self-confident, knowledgeable in their field, creative, responsible, self-motivated, team player, intelligent, humble, hard worker, and neat appearance.

LAUNCH A CAREER

After Joan completed her degree in architecture, she decided she wanted to pursue a career in computer animation. Because she had no experience in animation, she bought the basic software and spent several months training herself how to use it. Then she took her demo reel to a computer animation company that agreed to let her do an internship with them. When her internship was complete, the company hired her full-time, launching her career in computer animation. Joan's determination and flexibility in pursuing her career dreams eventually landed her the exact job she wanted.

When I completed grad school, one of my professor's parting words were: "Read everything you can about your field, and never stop learning." As you gain experience, work diligently to learn every detail about your current job and the one you would like to have in the future. Ask your boss if you may take on some additional responsibilities so you can gain even more experience. Instead of viewing your job as a daily hassle, look at your workplace as an expense-paid education.

> *Check out these internet sites for job postings: www.adguide.com, www.cweb.com, www.hotwired.com/webmonkey/jobs, www.4work.com, employment.yahoo.com, www.headhunter.com, www.jobweb.org, www.nationjob.com, www.americasemployers.com, www.careerexpo.com, www.careers.org, www.careerpath.com, www.monster.com, www.careermosaic.com, www.jobtrak.com.*

Once you have gained some experience in your field, you will be able to search for a position on your specific career path. Keep your eyes open for good opportunities that you can pursue. Instead of fearing a job change, see it as a new challenge that will help you develop your career.

Two years after I sat in the newspaper editor's dusty office asking for a typesetting job, I was offered a public relations position at a national cable television network. My short time working in low-paying grunge jobs paid off when I was offered this professional opportunity. The years I worked, planned, and prepared for my journalism career were all worth it when I sat down in my long-awaited office chair and looked at a desk full of press releases and writing resources.

The path you take can also land you in the job of your choice. By educating yourself and planning your career, you are on the path to success. And if you are continually open to learning new things and achieving high goals, you will succeed in the field of your dreams.

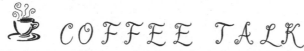 COFFEE TALK

1. What do you want to be when you "grow up"? What plans have you made to pursue your career goals?
2. Find examples in the Bible of people who had to go through a time of training before they pursued their career. For starters, check out Deborah (Jud. 4), Nehemiah (Neh. 1–5), David (1 Sam. 16–31), or Joseph (Gen. 39,41).
3. What steps are you taking to obtain your dream job? Why are you a qualified candidate for this job?

RESOURCES

Career Discovery Encyclopedia. Chicago: J. G. Ferguson Publishing, 1997.

Encyclopedia of Careers and Vocational Guidance. Chicago: J. G. Ferguson Publishing, 1997.

Jobs Almanac 1999. Holbrook, Mass.: Adams Media Corporation, 1998.

Messmer, Max. *Job Hunting for Dummies*. Foster City, Calif.: IDG Books Worldwide, 1995.

Plunkett, Jack W. *The Almanac of American Employers*. Houston: Plunkett Research, 1998.

- Seventeen -
THE RELOCATING WOMAN
Succeeding in a New City

COMMIT TO THE LORD WHATEVER YOU DO,
AND YOUR PLANS WILL SUCCEED.
PROVERBS 16:3

Every inch inside my hatchback car was filled with boxes, suitcases, bags, and the hangers I (Melanie) had stuffed into tight spaces. My passenger's seat and the floor were packed solid—I had somehow managed to squeeze in everything I needed. The rest of my belongings I had either sold or packed up and mailed.

My roommate, Sherri, helped me carry out my last items. Both of us looked a little haggard after staying up almost all night as I said good-bye to friends. In spite of my physical exhaustion, emotionally I felt fine. It had been only three weeks since I was offered an exciting job in Colorado, the state I had wanted to move to since I was a little girl. The last twenty-one days had been a whirlwind of packing, cleaning, sorting, wrapping up at work, and saying good-byes. I didn't have time to think about what it meant to leave my best friends.

I gave Sherri a big hug. It was sad to say good-bye to my roommate of three years, but I was doing okay. I got in my car and waved as I slowly backed out of the driveway, and I was still doing okay. I rounded the corner and suddenly I could no longer see my house anymore. I wasn't doing okay anymore. Sherri was completely out of view, and it hit me hard. Very hard! I was leaving Sherri and all my friends and the stability I had

had for the last few years. I was moving to a new state where I didn't know anyone. What was I thinking? For a moment, I wanted to swing the car around and say, "Forget it! This is where my friends are; this is where I'm staying."

But I didn't turn around, and for the next forty-five minutes, I cried nonstop. I passed my graduate school buildings, my office, and favorite restaurants. On to the interstate, I passed over Chesapeake Bay and before long the city was gone. It was just me and the long country road to Colorado.

The next four days in my car were really my good-bye to Virginia Beach. Memories flooded my mind, and I quietly appreciated each of my friends. During my years at the beach, I had tape-recorded funny answering machine messages that my friends had left me, and I laughed at their goofy greetings all the way across the state of Nebraska. By the time I arrived in Colorado, 2,200 miles after saying good-bye, I was emotionally prepared to start my new life.

One of the perks of being a single woman is that you have the freedom to pick up and move to a new city or state without many hassles. Your husband doesn't have to find a new job, and you don't have to find a school for your children. Do you like the ocean? You can move to California or the Carolinas. Are mountains your thing? Tennessee or the Rockies may be the place for you. Do you love quaint American towns? Why not head to New England? Does Anchorage have the perfect job opportunity for you? Check it out! If the idea of an artsy community with an abundance of mochas and cappuccinos excites you, Seattle may have your name written all over it. If you want a change of scenery or a career launch, do some research, visit your dream hometown, and if everything pans out, you can just do it!

SAYING GOOD-BYE

The hard part about making this leap, however, often comes when you have to say good-bye to the friends and family members who are dear to you. Maybe you can talk one or two of them into coming out with you so you can have an adventure together. When I moved to Colorado, my friend Jennifer decided she also wanted to head west. She quit her job the same week I left, and in a matter of days, she was in Vail working at the ski resort. The three-hour drive between us flew by as we faithfully traveled to spend weekends together (and as she attempted to teach me the art of snow skiing). Having her close by was important for me as I settled into my new home.

But what about the friends and family you leave behind (which will probably be most of them)? How do you say good-bye? My priority during my last three weeks in Virginia Beach was to spend time with every one of my friends. I did lunches, dinners, and late-night coffees where we talked about our present and dreamed about our future. The last night in Virginia, we had an all-night party at a friend's beach house, and I said good-bye to everyone for the last time.

We don't recommend that you live your new life thinking about how much fun you had in the past, but we do think you should collect memories of your friends as you move on. Take pictures, box up notes and gifts and maybe even a video from your good-bye party. You will treasure these memories in your new town. The beauty of technology is that you can easily keep in touch with your friends and family via phone and e-mail. My dad calls me once a week to catch up, and I see my family several times a year. One of my friends in Virginia Beach who is a video producer still keeps in touch by sending me occasional videotapes featuring several close friends. I love receiving his packages!

Just because you've left doesn't mean you have to be completely gone. You will probably visit your family on a regular basis. And every once in awhile, you will probably fly or drive back to visit with friends. Location certainly makes a difference in friendships, but your close friends will remain no matter where you live.

MOVING ON

The technical aspects of moving can sometimes be the most frustrating. Boxing up your stuff can be easy, but what do you do with it once it is in the box? How do you get from A to Z with as few hassles as possible? With a little planning, you should have a smooth and even fun moving experience.

Before the Move

When you decide it's time to make a move, start a list of the things you need to do before you relocate. On your list include things like:

• Determine your moving date and the arrival date in your new town.

• Find a new place to live.

• If you don't have a job at your destination, go to the library or get on the internet and locate all job openings. You may have to take a "survival" job before you land one for your career. Have your résumé and references complete and copied to mail or give away.

• Write a resignation letter to your boss giving your two-week notice.

• Cancel all of your utilities and cable, and call the utility companies in your new town to have them ready when you arrive. Get your new phone number, and pass it along to your friends.

• Order an inexpensive, new long-distance service.

• Keep a file of all your moving-related documents and expenses for a potential tax deduction.

• Gather all of your medical, insurance, school, retirement plan, and bank records. Also get phone numbers to contact your former health and financial professionals to transfer information to your new town.

• Decide if you will hire professional movers (can be expensive) or do it yourself with friends (have a pizza party as a thank-you). In some cities, the firefighters also help people move furniture for a fee. Call the fire station to find out.

• If you decide to use a moving company, ask acquaintances for recommendations and call the Better Business Bureau to shorten your list. They need to be reputable, reliable, and careful packers. Walk them through your house or apartment to show them what you are moving, and ask for a written estimate. Look over the estimate order for service—their contract with you— before you sign it so you agree on the terms. Also, consider purchasing moving insurance in case some things break, and be present on the moving day as they pack and load your belongings to ward off any problems.

• If you need a rental truck, check for discounts and make reservations.

• Decide on the best mode of transportation for your pet.

• If you are driving several states or across the country, have your car serviced before you hit the road.

• Get free boxes from a local department or grocery store, packing tape, scissors, and plenty of old newspaper to pack your things.

• Sort through all your stuff before you move it. Anything you don't need, you can sell, give, or throw away.

• To sell major items, take out a classified ad in your newspaper or put up an ad at your work or church. Other items can be sold at a garage or rummage sale.

• Cancel your bank account.

• Complete a "change of address" list to notify your out-of-state friends, credit card company, magazine subscriptions, car insurance (which you will have to eventually change), college and car loan offices, and college alumni office. Forward the rest of your mail by filling out a form at the post office.

Once you have your checklist of everything that needs to be done, you can start making calls and feel confident that you will have everything ready by your moving date.

The Move

When the week finally arrives for you to move, you will probably have a combination of emotions, including excitement and fear. Because you are prepared, however, you should be able to think clearly and make quick decisions as you pack and load your life's collections into a truck or car.

Before you start packing, map out your trip so you have the shortest drive possible to your new home. AAA gives free detailed maps and travel instructions to its members, and several websites will let you input your departing city and destination and then give you directions (like www.delorme.com/cybermaps). Also, decide where you will stay if it's an overnight trip. Our suggestion is that you stay with a friend along the way (it's much safer to have a loaded vehicle in a neighborhood or garage), or if you have to stay in a hotel, pack your valuable items in a separate box to take inside with you. Also, park in a well-lit lot and pay a little extra money to stay in a nice motel in a good neighborhood.

Then it's time to start packing. Number each box you pack, and then take inventory by writing the number and the box items in a moving notebook. Your unpacking experience will be easier if you put kitchen items together, bathroom stuff in the same box, and all of your linens under the same number. Wrap each breakable item carefully in newspaper or in your towels before you place it in a box. Put a combination of heavy and light items (don't fill it up completely with books) in each box so it will be easier to lift.

As you pack your home, keep the things you will need over the next week (hair spray, soap, work clothes) in a specific corner of your bedroom. This way you will avoid packing them unintentionally. Also, instead of heading to the grocery store, eat up the remainder of the food in your pantry or kitchen. After you finish packing a room, clean it thoroughly so you can get your deposit back. Even if there isn't a potential deposit to collect, it is considerate to leave your home or room clean for its next resident. Depending on your lease agreement, you may need to fill up any holes in the walls (get Spackle and a putty knife from your local hardware store) and have the carpets cleaned.

Once everything is in boxes, you are responsible for directing their transfer into a truck or car. If you don't have heavy furniture, you may be able to load the items easily into your vehicle. But if you have heavy items, please either ask for or hire help. It is not worth saving a little money on your move to spend hundreds of dollars on a chiropractor. During one of the almost twenty moves in my lifetime, my roommates and I offered pizza to any of the guys in my church singles' group who could help us load and unload a U-Haul. Would you believe six men showed up at our door that Saturday? The across-town move was complete in several hours.

If you are traveling across country, keep an eye on the forecast so you don't run into rough weather or snow storms. Better that you stay at a friend's and postpone your trip than get stranded on a lonely highway in a blizzard.

Once you have started on your journey, enjoy the drive. This is the time to reflect on your past, anticipate what lies ahead, and have a good talk with God. As you drive through beautiful parts of the country, enjoy the scenery and tune in to a local radio station to fully appreciate local life. Savor the quiet time before you launch into your busy new life.

After the Move

I'll never forget pulling into Colorado Springs after the long drive. Tiny pieces of snow were slowly falling from the dark sky, leaving me enchanted by my new western home. Even though I was exhausted, I was exhilarated that I was finally here.

If you arrive at your new town in the evening, get a good night's sleep before you start unloading your things. The next day you'll be refreshed and ready to complete your move. If you have hired someone to help you, patiently direct the move, and make sure the furniture is exactly where you want it so you don't have to move it again.

Because you have already had your utilities turned on, you should have lights and hot water. Over the next couple of days, unpack each box and put your things away. If you rush through this process, you will quickly become exhausted and want to re-arrange next week. If you have sold your furniture and haven't moved into a furnished home, find the local discount stores and start searching for new things (also look in the classifieds). Shopping may be a nice break from unpacking.

GETTING ADJUSTED

Once you have completed the bare minimum requirements of a move, it's time to get adjusted to your new hometown. So many things to learn, places to go, people to meet. It's time to get started. But where exactly do you start?

Finding Your Way Around

I remember vividly the shock I felt after I moved to Colorado. Three days after my move, I started my new job, and I was literally off and running. Easy errands like taking my clothes to the dry cleaner, getting my hair trimmed, or finding a new pair of shoes suddenly became intense missions. Every time I needed to do a simple task, I would have to quiz my coworkers and research the yellow pages before I ventured out to locate a reliable and economical business. I had taken for granted how easily I had done Saturday errands in Virginia, and I found myself in a whole new world.

It takes awhile to feel settled in a new area. You have to find a doctor, dentist, car insurance agent, a grocery store, an auto mechanic, and a decent pizza place. It's easy to feel over-whelmed. Instead of looking at everything you have to do at once, take challenges one at a time, dealing with your most pressing needs first.

The first step in getting settled is to ask coworkers, roommates, neighbors, and new friends for information. They'll be happy to rattle off the names of the businesses they frequent. Ask them why they recommend the business and what is the typical cost. The next step is to research local businesses in the yellow pages, newspaper, or on the internet. Call each company and ask specific questions about their services. The third step is to look on the bulletin boards of your church or workplace for ideas. Then the last step is to call the chamber of commerce and ask for a packet of local information. By asking questions and doing a little research, you should be settled quickly so you can start enjoying your new hometown.

GETTING STARTED

Put a local map in your car so you can drive around and begin feeling settled. Start shopping for a bank and set up an account. Find your local DMV, and get a new driver's license and license plates. Locate the nearest grocery store and gas station. Gather emergency numbers to put on your refrigerator. Get a phone book so you can put those yellow pages to work.

Making Friends

It was difficult for me to leave the surroundings of close friends and go into unknown territory. I remember sitting in my apartment one night watching TV sitcoms and begging God for a girlfriend. All I wanted was someone to go out with and chat over coffee, catch a movie, or even hike with on a Saturday. This was a lonely time in my life, but in a matter of weeks, God opened the doors for me to make friends. I'm so thankful for each of my new friendships.

The beauty of moving to a new community is that your former reputation has been washed away. You have a clean slate with these people, and they will never know that you've burned almost every meal you tried to cook, ended up in another state on the way to a church retreat, or forgot the words to your Easter morning solo (you still haven't lived that one down). If you want, this is the time to "recreate" yourself and try some new adventures. No one will ever know you just learned to surf or you hate public speaking. Next Saturday you can head to the beach, make dinner for your new friends, and confidently explain your views that night at a Bible study. If you don't attempt to bake something, they'll never know. All they know is the "new you."

As the new kid on the block, you have to be aggressive in making new friends. You have to ask people out to lunch, take brownies to your new neighbors, and introduce yourself at church. Also, be on the lookout for other new people in the area. They will be an excellent source of friendship and consolation, because you are in this new thing together. The joke about Colorado is that if you've lived here a week, there is always someone newer than you. Young people seem to move here in droves, and the best part is, they are all looking for new friends.

You will also have to ask to be included on occasion ("I heard you guys were going to a movie, do you mind if I tag along?"). That's okay. Just be friendly without appearing as desperate as you may feel ("Please, please, please let me go with you, don't make me stay alone in my apartment all weekend for the fourth weekend in a row, please!"). In no time at all, you will go home after work and your message light will be blinking. Hark, it's someone actually asking you out to dinner—you have arrived.

Getting Involved

Another way to meet new people is to get involved. Ask God to lead you to the church He wants you to minister in. Finding a church will open up a world of opportunities to put your gifts into action and introduce you to new friends who also are seeking God. It's a great way to get connected.

What else do you like to do? If you like to read, you may want to join a book group at the library. If sports are your thing, find a community or church team. Do you like to act or sing? Maybe you can join the local drama troupe or try out for a production. If you are politically motivated, is there a local campaign you want to support? As you look for ways to get involved, slowly put them on your calendar. We don't recommend filling your calendar to the point of exhaustion, but get involved in a ministry and activity or two, and you will soon feel like you belong.

Having Fun

It's amazing how many women move to a new area for the beach or mountains, and a year later when you ask them the last time they went swimming or hiking, they can't remember. Their calendar is so packed that they don't have time to enjoy what they moved for.

So don't forget to have fun. The first couple of months in your town are the best time to explore the museums, shop the outlets, walk on the beach, drive the mountain passes, and visit surrounding cities. As soon as you start making friends and getting involved, your time will be limited (that's a good thing!).

Get out, then, and enjoy your new state while everything is fresh. Try out some fun restaurants (even if you can only afford dessert), and go to the theater. Go to a sporting event, and then try out a new sport yourself. Is jazz the big thing in your town? Go with a friend to a jazz club. Appreciate the local flare. Do you know what's different about it than the town you came from? If not, get busy finding out.

After more than three years in Colorado, this is truly my home. There are days (like today) that I look back at my life in Virginia Beach with nostalgia. Life there was good, but my life today is even better. I have a good church, wonderful friends, and a whole mountain range to explore. I now know the best places to eat, where to get my hair cut, and who is the cheapest and best dry cleaner in town. I laugh when newcomers ask me advice about local businesses, because my three years have made me the expert. It wasn't long ago that I was asking all the questions.

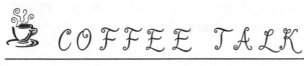

COFFEE TALK

1. If you have recently moved, what are you doing to make your new town feel like home? What have you done in the past?
2. How do these verses relate to moving? "It is the Lord who goes before you. He will be with you; he will not fail you or forsake you. Do not fear or be dismayed" (Deut. 31:8 NRSV). "Now may the God of hope fill you with all joy and

peace" (Rom. 15:13 NASB). "Casting all your anxiety on Him, because He cares for you" (1 Peter 5:7 NASB).

3. Do you remember the excitement of moving to your town? What new places do you still want to explore or activities do you want to get involved with?

4. What are you doing to befriend new people at your church or work?

RESOURCES

Furman, Leah and Elina. *The Everything after College Book: Real-World Advice for Surviving and Thriving on Your Own.* Holbrook, Mass.: Adams Media Corporation, 1998. Authors' note: We don't endorse this book in its entirety, but it has a very practical section on relocating.

Miller, Susan. *After the Boxes Are Unpacked.* Colorado Springs: Focus on the Family Publishing, 1995. Authors' note: This book is targeted toward married woman, but it is a good resource for single women dealing with the emotional trauma of a move.

Savageau, David, and Geoffrey Loftus. *Places Rated Almanac.* New York: Macmillan Travel, Simon and Schuster, 1997.

- *Eighteen* -
THE INSPIRED WOMAN
Pursuing Your Dreams

HOPE DEFERRED MAKES THE HEART SICK,
BUT A LONGING FULFILLED IS A TREE OF LIFE.
PROVERBS 13:12

What do I want to be when I grow up? I (Melanie) lay back on a grassy bank along the James River in Virginia and envisioned the multitude of things I could do with my life. I wanted to get a good job, write books, and explore our world. I thought about all the different ways those dreams could take place. Where was I going? What was I going to do with the rest of my life? My head started to ache as I pondered all of my options.

I was twenty-five and had just finished graduate school. As far as I was concerned, the sky was the limit. My résumé had gone to newspapers and magazines in places like Seattle, Anchorage, Honolulu, and Cape Cod, but my lifelong dream was to move to Colorado. In spite of my persistent résumé mailings, however, nothing seemed to be panning out for me to head west. Actually, nothing seemed to pan out at all, and I was becoming frustrated with my future. I really thought God should be working faster on my career.

On June 10, 1995, several of my friends from church and I were on a weekend retreat on the James River. The 1917 mansion we were staying in was filled with antiques and books from the beginning of the century, when the house was home for the Remwood family. The estate overlooked a canvas of dusty green trees and still water that created a pond before it opened into the river. A grassy trail, two bridges, and a gazebo led the mansion's guests down to the water.

And here I was. A guest of this incredible mansion with a future that seemed as murky as the brackish river water my friends were skiing in.

After a full day of fun and contemplation, I settled into my four-poster canopy bed and enjoyed the country breeze coming through the windows. I pulled out my Bible and prayed that God would give me some answers for my future.

Since we were staying by the James River, I decided to read through the book of James. As I began reading the first chapter, I sensed that God was talking to me. "If any of you is lacking in wisdom, ask God, who gives to all generously and ungrudgingly, and it will be given you. But ask in faith, never doubting, for the one who doubts is like a wave of the sea, driven and tossed by the wind; for the doubter, being double-minded and unstable in every way, must not expect to receive anything from the Lord" (1:5-8 NRSV).

I realized that was me. I lacked wisdom. I was double- and triple-minded. I was too fearful to give my dreams to God. I wanted to guard them selfishly and organize my life my way. After reading God's promise that night, though, I decided to put my future and my dreams into God's hands. He had given me the dream of becoming a writer, and in preparation, I received my degree in journalism. But I still had to wait on Him to show me the opportunities He wanted me to pursue.

Soon after that night at the estate, God opened amazing doors for me to get a dream job in Colorado Springs. The timing was impeccable. I had just completed school, I was ready to leave my job, and the dating relationship I was in came to a close. When I flew out West to interview for the job, they told me the position had been open for an entire year. I could have applied twelve months before, but the timing wouldn't have been right in my life. God's plan was much better than mine.

My dream didn't become a reality until I gave it back to God. I had to trust in Him to accomplish my aspirations instead of throwing out a hundred résumés to places I hadn't even explored. He guided my steps, and it was all in His time—and His timing was absolutely perfect.

WHY SHOULD YOU DREAM?

Do you remember those days as a little girl when you would close your eyes at night and dream about what you wanted to be when you grew up? Do you remember those hours you spent pretending to be a teacher, model, lawyer, mom, movie star, or beautician?

Dreams inspire and motivate us to pursue the talents God has given us. When I was growing up, I wanted to be an archeologist, journalist, or detective. My poor neighbors must have been concerned for my and my friend's well-being as we spent our summer afternoons digging up backyards in search of ancient bones or sneaking around their homes looking for clues to solve a mystery. After a day of digging and searching, my parents would let me use their old typewriter so I could write an article summarizing our day's finds.

My dreams of discovering new things launched my love of researching and exploring. My dreams of becoming a writer motivated me to get an education in journalism and spend hours with a pen and paper or computer to practice the art. When we dream about the future, we are inspired to prepare ourselves to accomplish our dreams.

Many children start developing their dreams when they are very young, when adults ask them, "What do you want to be when you grow up?" But not all children are encouraged to dream. My friend Edie recently returned from a two-week trip to Russia. She spent her vacation developing relationships with teenage Russian orphans and teaching them practical biblical insights. Talking to these orphans, she was surprised to find that none of them had any aspirations in life. They believed there was no reason for them to dream, and without dreaming they didn't have any motivation to develop their talents. Edie spent her time trying to give them a sense of hope for their future.

When we don't dream, we aren't disappointed when the dreams don't come true. It is easy to go through life without aspirations, but life quickly becomes stale. One of my favorite country songs is Garth Brooks' "Standing outside the Fire." He describes the difference between someone who maintains a safe but boring life outside the fire and someone inside the fire who takes risks in life to accomplish her dreams. Are you being molded by the heat of the fire or are you standing far away, afraid of being burned? Dare to take risks in life, and most important, dare to dream.

WHAT ARE YOUR DREAMS?

Do you want to be an artist or fly an airplane or travel to another country as a missionary? Have you always enjoyed taking care of children, making crafts, or exploring the outdoors? Do you love sewing, writing, singing, or playing the guitar? Maybe you've always wanted to perform with a drama team, open a bed and breakfast, run for a political office, or lead a Bible study at your church.

No dream is too big for God. The Bible is filled with stories of women with dreams of their own. The woman who touched Jesus' robe in Luke wanted to be healed of her illness. Esther may have dreamed about being queen, and Sarah and Hannah both wanted to have babies. After her husband died, Ruth dreamed about a secure future for her and her mother-in-law. Moses' sister, Miriam, desired to help lead Israel out of bondage.

What do you dream about? If you haven't recorded your dreams, write them in a special notebook or on a piece of keepsake stationary. These dreams could include your career goals, favorite hobbies, or relationships. If you were to glance at my dream list, you would find things like: writing novels that impact people's lives, starting my own public relations business, backpacking Europe, building a cabin in the mountains, learning how to ballroom dance, writing articles for travel magazines, getting married, and having a loving family.

My list is filled with things I dream about on a regular basis. A few of the items on my list are completely out of my control, while others I am able to accomplish with perseverance and determination. Some of the items are things I look forward to as I grow in the talents God has given me. Some are desires of my heart that only God can fulfill. Some are dreams that I have thought about since I was young.

What do you want out of life? What talents and desires has God put in your heart? And even more important, what are you doing to turn your dreams into reality?

HOW DO YOU MAKE YOUR DREAMS COME TRUE?

Wouldn't it be nice if we really could just wish upon a star to make all of our dreams come true? Since we can't guarantee that our dreams will come true, some of us don't even try. We are afraid of failing. It's much easier to not take risks in life and just get by than to get in the fire and pursue our dreams. But why should you settle for a dull life? By evaluating, planning, working hard, and reevaluating your dreams on a regular basis, you can make them become a reality.

Evaluate

The first step to making your dreams come true is to pull out your dream list and evaluate each item. Ask yourself: do I have the determination to pursue this dream? Your dream may require only a short time of education, or you may need to go to school for eight years. My dream of learning ballroom dancing will take up a lot less time than starting and maintaining my own public relations firm. Are you determined to stick with your dream even when you are tired, bored, or discouraged? Are you willing to pay the price?

While many dreams can be pursued through hard work, natural talent should also be a consideration. Do you have the talent to fulfill your dream? For example, if you desire to be a politician, you can take classes and practice to overcome stage fright and become a compelling speaker. If you want to play golf, you can learn how to swing and putt. However, if you want to be a professional drummer but can't keep a beat, you may want to pursue another one of your dreams.

As you evaluate your dreams, also determine which ones are completely out of your control to achieve. These are "heart desires." For example, do you have "getting married" on the list of things you'd like to do someday, but you haven't met a man yet with whom you'd like to commit? Is there a relationship in your life you'd like to mend, or do you want to be healed of an illness that has been plaguing you since you were young? Only God can make these heart desires come true.

Psalm 37:4 says: "Delight yourself in the Lord and he will give you the desires of your heart." If you'd like to get married someday, ask God to bring a special man into your life. If you're not able to mend a relationship, let God know the desires of your heart.

Spending time with God and talking to Him about what you want in life should be your umbrella as you evaluate, plan, and pursue your dreams. Ask Him about every dream you have, because He often redirects our dreams for something even better. He fulfills our dreams and heart's desires while He is accomplishing His purpose. For example, He may want me in Los Angeles instead of in a mountain cabin or working in an orphanage instead of writing magazine articles. If that's where He directs me, I pray that I will follow.

Plan

After evaluating, the second step is to put each dream on a separate piece of paper and write out your goals to accomplish them. To realize my dream of starting my own business, I have created a step-by-step plan of how to save money, purchase computer equipment, write marketing materials, generate clients, and pay my taxes. To plan for my backpacking trip to Europe somday, I have a box filled with price information, potential travel itineraries, and beautiful color magazine clips of my dream destinations.

As you look at your dreams, ask yourself questions like: What kind of training do I need? Do I know anyone who has done this before whom I could get advice from? How much will it cost? How much practice do I need? If I start today, how long will it take for me to accomplish my plan? Often, when you break a large dream down into bite-size goals, you can suddenly see a way to accomplish it. With your planning and evaluation, you should be ready to start working to achieve your dream.

Work Hard

I have always been fascinated by Olympic ice skaters. When I was a little girl, I determined that I also was going to skate someday for a medal. I spent hours practicing on the ice and dreaming of the day I would compete.

When I was nine, my family and I headed to Lake Placid in New York to see the site of the recent Olympics. We walked around the grounds and stopped at the training rink for ice skaters. The woman who gave us our tour told us that these young women and men practiced daily to compete for the Olympics. Most of them didn't have much of a social or personal life because they were so focused on being the best in the sport and winning the gold. My ice skating dream died that day, because I didn't want to spend the majority of my life on a rink. But I still admire Olympic athletes' determination.

The third step to pursuing your dreams is to work hard. Evaluating and planning are usually the easiest stages because, like dreaming, you don't have to accomplish anything. But this step requires you to start learning and practicing your dream. I wasn't willing to pay the price to become an Olympic ice skater. My dream was only of the glamour and prestige of winning a medal, and I hadn't taken into account the hard work that would be needed.

We need to work diligently at accomplishing our dreams. If you want to be a writer, this would be the stage where you begin submitting articles to newspapers and magazines to get published. If you want to be an actress, you need to be auditioning for local plays and commercials. If you want to travel to another country, you need to research your trip and start saving for this adventure. If your goal is worth achieving, it is certainly worth working hard for.

Reevaluate

The last step in pursuing our dreams is to continually reevaluate the goals we have set out. In high school I decided that one of my dreams was to be a singer. Anyone could be in the glee club at our school, so I was there for every practice. The first time I tried out for a solo part I didn't make it. Not to be deterred, I tried out again for another solo part, and this time the teacher asked me if I could start singing "a little quieter." The last time I tried out, he finally gave me a part to appease me, but when I actually heard myself singing in the speakers, I opted to never try out again. I still love to sing but do all of my performances either in my car or my bedroom (after shutting the door). I am not a talented singer and decided to spend my life pursuing dreams that came a bit more naturally.

If I had decided to continue pursuing my dream of being a vocalist, I would have been frustrated to see that dream die. While God wants us to be determined in our dreams, He also wants us to be flexible as we follow Him.

"Whatever you do, work at it with all your heart, as working for the Lord, not for men, since you know that you will receive an inheritance from the Lord as a reward. It is the Lord Christ you are serving" (Col. 3:23-24). Whatever your dreams and goals are as you follow Him, continually evaluate, plan, and work hard to achieve them. Then, as you reevaluate your dreams, ask yourself questions like: Am I still willing to work hard to achieve this dream? Is God directing me to another location or even vocation? Where do I see myself in five or ten years? Do I want to continue pursuing this dream? Maybe you've decided to compose music instead of play in a band. Or maybe you like teaching adults instead of children. It's okay to change your dreams after much thought and prayer, but never stop dreaming. And never stop pursuing those dreams.

When I was twenty, I started to seriously think about what I wanted to do with my life. I was torn between the little girl I had been and the woman I was becoming. One February night in my college dorm, I penned this poem:

> As a little girl, I would put down my dolls
> I would put down my books and my games to go some-
>   where by myself to pray
> And to dream.
> I prayed prayers that I knew could be answered, because
>   I prayed to a God who was listening to me
> I dreamed dreams that everyone else thought were
>   impossible but me
> They were my dreams.
>
> I could dream anything I wanted
> No one else would know what I desired—my dreams
>   were all mine, mine and God's

As a little girl, I looked out into the big world and the
    big people
It seemed so far off—like I would never grow up
Being big and living life would never happen.
Now, I look in the mirror
I've grown up
I'm the woman the little girl looked up to.

I still dream
Yet, now my dreams are coming true
God has given me life and made it so special
My dreams aren't easy—
The biggest dreams in life are the hardest to reach
They are the most important.

At times, I still feel like that little girl lying on the grass
    and looking up into the stars
At times, I long to be that little girl again
Free to dream what I want—for dreaming isn't hard
It's accomplishing those dreams that is hard
It takes an effort that makes me want to crawl back into
    my shell and hide
It's a reality that makes me want to crawl under my
    covers, away from the dark and unknown
I could watch the world from the inside
Watch my life go by.

Someday, my life will be over
I won't be dreaming anymore
I won't go out into the night to look at the stars
The little girl must grow up

She's done her dreaming and now she must do the ultimate
She must do what she has dreamed.

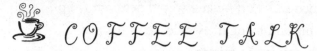 *COFFEE TALK*

1. What are the dreams God has given you? How do you plan to accomplish them?
2. How have your dreams changed since you were a little girl?
3. Are there any childhood dreams that you should revive and pursue?